‘MORI

For Ian, Harry, Max and Declan

'More than an Ally'?
Contemporary Australia–US Relations

MARYANNE KELTON
Flinders University, Australia

Routledge
Taylor & Francis Group
LONDON AND NEW YORK

First published 2008 by Ashgate Publishing

2 Park Square, Milton Park, Abingdon, Oxon OX14 4RN
711 Third Avenue, New York, NY 10017, USA

Routledge is an imprint of the Taylor & Francis Group, an informa business

First issued in paperback 2016

British Library Cataloguing in Publication Data
Kelton, Maryanne, 1959-
More than an ally? : contemporary Australia-US relations
1. Australia - Foreign relations - United States 2. United States - Foreign relations - Australia 3. Australia - Military relations - United States 4. United States - Military relations - Australia
I. Title
327.9'4'073

Library of Congress Cataloging-in-Publication Data
Kelton, Maryanne, 1959-
More than an ally? : contemporary Australia-US relations / by Maryanne Kelton.
p. cm.
Includes bibliographical references and index.
ISBN 978-0-7546-7367-5
1. United States--Foreign relations--Australia. 2. Australia--Foreign relations--United States. 3. United States--Military relations--Australia. 4. Australia--Military relations--United States. I. Title.

JZ1480.A57A854 2008
327.94073--dc22

2007046434

ISBN 978-0-7546-7367-5 (hbk)
ISBN 978-1-138-26765-7 (pbk)

Transferred to Digital Printing 2014

Contents

List of Abbreviations

AAFTAC	American Australian Free Trade Agreement Coalition
ABA	Australian Biotechnology Association
ABARE	Australian Bureau of Agricultural and Resource Economics
ABC	Australian Broadcasting Corporation
ABM	Anti-Ballistic Missile (Treaty)
ABRI	Angkatan Bersenjata Republik Indonesia (Indonesian military)
ACSI	Australian Coalition of Service Industries
ACTU	Australian Council of Trade Unions
AD	anti-dumping
ADF	Australian Defence Force
AFL–CIO	American Federation of Labor–Congress of Industrial Organizations
AFP	Australian Federal Police
AFTA	ASEAN Free Trade Area
AGPS	Australian Government Publishing Service
AIA	Advanced Informed Agreement
AIDC	Australian Industry Development Corporation
ALP	Australian Labor Party
AMF	Asian Monetary Fund
AMS	Agreement on Maintaining Security (Australia–Indonesia)
ANAO	Australian National Audit Office
ANZCERTA	Australia–New Zealand Closer Economic Relations Trade Agreement (sometimes referred to as CER)
ANZFA	Australia New Zealand Food Authority
ANZUS	Australia–New Zealand–US alliance
APEC	Asia Pacific Economic Cooperation
APMA	Australian Pharmaceutical Manufacturers Association
ARC	Australian Research Council
ARF	ASEAN Regional Forum
ARIES	Airborne Reconnaissance Integrated Electronic System
ASC	Australian Submarine Corporation
ASEAN	Association of South East Asian Nations
ASEM	Asia–Europe Meetings
ASIS	Australian Secret Intelligence Service
ASPI	Australian Strategic Policy Institute
ASI	American Sheep Industry
ASW	anti submarine warfare
AUSFTA	Australia–US Free Trade Agreement
AUSMIN	Australia–US Ministerial (meetings)

AUSTA	Australia–US Trade Agreement
Austrade	Australian Trade Commission
AWB	Australian Wheat Board
C3I	Command, Control, Communication and Intelligence system
CAP	Common Agricultural Policy
CBD	Convention on Biological Diversity
CCS	Combat Control System
CEO	Chief Executive Officer
CER	Closer Economic Relations (between Australia and NZ)
CFO	Chief Financial Officer
CGT	capital gains tax
CIA	Central Intelligence Agency
CIE	Centre for International Economics
CITAC	Consuming Industries Trade Action Coalition
CNO	Chief Naval Officer
COTS	commercial off the shelf technology
CPD	Common Parliamentary Debates
CROs	Contract Research Organisations
CRUCS	*Collins* Replacement/Upgraded Combat System
CSFs	colony stimulating factors
CSIRO	Commonwealth Scientific and Industrial Research Organisation
CSL	Commonwealth Serum Laboratories
CVD	countervailing duties
DAO	Defence Acquisition Organisation
DFAT	Department of Foreign Affairs and Trade
DIO	Defence Intelligence Organisation
DSD	Defence Signals Directorate
DSMAC	Digital Scene Matching Area Correlation
DSTO	Defence Science and Technology Organisation
DTSI	Defence and Trade Strategic Initiatives
EC	Economic Community
EEC	European Economic Community
EEP	Export Enhancement Program
EFS	Export Facilitation Scheme
EU	European Union
EVSL	early voluntary sectoral liberalization
FAO	Food and Agricultural Organization
FDA	Food and Drug Agency (US)
FDI	foreign direct investment
FTA	Free Trade Agreement
FTAA	Free Trade Area of the Americas
GATS	General Agreement on Trade in Services
GATT	General Agreement on Tariffs and Trade
GMO	genetically modified organism
HDW	Howaldswerke-Deutsche Werft
HAS	Hollandse Signaalapparaten

ICC–OFFP	Independent Inquiry Committee–Oil For Food Programme
ICS	Import Credit Scheme
IKL	Ingenieur Kontor Lubeck
IMF	International Monetary Fund
INTERFET	International Force East Timor
IP	Intellectual Property
IPEG	Intellectual Property Rights Experts' Group
IPO	Initial Public Offering
IPR	Intellectual Property Rights
ISCMMS	Integrated Ship Control Management and Monitoring System
IT	Information Technology
ITR	Invitation to Register Interest
JCPAA	Joint Committee of Public Accounts and Audit
JMSDF	Japan Maritime Self Defence Force
LMO	Living Modified Organism
MAI	Multilateral Agreement on Investment
MEF	Marine Expeditionary Force
MFN	Most Favoured Nation
MPR	Majelis Permusyawaratan Rakyat (the Indonesian Parliament)
NAFTA	North American Free Trade Agreement
NASDAQ	National Association of Security Dealers Automated Quotes
NATO	North Atlantic Treaty Organization
NFF	National Farmers Federation
NGO	Non Government Organisation
NHMRC	National Health and Medical Research Council
NMD	National Missile Defence
OASITO	Office of Asset Sales and IT Outsourcing
OECD	Organization for Economic Cooperation and Development
ONA	Office of National Assessments
PACOM	Pacific Command (US)
PBS	Pharmaceutical Benefits Scheme
PDS	Project Definition Study
PHON	Pauline Hanson's One Nation
PhRMA	Pharmaceutical and Research Manufacturers of America
PIAA	Pharmaceutical Industries Action Agenda
PIIP	Pharmaceutical Industry Investment Programme
PMV	passenger motor vehicles
RAAF	Royal Australian Airforce
RAN	Royal Australian Navy
R&D	Research and Development
RMA	Revolution in Military Affairs
RTA	Regional Trade Agreement
SAS	Special Air Service
SDSC	Strategic and Defence Studies Centre (Australian National University)
SEATO	South-East Asian Treaty Organization

SIGINT	Signals Intelligence
SIS	Secret Intelligence Service
SLCM	sea launched cruise missile
TA	Trade Agreement
TCF	textiles, clothing and footwear
TDHS	Tactical Data Handling System
TERCOM	Terrain Contour Matching
TGA	Therapeutic Goods Administration
TMD	Theatre Missile Defence
TNI	Tentara Nasional Indonesia
TPA	Trade Promotion Authority
TPM	trigger price mechanism
TRIMs	Trade Related Investment Measures
TRIPs	Trade Related Aspects of Intellectual Property
UKUSA	United Kingdom–United States–Australia (intelligence agreement)
UN	United Nations
UNAMET	United Nations Mission in East Timor
UNMOVIC	United Nations Monitoring and Verification Commission
UNSC	United Nations Security Council
UNSCOM	United Nations Special Commission
UNTAET	United Nations Transitional Administration in East Timor
USITC	United States International Trade Commission
USN	United States Navy
USP	United Sheep Producers
USTR	United States Trade Representative
VERs	voluntary export restraints
WIPO	World Intellectual Property Organisation
WMD	weapons of mass destruction
WTO	World Trade Organisation

Acknowledgements

I am indebted to a long list of people who have assisted me with this book. Not only do I owe Richard Leaver an intellectual debt but also I have been the fortunate beneficiary of his expertise and commitment to the project. My thanks also to John Fitzpatrick for his long-term support. My gratitude goes to Leonard Seabrooke not just for his decisive advice on conceptualisation of the issues but also for his relentless backing and excellent good humour. I am particularly grateful to Andrew O'Neil and Alex Stephens who thoughtfully read through the entire manuscript and provided indispensable advice. I am grateful also to Don DeBats, Martin Griffiths and Carol Johnson for their expert comment on various draft chapters, in addition to their encouragement for the book. I am appreciative of Liz Kelton's and Robert Fitzsimons' expertise and efficiency in commenting on the manuscript. I thank Ann Capling, Peter Burns, Bill Tow, George Crowder, Rick DeAngelis, John Summers, Lionel Orchard, Noel Tracy and Anthony Langlois for their support of my research. This book has been written with the endorsement and interest offered by The School of Political and International Studies at the Flinders University of South Australia. Within the School, Julie Tonkin and Sonja Yates have provided valuable ongoing administrative assistance for the project. I am very grateful for the support given to this project by Kirstin Howgate and her team from Ashgate Publishing.

I have been struck by the remarkable generosity and graciousness of those people who have assisted me with the case studies. Many kindly agreed to review and discuss the drafts. I have learnt much and enjoyed the ensuing discussions. I wish to thank Lyall Howard for reviewing the chapter on the early trade disputes. Mark Laurie, Suzanne Farquhar, Anne Holmes, Anthony Taubman, Richard Wadley, Richard Walmsley and Anya South all assisted with the biotech study. Roger Creaser, Mike Deeks, Paddy Hodgman, Andrew Mack, Andrew Millar, Hans J Ohff, Rob Walls, Horden Wiltshire and Kim Beazley, reviewed the *Collins* chapter. Gary Hufbauer provided insights into the provision of exclusions to the steel tariffs and David Goodwin commented on that chapter. I.M. Destler offered incisive assessments of the US environment for the Trade Agreement analysis. My thanks to Kurt Campbell for his analysis of the broader alliance relationship. I remain indebted to Peter Field for his advice, particularly on the trade issues, but also as some of the research has been the beneficiary of his corporate experience and intellectual rigour. Other members of the Australian and US bureaucracy, industry, academia and retired officials of the armed forces who wish to remain anonymous have also assisted either through interviews or via reviews of drafts. Not all have agreed with my interpretations, but all have nonetheless been interested analysts and helpful with their assistance. I acknowledge their preparedness to share their expertise and encourage debate. To John McCarthy and Stuart Harris, who were interviewed themselves, I also thank for their time and assistance in organizing interviews of others both here and in Washington. Any flaws in the book are exclusively my responsibility.

I thank Moira Gallagher, Helen Jones, Jill Kelton and Anne Spencer for their intellectual and personal support. Thank you to Helen Beikoff, Jennifer Bracht, Sue Bowker, Rosemary Coorey, Chris deSilva, Sue Dooley, Robyn Eaton, Robyne Garrett, Bill Haskett, Janet Maitland, Jan Marshall, Colleen Moriarty, Tim Morris, Linda Petfield, Jane Riordan, Tina Saunders, Anya South, Jenny Young and the Fitzsimons and Haskett families. Thanks also to Michael Coats, Leonie Hardcastle, Vandra Harris, Aaron Jackson, Tanya Lyons, James Manicom, David Scott Mathieson, Seth Nicholls and Greg Shepherd for their intellectual collegiality.

I could not have written this book without the love and support of my family. I am deeply grateful to Ian, Harry, Max and Declan Jamieson, my parents Pat and John, together with Steve, Liz, Jake, (dec) Jill Kelton and families.

Sections of the book have appeared in some form in two previously presented pieces: 'New Depths in Australia–US Relations: The *Collins* Class Submarine Project', *Canberra Papers on Strategy and Defence* No. 162, Strategic and Defence Studies Centre, Australian National University, 2006; and 'The AUSFTA and the Current Alignment of US Trade and Security Strategy', *Paper presented to the Australasian Political Studies Association Conference*, University of Tasmania, Hobart, 29 September–1 October 2003.

Introduction

Threat Mediation in Australian Foreign Policy

When the Howard government was first elected in March 1996 on the campaign pledge of upgrading the Australia–US alliance, few could have imagined the extent to which its promises would be realised. Yet, after eleven years in office, Australia's Howard government had significantly intensified the alliance. By 2007, Australia had supported US global strategic policy and, with the US, was at war in Afghanistan and Iraq. Australia had given in-principle support for the US Missile Defence programme and approved US equipment and supply basing in northern Australia. The US encouraged Australia's acceptance of an active regional security role and cited Australia's leadership of the UN peacekeeping force in East Timor as a model for its allies' regional engagements. Australia too, embraced further economic integration with the US and in 2004 signed the Australia–US Free Trade Agreement. The government thus had implemented bilateralism as Australia's preferred foreign policy diplomatic track.

Yet, the success of this strategy, particularly in the delivery of trade outcomes and its effect in inflating Australia's defence ambitions, remained questionable. Though Prime Minister John Howard and his conservative government could espouse the similarity of cultural values and interests and intensify the support it offered the Washington, US domestic preferences remained as a key determinant of American foreign policy. Even though the Howard government changed from a policy which was solely reliant upon its cultural relationship with the US to one which provided material support for the US military response to the 11th September 2001 terrorist attacks, it appeared that reciprocity in foreign relations still only remained possible where interests coincided.

There is no doubt that the US has been an invaluable ally for Australia.[1] In its provision of pivotal support for Australia's defence in World War II and its intervention in East Timor in 1999, the US demonstrated at once the substance of the alliance for Australia. For Australia, the alliance with the US extends the possibilities for the maintenance of its position in a region where some states' population, military capacity and economic status will increase dramatically. However, Australia's recent attempts to manage its international situation, particularly vis-à-vis the US, have demonstrated the structural fragility of its policy choices. This has been evident predominantly in the delivery of trade outcomes. In its early trade disputes

1 Ron Huisken, 'Inquiry into Australia's Defence Relations with the United States: Submission No. 10', Joint Standing Committee on Foreign Affairs, Defence and Trade, Defence Sub-Committee, Australian Parliament, Canberra, March 2004, p. 1.

with the US over an Australian leather manufacturer's increased share of the US automotive market and the imposition of US tariffs on the export of Australian lamb, the Howard government was unable to leverage on its special relationship to exact promised material gain in its trade negotiations. Although the US signed the free trade agreement with Australia, and though it is too early to determine the financial success of the deal, the negotiations clearly failed to meet the government's initial expectations for the agreement. These outcomes reflect both the exigencies of power in bilateral negotiations for any small government, in addition to a misplaced belief that a cultural affinity would deliver material gain.

Australia's non-strategic location has also lessened the likelihood of great power commitment in the relationship. While small states in the Middle East or in Northeast Asia may have been crucial to UK or US grand strategic plans or vital to their economic hegemony, Australia's remote location and small population has denied it leverage on either geostrategic or economic grounds. Thus, when confronted by domestic lobbying of the US administration, little advantage could be exerted by the Australian government. Even if Australia were to link trade with security, this attempted construction of advantage in its foreign policy space may not be enough.

Space in the realm of foreign policy-making has been divisible by three. These establish a) the state's role in the international system, b) the external needs of the society as they interconnect with the foreign arena and c) the interests of the governing party.[2] In order to explain the Howard government's preference for bilateralism I examine the management of the first two spaces by the third. The government has endeavoured to ameliorate, if not maximise, its international and domestic situations while concurrently ensuring its electoral survival. The Howard government, as is the case with most, was in the business of risk management. Therefore, I examine the conduct of current Australian foreign policy as it exposes the Howard government's arbitration of the international and domestic spaces, or as I interpret them here, as threats, while simultaneously guaranteeing its electoral survival.

Of necessity, the party in power must mediate these threats in order to preserve its position. Governments of all persuasion in Australia's history have endeavoured to do so. To manage both government and incumbency entails a concerted effort to shore up middle Australia's constituency through adept management of both the international threats and domestic understandings of these threats to its survival. Consequently, the government has become a threat manager, or mediator, in a situation where it simultaneously managed both the international settings and its domestic situation. The central aspect of the Howard government's choice in this role has been to pursue an asymmetrical bilateral relationship with the United States. My main concern then in this book is to analyse why and how this government chose to upgrade Australia's relationship with the US, and to examine the consequent effects.

---

2 Allan Gyngell and Michael Wesley, *Making Australian Foreign Policy*, Cambridge University Press, Cambridge, 2003, p. 23 and pp. 246–48.

Australia in the International Environment

In 1996, the intensification of the US alliance arose at a time of change and uncertainty in the international environment. Both enduring and new crises fortified the Coalition's public prioritisation of the alliance. Over time Australian governments had done much to address a situation where perceived chronic threats to Australia's international circumstances traditionally emanated from its isolated geography, small population, sizable territory, resource orientated economy and a neighbourhood to the north that had been culturally remote and strategically separate from Australia's heritage. More acute issues for Australia over the past decade now included the continued uncertainty of the post Cold War security environment and, after 1993, a parallel waning of multilateral institutions to cater for and accommodate this change. While this was clearly demonstrated through the Iraq crisis in the UN Security Council in 2003, where the UN was asked either to support the US military intention, (and thereby be perceived to succumb to US pressure) or deny support (and invite irrelevance), it is arguable that this fiasco was long in construction. More specifically, after Australia's intervention in East Timor and the attacks in Bali and New York, Australia's security concerns also became focused on the spread of terrorist assaults. As parts of Southeast Asia were regarded in some quarters as ripe to spawn and activate groups antithetical to the US and its allies, Australia's region assumed a more threatening form. Prior to this, President Suharto's resignation in 1998 and the deaths of approximately 2,500 people in Indonesia, together with the instability in East Timor and the Southwest Pacific provided the sources of concern in Australia's immediate security environment. Further afield, the rise of China, and instability on the Korean peninsula presented new sources of tension.

Against these anxieties, Australian governments and their bureaucracies had creatively and intelligently maximised opportunities. Australia's economic performance had improved dramatically. Partial transformation of the economy resulted in a strengthening and repositioning, yet ultimately the economy would always remain responsive to international financial and economic trends. Although the dollar strengthened against the greenback by 2003, this was generally acknowledged as a reaction to the weakening of the US economy and the alteration in fiscal policy and subsequent retreat from a strong US dollar policy. By mid-2007, the Australian dollar's strength was bolstered by the vigour of international commodity prices and Australia's capacity to provide raw materials to its northeast Asian trade partners. The Australian economy weighed in at sixth in the region but given present indicators and current levels of growth, it would drop to eleventh by 2050. Ongoing attention to its performance was necessary.

Asia's financial crisis of 1997/8 initially posed significant threats to Australia's economic health, not just because of the contagious nature of the currency market collapse but also because of the cessation of the sustained economic growth to the north that was underpinning Australia's export market development. Stubborn stagnation in the Japanese economy for most of the 1990s and its durability in the early part of the twenty-first century were unwelcome factors for all. Moreover, the prospects of this economic crisis translating into instability in the security sphere, particularly in non-traditional areas, raised further concerns for Australian policy-makers. Mitigating these anxieties, however, was the temporary reduction in state capacity to persist in arms purchasing. Regional disorder in the late 1990s nonetheless provided a challenging environment in which to enact both foreign economic and security policy.

Early in Howard's tenure, it also became apparent that Australia's interest in regional integration was experiencing difficulties in reciprocation. Prior to 1996, Malaysian President Mahathir Mohammed had been a consistent antagonist in Australia's efforts to secure a place in regional dialogues. After that time, The Philippines and Indonesia joined Malaysia in registering opposition to Australia's membership of regional forums, including ASEM (Asia–Europe Meetings) and ASEAN+3.

Explicit rejection aside, it was noticeable that in 1996 China also circumscribed the avenues through which Australia might seek to engage with the region. Arguably, China's behaviour in the mid-1990s created some of the preconditions for Australia's pursuit of choices other than those regionally focused. These included China's confrontational approach to the Taiwanese elections, its testing of nuclear weapons and aggressive claims to territories in the South China Sea, together with the deficiencies of any commensurate regional forums to contest or discuss these actions.[3] China's actions assisted in reinforcing the Coalition's preferences to refocus Australia's foreign policy on the US. At the outset of the Coalition's tenure, any desire to embrace relations with China was hamstrung by Chinese behaviour.

It is possible, too, that in June 1996 resultant concerns over Chinese behaviour prompted Alexander Downer, in talks with Yukihiko Ikeda (then Japanese Foreign Minister), to suggest that Japan take a more forthright role in regional security.[4] US Secretary of State, Warren Christopher, in commenting upon US engagement in the region in the mid-1990s, referred to Australia as its southern anchor.[5] China's ambassador to Australia, however, made clear that China regarded Australia's endorsement of US activity as unacceptable. These views were exacerbated by the tensions resulting from the cancellation of Australia's Development Import Finance Facility (the DIFF scheme); and Minister for Primary Industries, John Anderson's visit to Taipei. Australia's welcome of the Dalai Lama caused a further deterioration in relations. Australia's support of US intervention in Kosovo was opposed by Beijing. US bombing of the Chinese Embassy in Belgrade and then the Chinese capture of a US spy plane ensured that tension was a durable feature of the relationship. China's characterisation as the 'crab's claw' of US strategy in East Asia remained unpalatable for the Chinese.

---

3 Ann Kent, 'Australia and China, 1991–95: Asymmetry and Congruence in the Post-Cold War Era', in James Cotton and John Ravenhill (eds), *Seeking Asian Engagement: Australia in World Affairs 1991–95*, Oxford University Press in Association with The Australian Institute for International Affairs, Melbourne, 1997, p. 171.

4 Mohan Malik, 'Australia and China: Divergence and Convergence of Interests', in James Cotton and John Ravenhill (eds), *The National Interest in a Global Era: Australia in World Affairs 1996–2000*, Oxford University Press, South Melbourne, 2001, p. 112.

5 Linda D. Kozaryn, 'More US Training Planned Down Under', American Forces Information Service News Articles, August 1996, p. 1.

Later in the decade, however, the government endeavoured to redress this issue. Alexander Downer attended the handover of Hong Kong to China, despite the US boycott. Chinese President, Jiang Zemin, Vice Premier Zhu Rongji, and Defence Minister Chi Haotian, were welcome visitors to Australia. This was followed by the visit of three Chinese warships. Australia also withdrew its sponsorship from the UN Commission on Human Rights resolutions. Instead, it was agreed that China's human rights conduct should be discussed bilaterally. Its successes were assisted at the turn of the century by China's appetite for Australian coal, iron ore, LNG and uranium resources. Nuanced diplomacy on the part of Australian officials was also required to manage the continued tension between the US and China. The new strength of Howard's position with China was marked by Hu Jintao's address to the Australian parliament in 2003 and his efforts to proclaim China's benign rise in the US. Yet, as Howard became more comfortable with China's rise and Australian supply of raw materials, it was Australia's capacity to manage both the Chinese and US relationships in tandem that became more conspicuous.

In the international arena, then, the Howard government from 1996 onwards, encountered a raft of risks both economic and strategic with which it needed to contend. For the Coalition, this was complicated by the rise of Hansonite right-wing domestic politics.[6] While Chinese bellicosity at the beginning of the Howard incumbency provides a partial explanation for the Coalition's endeavours to reaffirm Australia's US ties, it is inadequate in explaining its complete motivation. Instead, while the Coalition chose to upgrade these relations as a response to broader international and domestic demands, the upgrade itself raised some questions internationally. Successive Australian governments' management of intimacy with the US required deft diplomacy. It was all too easy for Australia to be perceived as a US service provider even where this was not so. This interpretation to some extent would become self-fulfilling where Australia aligned itself with US preferences and thus either alienated or spurred defensive behaviour in other states or provoked disaffected stakeholders, particularly within the region. Nevertheless, it is still evident that through the US bilateral system of alliances in the Pacific, which includes treaties with Japan, South Korea, Thailand, Singapore, and The Philippines, many local governments were anxious to maintain the US presence in the region. The complicating issue for Australia, as was evident during the Keating government, was that US engagement in the region was never a certainty.

Domestic Demands

Co-existing with these international risks for the Coalition to manage were related domestic pressures. Electoral survival required that the Coalition successfully deal with its constituents' perceptions of security: physical, economic and psychological. It demanded that the government implement a successful foreign economic policy that could sustain Australia's standard of living and, ultimately, quality of life.

6 Pauline Hanson representing the One Nation Party was elected to Federal Parliament on a platform that exposed Australia's xenophobic fears.

Pressures then evolved from the more direct needs of its constituents for quality government-assisted services. Provision of health, education, and employment were vital concerns of the people that could be aided through a successful foreign economic policy. Yet the articulation and explanation of this eventually had proved elusive for the Hawke-Keating governments. The indirect nature of the relationship between international policy and the immediate benefits for ordinary Australians was difficult for governments to explain, especially given media sound byte stipulations.

Much weight had been placed by the previous Labor government on Australia's role as a 'good international citizen' and its role as a middle power in the international system. One section of the population would still carry with it a sense that Australia, as a privileged society, had an inherent responsibility to assist others in the system. Australia's role in the Cambodian peace process was demonstrative of this. Its construction of the Canberra Commission on nuclear disarmament, its role in multilateral services negotiations, and its Cairns Group leadership, were all indicative of the possibilities of niche diplomacy. Sections of the Australian electorate would continue to be influenced by this agenda and still feel the need to embrace a continued role for Australia in international affairs either in niche diplomacy and/or as the good international citizen. This would also extend to assisting the East Timorese peoples in repelling the terror imposed via renegade Indonesian repression. Concurrent with this view was an independent streak in the community that decried comprehensive dependence upon another state. Although Australians were often perceived as a natural cultural partner for the US, this was more nuanced than initially suggested. The Lowy Institute's survey of Australians in 2005 revealed the undercurrents of policies that reflected concerns regarding the turns in US foreign policy and possibly unfulfilled expectations regarding the free trade agreement. In 2007, while three-quarters of those surveyed had a favourable opinion of Americans, less than two thirds had a favourable opinion of the US.[7]

Early in Howard's term in office, it was perhaps ironic that an independent member of Federal parliament should become a threat to the conduct of foreign policy. Pauline Hanson, elected as the independent Member for Oxley in Queensland and espousing an economic nationalism and xenophobic populism, altered the boundaries of the debate about Australia's relationship with Asia. For a while, Hanson's erroneous criticisms of the 'privileged place' of Aborigines in Australia and the 'hazards' of Asian immigration captured the attention of both alienated voters and Federal politicians. Hanson had given voice to those affected by the dismantling of the 'Australian settlement'; to those disaffected by the change wrought by the Hawke–Keating restructuring of the economy and engagement with Asia. Hanson and her One Nation Party emerged to occupy a fissure that had been expanding over the previous decade with ominous implications for national governments.[8]

---

7 Ivan Cook, 'Australians Speak 2005: Public Opinion and Foreign Policy', *Lowy Institute for International Policy*, Sydney, 2005. Alan Gyngell, 'Australia and the World: Public Opinion and Foreign Policy', *Lowy Institute for International Policy*, Sydney, August 2007.

8 Rick DeAngelis, 'Xenophobic Populism and Pauline Hanson's "One Nation": A Comparative Perspective', *Policy, Organisation and Society*, vol. 16, Winter, 1998, p. 6.

Threat Mediation

As the incumbent Party, it was then imperative for the Coalition to negotiate or mediate between these two sets of threats. It was also necessary, given that the Coalition regarded itself as best able to deliver on security and wealth that it should seek to retain government. Consequently, in the mediation process between international and domestic threats, foreign policy differentiation was valuable. By 2003, Allan Gyngell and Michael Wesley had observed that:

> while foreign policy used to be thought of as bipartisan or separate from the inter-party process in Australia, foreign policy makers are increasingly finding the need to be mindful of the political implications of foreign policy developments as they monitor the policy space.[9]

Progressively, foreign policy was regarded as a fertile arena on which to cultivate rule. Appealing to the electorate, via successful arbitration in defence and foreign economic policy, would assist in the maintenance of domestic power. In this process in 1996, mediation was framed through the test of 'national interest'. In breaking the supposed Hawke/Keating nexus, the Coalition proclaimed that: 'It is vital that Australia re-affirms and upgrades the importance of the security alliance with the United States as its contribution to assisting in US involvement in the entire region.'[10] As Hugh White observed of Howard, 'the chance to remodel the US relationship probably had both national and political attractions.'[11]

This direction was explored in the 1996 pre-election document, 'A Confident Australia'. Australia was envisioned as a country that was:

> Cooperative, economically competitive and secure, [it would be] fully engaged with the East Asian region, while maintaining and developing important links with countries beyond the region.[12]

Motivated by 'enlightened realism', it would entail 'a commitment to practical measures to advance Australia's national interests within a framework of liberal values, the rule of law and practical international co-operation'. While the Coalition documented the correctness of a bipartisan approach to foreign policy, it nevertheless realised the 'considerable scope for changes to the style and conduct' of foreign policy. Avoidance of the following actions was integral in this practical approach:

---

9 Allan Gyngell and Michael Wesley, *Making Foreign Policy*, Cambridge University Press, Cambridge, 2003, p. 23.

10 Federal Coalition, 'A Confident Australia: Coalition Foreign Affairs Policy', Melbourne, February 1996, p. 10.

11 Hugh J. White, 'Mr Howard goes to Washington: The US and Australia in the Age of Terror', *Comparative Connections, Pacific Forum CSIS*, 2nd Quarter 2003: Occasional Analysis: Australia–US Relations, p. 3.

12 Federal Coalition, 'A Confident Australia', 1996.

> Actions and policy initiatives which are based on inflated expectations or an exaggerated perception of our likely influence and which can be seen as meddlesome and with little chance of outcomes favourable to Australia's interests.[13]

This difference was highlighted three years later in Coalition foreign affairs and trade policy documents as 'Advancing Australia's Interests' explored the inadequacies of the ALP's record.[14] Achievement of both the vision and the maintenance of the position of power by which to ensure its implementation also required some restructuring of policy processing. Past Prime Ministers Gough Whitlam, Malcolm Fraser and Paul Keating were vitally enthused by the opportunities of foreign policy. Robert Menzies too, revealed himself as a master mediator of international and domestic threat. Bob Hawke, together with Keating, understood that the threats posed by the global economic situation required domestic attention. If Prime Minister Howard was initially more predisposed to the domestic policy arena, he was soon to realise the benefits of managing international policy and its bearing on domestic outcomes. Revealingly, the role of the Prime Minister's international advisor had become increasingly significant since its establishment in the 1980s.[15]

Perceiving that the pace of economic change enacted by the previous government was too rapid or unexplained for the Australian population, and cognisant of the present international and domestic threats, the government needed to navigate a way forward that was most appropriate for Australia's international predicament and would suffice for middle Australia. In security policy, while the US alliance remained a constant, previous governments also had endeavoured to pursue cooperative security arrangements with regional states. Consequently, a more independent security culture emerged through the 1980s.[16] Through the recent past, in foreign economic policy, Australia had opted to sustain a multilateral approach, reinforced with a regional emphasis. Integration of these two orientations became part of a more extensive policy direction to 'enmesh' or 'engage' with Asia.

Success in the 1996 election presented the opportunity for the Coalition to impose its own thinking upon how best to manage Australia's predicament. Historically, the Coalition Parties had always demonstrated their interest in bilateral relationships. Prior to the Howard government's election in 1996 the Coalition had provided further indications of their preferred diplomatic choice through their election strategy to upgrade relations with the US. For John Hewson and then for Howard, this type of diplomacy was perceived to deliver material gains in addition to embodying

---

13 Federal Coalition, 'A Confident Australia', p. 1.

14 Federal Coalition, 'Advancing Australia's Interests', authorised by Lynton Crosby, Melbourne, 1999, p. 5.

15 Allan Gyngell and Michael Wesley, 'Interweaving of foreign and domestic policy: international policy', in Glyn Davis and Michael Keating, *The Future of Governance: Policy Choices*, Allen and Unwin, St. Leonards, 2000, p. 225.

16 Graeme Cheeseman, 'Australia: the White Experience of Fear and Dependence', in Ken Booth and Russell Trood (eds), *Strategic Cultures in the Asia–Pacific Region*, Basingstoke, Macmillan, 1999, pp. 273–74 and Richard Higgott and Kim Richard Nossal, 'Australia and the search for a security community in the 1990s', in Emanuel Adler and David Barnett, *Security Communities*, Cambridge University Press, Cambridge, 1998, p. 281.

heightened value in electoral terms as Labor had clearly cornered the multilateral and regional markets. Not only was this the Coalition's pre-election tactic to differentiate itself from the ALP's multilateralist strategy, its continued emphasis on a traditionalist approach[17] to security relations underscored its pre-election analysis of political advantage. In part, it perceived that where the Keating government had failed was in its inability to communicate the benefits of its multilateral and regional international activity to its domestic constituency. However, in practice the Hawke/Keating governments had not demoted the importance of the US alliance, instead Labor government rhetoric situated the alliance amongst both its regionalist and multilateral strategies.

At the time, in comment upon this issue, William Tow noted that in 1996 even US policy officials were 'puzzled' by the Coalition's zeal for upgrading the relationship.[18] Rhetoric is a potent tool, nevertheless, and perception a powerful dynamic for any government. Astutely, Howard had sensed that Hanson had voiced 'the fears and concerns and the sense of insecurity that many Australians feel at a time of change and instability'.[19] Though one manifestation of this was the dogmatic defence of Australian sovereign borders (as the refusal of assistance to the Tampa's asylum seekers in 2001 evidenced), it was also about refocusing policy on alliance relations. A renewed emphasis on the traditional US relationship, Australia's contemporary cultural partner, could be driven to allay the supposed anxieties of middle Australia. It could also provide an alternate refuge if engaging with Asia became problematic. The ANZUS Alliance would be upgraded and more broadly, bilateralism installed as the foundation stone of Australia's international relationships.[20] Concurrent with the installation of bilateralism was the testing of Australia's multilateral commitments against the national interests.

Foreign Policy Options

It is clear that the government pursued all its options for international diplomacy: multilateralism, regionalism, bilateralism, and unilateralism. Yet for a country of Australia's size, with limited resources in foreign diplomacy and less after the election of the Coalition in 1996,[21] only so much was possible. By allocating precedence to

17 Michael Wesley and Tony Warren, 'Wild colonial ploys? Currents of thought in Australian foreign policy', *Australian Journal of Political Science*, Canberra, vol. 35, no. 1, March 2000, pp. 9–26.

18 William T. Tow, 'Introduction', in William T. Tow (ed.), *Australian–American Relations: Looking Toward the Next Century*, Macmillan in association with the Australian Institute of International Affairs, South Yarra, 1998, p. 2.

19 John Howard, 'Fair Australia', Address to the Australian Council of Social Service, Sydney, 13 October 1995.

20 Department of Foreign Affairs and Trade, 'In the National Interest: Australia's Foreign and Trade Policy White Paper', Canberra, 1997, pp. 53–59.

21 David Goldsworthy, 'An Overview', in James Cotton and John Ravenhill (eds), *The National Interest in a Global Era: Australia in World Affairs 1996–2000*, Oxford University Press, South Melbourne, 2001, pp. 14–16.

multilateral and regional efforts, the government would have maintained the Labor initiative and remained basically indistinct in policy terms. Through a multilateral focus, other states' qualms over the development of a US-led hegemonic bloc would continue to be allayed. Some of China's concerns that Australia would provide an appendage to the US presence in the region would be annulled. Bargaining strategies would continue to operate through the largely predetermined processes of global institutions. Other states' fears would be eased by the perception of predictability of state behaviour. Nevertheless, while international pressures would be diminished, domestic concerns remained foreboding. Although often rightly acknowledged as a model of what is possible in multicultural social tolerance, Australia nonetheless traditionally has sought security with conventional partners. Continued adherence to multilateral processes, and undertakings with a deluge of diverse states, drained the ongoing capacity of Australia to remake itself. Change management was a thorny and taxing domestic exercise as the Hawke–Keating enterprise discovered.

Alternately, reinvigorated bilateral engagement, particularly with the US, would serve to allay domestic pressure, as an alliance with a global hegemon with familiar cultural predispositions seemingly offered the prospects of stability and certainty. A perception existed that bargaining would not need to be process-bound. Instead, reliance on the personal familiarity of the cultural connection could be the means by which results could be achieved. Immediate relief from cosmopolitan demands was thus proffered to the electorate and threats dissipated.

Internationally however, as later exemplified in USTR Robert Zoellick's formulation of US trade policy, countries would compete for liberalising trade deals with the US. Australia would not be the only state to solicit bilateral deals and this would further the competitive practice. Thus, an exclusionary process was fortified.

Choosing bilateralism for the Coalition thus meant it was mediating between the international and domestic threats where it was firmly focused on the exigencies of the domestic contest. As such, it was prepared to snub some threats in a plural international setting in favour of association with the hegemon with similar cultural preferences. However, whether the culturally bound bargaining that would eventuate could deliver in the way that the Coalition envisaged in 1996 was far from certain.

Alliance Upgrade

New partners in the upgraded relationship with the US were both the trade and security dimensions. The new bilateralism eventuated with the attempt to overlay trade relations on the enduring ANZUS alliance. Ironically, however, the Coalition chose to model its trade policy on American 'aggressive bilateralism'. Limitations of size remain the obvious restraint upon the likely success of a bilateral policy with commensurate emphasis on reciprocity. Commanding approximately one per cent of global exports, Australia has limited options to exercise any kind of leverage in two-way trade relationships. Though it initially represented a retreat from the liberalised free trade processes emphasised through APEC [22] by 1998, it appeared that the APEC Bogor Declarations were unlikely to be realised. The Coalition's bilateralist policy, nonetheless, had predated the obvious demise in APEC trade outcomes.

Diversification away from the 'Asia only' focus, as the Coalition espoused, also involved pursuing opportunities more widely. As the Asian Financial Crisis hit in June 1997, Australia's isolation from the crisis vindicated the Coalition's expanded trade policy tactics. Further, its intent on upgrading the US relationship was given impetus by way of the difficulties for enhancing relationships elsewhere. Internationally, the Uruguay Round of Multilateral Trade Negotiations was completed just three years earlier, yet Europe retained its intransigence on the Common Agricultural Policy (CAP). With the eventual failure of the WTO Seattle talks in 1999, the government sensed an affirmation of its bilateral approach.

Once elected, the Howard government endeavoured to implement the rhetoric of its campaign strategy to elevate relations. Defence Minister at the time, Ian McLachlan, immediately expressed support for US action in the Taiwan crisis. In Sydney at the 1996 AUSMIN talks, Australia offered to preposition US military equipment, although this was not accepted by the US. Instead, training exercises were initiated, intelligence interconnections were upgraded and the lease on Pine Gap extended. Resultant from these talks, a Joint Security Declaration, The Sydney Statement, reaffirmed US commitment to the region and Australia's shared role in promoting stability and affirming democratic values. The two governments professed that:

> Australia and the United States place enduring value on the alliance because of its significance in maintaining and consolidating Australia's capability for self-reliant defense, and because it constitutes a crucial element in the United States' permanent presence in the Asia–Pacific region.[23]

As later exposed, however, this 'practical bilateralism' would have its obligations. William Cohen, US Defense Secretary (1997–2001), soon made clear that if Australia were to become fully interoperable with the US then this would entail a dramatic investment in defence spending.[24] Richard Armitage, later Deputy Secretary of State (2001–2005) in the Bush Administration, reminded Australia of the reciprocity needed in these arrangements and that ANZUS was not alliance *à la carte*. In 1999, Armitage had stated that at some point Australia might need to choose whether it would support the US in defence of Taiwan and in which case it would need to be prepared militarily to do so.[25]

However, in 1996 the immediacy and necessity of the intensification of the relationship was not necessarily apparent to the US. What was apparent was that

---

22 David Robertson, 'Reciprocity and Protectionism in Australia's Trade Policy', *Agenda*, vol. 4, no. 2, 1997, pp. 138–140.

23 US Department of State, 'Australia–US Joint Security Declaration: A Strategic Partnership for the 21st Century', jointly released in Sydney, Australia, 27 July 1996, p. 1.

24 David Goldsworthy, 2001, p. 21.

25 Richard Armitage quoted in Peter Hartcher, 'Australia urged to take China conflict role', *Australian Financial Review*, 31 August 1999.

the Howard government's national interest framework was at variance with the Clinton Administration's rhetoric on the new security agenda, the environment, and human rights issues. Moreover, it was clear that both Clinton and Howard were, in demeanour at least, very different leaders. What is more, in seeking to implement its new proactive trade bilateralism in its relationship with the US, it was not apparent what would be the catalysts for success. The Howard government's culturally bound bargaining proposition failed to resonate with the US. Its attempt to utilise its special relationship with its alliance partner was not significant enough to overwhelm the potency of US domestic interests. Not surprisingly, in this asymmetric bilateral relationship with the US, Australia had little with which to exact leverage. What was needed was traction.

In 1998, Howard committed 110 SAS troops, 120 intelligence and medical specialists and two RAAF Boeing 707s, to the proposed US led, but UN backed, force to ensure Iraq complied with its UNSCOM agreements. This was a precursor of his support for US intervention in Iraq in 2003. Conflict was averted in this instance and Howard used the opportunity to assert that 'it was to the credit of the United States and her allies, such as Australia', that it was.[26] While Clinton thanked Australia for its supportive offers, it was the election of George W. Bush in 2000 that provided the opportunity for grip.

Deaths of nearly 3000 people in the terrorist assaults on the US in 2001 activated 'Operation Enduring Freedom' in Afghanistan. Australia invoked the ANZUS treaty and Howard stated Australia's commitment to assist the US. Australia deployed approximately 1,550 military personnel in Afghanistan. In defence procurement, Australia abandoned the usual selection procedure and signed onto the ambitious Lockheed Martin Joint Strike Fighter Project and the Raytheon submarine combat system development project. Further terrorist attacks in Bali in 2002 reinforced Howard's commitment to the mutual response in 'the war against terror'. Following this, in March 2003, Howard joined 'the coalition of the willing' by committing over 2,000 military personnel to the war in Iraq and assumed the role as a joint occupying force post war. Over the following two years, Australia's commitment was scaled back to 880 personnel. However, in February 2005, Howard committed another 450 troops to the Al Muthanna province in southern Iraq, and did not rule out further deployments. These troops replaced the 1,350 Dutch troops deployed in the province to provide security for Japanese engineers. Howard recounted that the request emanated from the Japanese who were restrained in the commitment of combat troops and was supported by British PM Tony Blair. There is no doubt, however, that Australia remained under sustained pressure from the US to re-engage significant numbers of combat troops in Iraq. By mid-2007, Australia's Operation Catalyst in Iraq comprised approximately 1,575 Australian Defence Force (ADF) personnel and its contribution to the International Security Assistance Force through Operation Slipper saw 970 members of the ADF serving in Afghanistan.

Given the benign security environment in the late 1990s it was also apparent that if the Howard government's first efforts at upgrading its relationship with the US

---

26 Dennis Shanahan and Don Greenlees, 'SAS Troops Play Waiting Game in Gulf', *The Australian*, 24 February 1998, p. 1.

were only superficial, and the results of its trade policy bilateralism by 2000 had not altered its $13.6 billion trade deficit with the US,[27] then the new US bent for military intervention would provide an opportunity for an Australian niche connection between trade and security policy.

Much has been written on alliance relations with many analysts pointing to the crucial benefits for Australia in access to US intelligence and defence science, but also to its enhancement of Australia's regional environment and status. However, the alliance relationship is not confined to security interaction as relations transpire through a diverse set of experiences. Precisely because of the value of the alliance, it is important for Australia to manage these relationships well. Precisely because it is an asymmetrical relationship, this is not an easy task for Australia. Consequently, my intention as stated is not to critique the alliance. It is, instead, to analyse *why* and *how* Australia chose to upgrade the alliance relationship with the US. Further, I consider the subsequent results through a range of sectors.

This book aims to provide a means by which the Howard government's interest in emphasising the US relationship can be understood. There is a scarcity of literature that explains the alliance behaviour of small states in remote locations. As I have described in the earlier sections of this chapter, I consider the government's role in mediating both the international and the domestic demands placed upon it and its resultant choice to foster its bilateral relationship with this superpower. I have also considered what might be achieved in this process. The government has made specific and rational choices within an Anglo cultural context. The introduction lays the foundation of this approach, while Chapter One builds on this base. In the first chapter, I argue that the Howard government has pursued this bilateral option because of the way it perceives threats. Interpreting threats for this government has been both materially and culturally informed. Therefore I have not employed a rational actor game-theoretic model, because the government's ability to choose rationally has been bounded by its perception of what choices the domestic electorate will tolerate. It is a threat mediation argument that incorporates both material and cultural motivations and considers these in response to both the international and domestic environment. It is not, then, the traditional and unitary assessment of threat perception as often discussed in Australian foreign policy literature. This chapter concludes with an analysis of the bargaining process employed.

Having explained the government's choices initially, I then present the case studies to show both the government's intentions and outcomes in upgrading the relationship. Chapters Two to Seven to demonstrate how the government managed to intensify the relationship with the US and, in the process, how it arbitrated between its international and domestic environments. I examine the specific effects of this bargaining process. In Chapter Two, I analyse the initial unsuccessful attempts of the government to exercise its special culturally informed bargaining tactic with the US to resolve the Howe leather and lamb disputes. This was the first indication that a trade policy built solely on a shared identity would not suffice in international bargaining. The Howard government may have expected that its cultural associations

27 In 1996, this figure was $12 billion. Source: Australian Trade Commission, Annual Reports, 1996–1999, Canberra.

with the US would determine policy but in the US, it was clearly inadequate in countering US domestic interests. Australia needed to exact more leverage if it was going to deliver to its domestic constituency.

Parallel to this in Chapter Three, the Prime Minister's exhortation that the US should provide troops to assist its long time ally, Australia, in restoring peace in East Timor was met initially with a cool response from the Clinton Administration. Nevertheless, the political and economic leverage that the US did apply in persuading Indonesia to allow an Australian-led UN force into Timor reinforced the importance of a culturally close but, more importantly, materially powerful friend – caveats notwithstanding.

I continue with this siren call of the US in two industrial sectors. The first of these, in Chapter Four, examines a completely different and not much discussed sector: biotechnology. Through this chapter, I explore the structural power of the US, not only with its availability of capital and market lure, but also in its ability to impose preferences upon Australian policy. It is here that the asymmetrical bargaining power not just of the government but also of transnational actors is considered. Here the Australian government has the reverse and difficult task of managing the power of the US transnationals in the international arena together with the Australian population's need for affordable, quality health care. This is coupled with the desirability of fostering a sustainable, vibrant, knowledge-based economy where the US can play a vital role. Part of this discussion concerns bilateral intellectual property negotiations. This chapter highlights some of these issues that ultimately may become some of the most contentious long-term issues in the prospective Australia–US Free Trade Agreement (AUSFTA). I conclude with an investigation of some of the indications of the Australian government's inclination to follow the US *modus operandi* in multilateral forums.

Chapter Five reveals how the government achieved much greater intimacy with the US through Australia's *Collins* class submarine project. Here is an example of the difficulties governments encounter in the endeavour to mediate sometimes contradictory pressures. I explore how a remarkable naval project, earmarked initially to develop an independent shipbuilding industry, was politicised in the domestic arena to create both a supposed 'messianic' role for the Coalition and a US function in 'resuscitating' the venture. It remained, nonetheless, that the *Collins* submarines were an acknowledged highly desirable technological and force structure asset both for Australia and for the US Navy to acquire. The government and some sections of the Australian Navy aspired to lock into the larger parent force and the US snaffled the offer. Australia turned quickly to US assistance, readily exchanging shipbuilding independence for alliance reassurance.

Chapter Six examines the government's motivations for supporting the US in military intervention in both Afghanistan and Iraq. Despite the government's initial claims that its military deployment in regions outside Australia's immediate area of interest was to rid Iraq of weapons of mass destruction, alliance relations and the protection of its lucrative wheat trade with Iraq eventually surfaced as key issues in its decision-making.

Through Chapters Seven and Eight, I consider whether government support for US security aims produced better results in the trade relationship. These two chapters also demonstrate how a change of President and administration in the US can significantly affect relations for Australia. Chapter Seven examines the initial imposition of steel tariffs by the US administration and the Australian government's efforts to use its US relationship to reduce these for Australia. Once again, the power of the US domestic constituency is revealed as integral in the construction of US policy. While the role of the Australian transnational BHP Billiton is shown to be crucial in ameliorating the tariff impact upon Australia, the government was keen to display to its constituents the value and responsiveness of its cultivated alliance friendship. Chapter Eight extends this with an examination of both parties' motivations for the Australia–US Free Trade Agreement (AUSFTA). In particular, I consider the overlay of security and trade links through the proposal. I examine whether the government's support for US military intervention in Afghanistan, the 'War on Terror', but, more significantly, the War in Iraq not only tightened the binding ties but also delivered on trade outcomes. Thus, I consider whether this interpretation of threat and bilateral strategic choice, oriented to produce domestic economic outcomes, has been successful. If, toward the end of 2003, it may be said that the US was becoming increasingly dissatisfied with Australia's lesser role in Iraq, what then would be politically persuasive in the US to complete the FTA deal? At this point, I reconsider the coalescing power of US commercial interests in providing the impetus to overcome the US agricultural lobby's opposition to any concessions. So I return to the issue of intellectual property, as examined in the biotechnology chapter, but also of the commercial appeal to US manufacturers and investors as providing the credible capital for US interest in the deal. Ultimately, however, an assessment of the political value of the alliance for the government provides an understanding of the government's preparedness to sign a deal that was much less profitable than anticipated.

To what end, then? The Howard government constructed foreign and trade policy through the arbitration of international and domestic demands. By prioritising the domestic settings, its deployment of a bilateral upgrading of its US ties initially mandated a trade bargaining that was culturally bound. This was initially unsuccessful however. Guided by traditional assumptions about the world, nonetheless, the government persisted with this approach, eventually securing an intersection of trade and security policy that provided greater traction in alliance relations. Undoubtedly, this policy has been assisted by the synchronisation of actors in alliance affairs, but it has also been aided by the structural fragility of international institutions and processes during this period. Ultimately, however, it remains that the success of bilateralism as a strategy with the US and the delivery of successful outcomes for Australia rests on a convergence with US domestic interests.

Chapter 1

Integrated Threat Perception and the Intensification of the US Alliance

In 1996, the Howard government instituted a policy that gave precedence to a bilateral approach in foreign diplomacy that prioritised the US. Underlying this bilateral predilection for the Coalition were its assumptions about global relationships that were at once both material and cultural in orientation.[1] By pursuing a policy that deployed both material and cultural capital, the Coalition fostered an approach that resonated on inherited and conservative security preconceptions within the Australian electorate. Accomplishment of this for the Coalition resulted in a reaffirmation of the centrality of the US alliance in both foreign and security policy.

Hence, one of the Coalition's pre-election themes (while acknowledging its regional cooperation) was to upgrade the alliance. Howard later confirmed:

> The maintenance of strong bilateral relations remains a cornerstone of this government's foreign policy approach...The relationship we have with the US is the most important we have with any single country...[t]his is not only because of the strategic, economic and diplomatic power of the US. But of equal, if not more significance, are the values and aspirations we share.[2]

What, then, are the origins of this Coalition strategy? What is the theoretical and historical context that has informed this convergence of security and trade policy focus upon the United States and the parallel emphasis on a bilateral approach as the vehicle by which to enact these relations? Furthermore, under what conditions is this asymmetric bilateralism likely to be successful? In responding to the demands inherent in these questions it is my intention here to analyse one set of alliance relations between states. These relations underpin the Howard government's approach to foreign and trade policy and have been central to the development of policy in this period for Australia.

Solving these puzzles requires a specific exploration of the material factors in alliance considerations and also a discussion of the historical, cultural, and domestic explanations. The first of these is the 'dependent ally' thesis. Pervasive in Australian foreign policy literature is the understanding that Australia has traditionally been dependent upon a powerful patron. This is at once an historic and geographic legacy. However, while it embodies explanatory power in clarifying the origins of

---

1 Chris Reus-Smit, 'Lost at Sea: Australia in the Turbulence of World Politics', *Working Paper*, 2002/4, Department of International Relations, RSPAS, ANU, July 2002, p. 3.

2 John Howard, 'Australia's International Relations – Ready for the Future', *Address to the Menzies Research Centre*, Canberra, 22 August 2001.

the strategic importance of the US for Australia, it is not illuminating enough, in this instance, of the change in emphasis between the Hawke/Keating and Howard governments. A focus solely on Australia's path dependence does not adequately explain Australia's evolution as a state, nor the government's motivations.

Second, recent thinking by international affairs scholars emphasises the significance of culture and identity. An analysis of culture and identity is important in orienting the Howard government's security and trade policy to the US, yet as a total explanation, the omission of material and strategic dynamics renders it incomplete. This may provide some insights into why the Coalition deemed that its solution to its trade disputes could turn solely on a cultural axis. Third, domestic electoral considerations play some role in determining actors' choice of policy. Most certainly, John Howard repudiated the Keating endeavour to lead Australia to a new understanding of the necessity for regional engagement. Sensitive to the resistance of the electorate to dramatic change, Howard offered solace in the familiar. Yet, once again, this can only be part of the story.

To explain sufficiently the need to prioritise an asymmetrical bilateral alliance, I argue that this Howard government policy solution is based on managing perceptions of threat, both international and domestic. Thus, as stated in the introduction, the analysis ranges over three levels, with the government mediating the international and domestic. My argument incorporates an understanding of the exigencies of Australia's vulnerabilities, its past relations and inherited identity. It is informed by both material and cultural dynamics. At the conclusion of this chapter, however, I consider the difficulties of a bargaining position that is culturally enclosed or that which rests solely on a cultural dimension.

Prior to this, an explanation for my focus on aspects of the alliance security debate is necessary. A study of the security landscape is crucial to the discussion as the Howard government utilised the alliance relationship as the cornerstone for the management of the interplay between its international and domestic situation. Its bilateral relationship upgrade was channeled along the preferred conduit of its alliance relations. Furthermore, in the past, Australian governments have typically allowed the security agenda to dominate relations with the US. Contentious trade issues have traditionally been subordinated to the high politics of the security realm. When the first Howard government pursued this policy, its trade outcomes with the US were dismal. Thus, in its second term the government sought to utilise the perceived strength of its alliance security relations to either enhance trade outcomes or to impose alliance preferences on defence projects and purchasing. Trade had been contextualised by the security environment and to some extent driven by it.

Alliances and Threat Perception: An Integrated Approach

The Howard government's choice of an upgraded asymmetrical bilateral alliance is best understood through a conceptualisation of threat perception that also deploys the most appropriate characteristics of the dependent ally thesis, the cultural connections and the domestic considerations. The dependent ally legacy, the cultural orientation and the domestic responsiveness are all factors that are incorporated into a model that places the government as mediator of perceived threats from above and below. These perceptions of threats and the government's proposed solution are also culturally informed. My analysis of the government's behaviour, however, is primarily materially premised and presumes rational behaviour within a culturally contextualised environment.

As the discussion in the introduction explains, the exigencies of Australia's size and geography make Australians much more concerned about traditional security threats in their regional environment. More recently for the Howard government, international threats have emanated from the right and left of the political spectrum. They have concerned terrorist assaults, China's great power intentions, Pacific island state weakness, international institutional fragility, Australia's exposure in the international financial economy, maintaining growth in a resources based economy, the effects of the Asian financial crisis, regional instability and a consequent increase in new security issues. How these threats could be managed has also been affected by the need to deal with threats from below. These have included both the desire for international independent activity from some sections of the population and the domestic electorate's wont to have its immediate concerns in employment and prosperity, healthcare, and education met.

By prioritising these domestic concerns of international origin and placing them in a cultural framework, the government could reasonably choose a bilateral relationship with a powerful US. More specifically, this perception of threat was used in the design of this policy outcome. Defined simply, threats are 'an anticipation of harm', even where the perceived opponent does not intend harm. This perception may incorporate 'the loss of something of value, such as territory and population, restriction of sovereignty, economic assets, and political constitution.'[3] Misperception of threat, also, is a common occurrence in international affairs.[4]

While there has been much discussion on the nature of threat perception, two scholars, Glenn Synder and Stephen Walt, link these perceptions to the formation of alliances, which is at the heart of the Australia–US discussion here. Most definitions of alliances are akin to the 'formal or informal commitment for security cooperation between two or more states...the defining feature of any alliance is a commitment for mutual military support against some external actor(s) in some specified set of circumstances'. As such, they are exclusive arrangements, with states committed militarily to support each other against another in specific circumstances.[5]

Early assessments of alliances were based on materialist calculations of costs and benefits with military power cited as the defining criterion in the assessment. However, particularly as the ANZUS Alliance was constructed at the conclusion of Japanese aggression in the Pacific War and the onset of the Cold War, and has endured for some considerable time, Stephen Walt's contention that greater explanatory power

3 Klaus Knorr (ed.), *Historical Dimensions of National Security Problems*, University of Kansas, Lawrence, 1976, p. 78.

4 Robert Jervis, *Perception and Misperception in International Politics*, Princeton University Press, Princeton, 1976.

5 Stephen M. Walt, 'Why Alliances Endure or Collapse', *Survival*, no. 1, Spring, 1997, pp. 157–58.

can be generated by the introduction of threat perception as the focus of analysis, rather than power per se, is more useful. Although it may be noted that the US signed the ANZUS pact to reciprocate Australia's signature of the Japanese Peace Treaty, it has more generally been understood that the ANZUS Treaty acts as Australia's hedge position against (diplomatically) unspecified threats to its security. As Foreign Minister Downer noted in August 1999, 'ANZUS continues to serve as an effective deterrent against attack on Australia'.[6] He reiterated in 2001 that:

> from the outset, ANZUS was conceived as a security pact flexible enough to be relevant to a range of challenges. Initially, this was Australia's concern to be protected against the threat of a militarily resurgent Japan. Then, in the Cold War, it was protection against the threat of Communist expansion.[7]

In sum, this conceptualisation of Australia's position is reflective of the 'security dilemma' where no state can be sure that another's intent is either defensive or offensive.[8] Arguably, states ally to maximise their security for one of two reasons. Either they act to balance against the threat, or bandwagon with the threat itself, thus removing the threat for aggression. Moreover, in the balancing and bandwagoning process in the Middle East, regional states were less likely to seek security with each other. Instead they were much more inclined to seek superpower assistance. Power capabilities and geography suggest that not only do superpowers offer exceptional power capacity, but if the threatened state were to balance with another in their region, then potentially their neighbour would become too strong.[9]

In grappling with the determinants of location and ideology, Walt contended that regional states are always more concerned with the threat posed by geographically proximate powers, rather than the strongest powers in the international system and that these threats invariably produce balancing behaviour. Attributing this to a function of size, Walt suggested that regional states were concerned with their immediate interests and were unable to vitally affect the global balance, so they only ally with those most *willing* to assist them.[10] In WWII as the US became involved, it was more likely to assist Australia. And in the Vietnam conflict, for the US, the global balance was significant, but for Australia, the 'loss' of South Vietnam was an immediate regional threat. It remained then, that in these joint conflicts, US interests coincided with Australia's.[11]

---

6 Alexander Downer, 'Australia and the United States: Old Friends and New Priorities', *Speech by the Hon Alexander Downer MP, Minister for Foreign Affairs, to the American Chamber of Commerce*, Sydney, 5 August 1999.

7 Alexander Downer, 'The Australia–United States Alliance and East Asian Security', *Speech at the University of Sydney conference*, Sydney, 29 June 2001, p. 3.

8 Glenn H. Snyder, 'The Security Dilemma in Alliance Politics', *World Politics*, vol. 36, no. 4, July 1984, p. 461.

9 Stephen M. Walt, *The Origins of Alliances*, Cornell University Press, Ithaca, 1987, p. 266. Principally the work entails a discussion of Middle East politics from 1955 to 1979.

10 Stephen M. Walt, 1987, p. 162 (my italics).

11 Stephen M. Walt, 1987, pp. 214–17.

The Australia–US alliance has survived and the government has given it precedence not only because threat perception survived, but also because this was supplemented by a preference for a culturally similar ally and an intent that it should resonate in the domestic political environment. For the US, the collapse of the USSR in 1990 wiped clean one of the principal sources of threat, but this did little to alter the sources of Australia's regional threat perception. As a consequence, the US alliance became further entrenched as a pillar of Australian foreign policy. Even when Australia chose to pursue a more independent defence policy in the late 1980s and reorient itself to its immediate regional concerns, it was still couched within the alliance framework. Defence papers gave priority to the defence of Australia and its northern littorals. The sea air gap through the island chains of the Solomon Islands, Papua New Guinea, Irian Jaya, and the Indonesian archipelago assumed greater significance than the more remote concerns of its larger allies. Nevertheless, Defence Minister Beazley's 'self-reliance within alliance' theme, demonstrated that even Australia's enthusiasm for a more independent posture would still be couched under the auspices of larger power capabilities. It was argued too that despite the endeavours to establish more cooperative security regimes, including the promotion of the ASEAN Regional Forum within the region by Gareth Evans and his department, the defence establishment was still captive of the 'old-style realist' thinking.[12] Moreover, in 1993 the aim of the Defence Department's *Strategic Review* was for the establishment of a 'strategic partnership' with Southeast Asia to 'support a continued commitment by the United States to the region'.[13]

Later in the 1990s, a more pessimistic assessment of regional danger asserted itself. Australia's 1994 Defence White Paper reiterated the dynamic nature of regional security and the need for continued vigilance. However, the crucial difference here was that Keating sought assiduously to do this with Asia. In 1993, the Keating government announced that '(m)ore than with any other regional nation, a sound strategic relationship with Indonesia does most for Australia's security'. The subsequent negotiation of the Agreement to Maintain Security with Indonesia, in addition to its traditional partner, testified to this.[14] While judgement remained reserved on the substance of these policies, under the Howard government,

> Australia's defence policy-makers [were] seeking a strategic partnership only with Asia, they continue[d] to stress the importance of military deterrence, they remain[ed] concerned over the possible intentions and actions of northeast Asian powers such as China.[15]

---

12 Richard Higgott and Kim Richard Nossal, 'Australia and the search for a security community in the 1990s', in Emanuel Adler and David Barnett, *Security Communities*, Cambridge University Press, Cambridge, 1998, p. 275.

13 Department of Defence, *Strategic Review*, Australian Government Publishing Service, Canberra, 1993, pp. 22–23.

14 Paul Keating, *Engagement*, Macmillan, Sydney, 2000, pp. 141–146 and 156–57.

15 Graeme Cheeseman, 'Australia: The White Experience of Fear and Dependence', in Ken Booth and Russell Trood (eds) *Strategic Cultures in the Asia–Pacific Region*, Basingstoke, Macmillan, 1999, pp. 290–91.

Even prior to 2001, it was judged that defence cooperation rather than cooperative security was the Howard government's preference.[16] The perception of threat was thus significant in the determination of behaviour.

The Howard government's perception of local threats and consequent response to affirm alliance relations intersected with US ambitions, and was given much greater emphasis by al-Qaeda's terrorist attacks in 2001. In Chapter Six, I explain that one of Howard's primary motivations for deploying military forces in Iraq and Afghanistan concerned the maintenance of alliance relations.

Disintegration of the USSR had allowed for a redefinition of US interests globally and locally, including a greater focus in East Asia. With the economic rise of the region, attendant increases in military expenditure and an expectation that at some point China would seek to reassert its great power status, the US became reoriented to its Pacific relations. Through the maintenance of its Pacific alliances, the US managed its interest in the region. Warren Christopher's description of Australia as the 'southern anchor' of US strategic policy in Asia remains illustrative of this instrument.[17] The US too, had valuable military intelligence interests in Australia to maintain. In later years the Bush Administration declared that China was its strategic competitor, not partner. At once this dismissed the Clinton Administration's endeavours to 'engage' with China as a 'partner'. US threat perception was then refocused within the region. The 1996 Sydney Statement affirmed US commitment to the region. However, with the change in Administration in 2000, US policy had toughened. Much had been made of the US neoconservative ascendancy in this Bush Administration, especially since the terrorist assault on New York and Washington. With this alteration of the global security environment, which included the US response through Afghanistan and Iraq, the US preference for unilateralism tested the strength of the international security institutions. For a while, exceptionalism in the US asserted its supremacy and the US undertook military activities that would only require the assistance of those who would support its ambitions. Australia, newly alert to the threats posed within the region and beyond, and of the leverage of US might as evidenced in the East Timor crisis, was keen to affirm its relationship with the US. Australia remained as one of the few countries which had deployed troops in both the Afghanistan and Iraq operations. Moreover, through the 2003 and 2007 *Defence Updates* the government eventually exerted its intent to refocus the ADF to become a US global partner. It was also eager to display its responsiveness to a 'terrorist crisis' and continue to engage middle Australia. So, in the reorientation to the US, the Australian government acted upon its understanding that the US, with its unrivalled military capability, would be integral to the provision of security.

16 Graeme Cheeseman, 1999, pp. 290–91.

17 Warren Christopher, 'The US and Australia meet the challenges of the new millennium', speech by US Secretary of State, transcript, 29 July 1996, p. 1.

The 'Dependent Ally' Inheritance[18]

While the primary driver for the government's alliance upgrade was related to its material threat assessments, any explanation of the government's motivation must also include an historical component. The geostrategic bequest for Australian governments reveals that Australia's need for a powerful patron has been pervasive in its history. Because of the United States' place in Australia's historical and cultural legacy, it would also be an ideal relationship with which to mediate the government's perception of threats both from above and below.

Despite the Australian landmass being chosen in 1788 because it was a location that was geographically remote from Britain, the white settlers in Australia were acutely conscious of the alien nature of the indigenous Pacific and Asian environment. However, with its British heritage, Australia's foreign policy concerns within the region were duly affected by imperial foes in the context of the prevailing international system. Australia thus functioned as an imperial strategic base in the Pacific and as a port *en route* to Asia. But this tripartite relationship was to be problematic for Australia. Australia's proximity to Asia for trade purposes and eventually its acquired regional expertise was of benefit to both the UK and the US. Ironically, throughout its history, part of Australia's value to its hegemonic patrons was its place in the region. As former PM Gough Whitlam later interpreted Australia's relationship with the United States:

> (t)he United States alliance is essential. Co-operation with the United States must be maintained… More than any other country in the area Australia is able and bound to interpret the United States to the countries of the region and to interpret those countries to the United States. [19]

Yet this role would require a confidence to step beyond the familiar and overcome the perception of threat the region traditionally embodied for it.

By Federation, emerging and increasingly mobile powers in Asia had intensified concerns in Australia. Geopolitical fears with origins in race and religion, coupled with the need for Australian military security as a response were prevalent in Australia. Both a strategically uncertain and culturally unfamiliar environment played to a dependency mentality. Security was sought in an English-speaking world with cultural ties to its Anglo heritage. Hence, Australia's support of both British and then US security aims was an endeavour to create security from the miasma of ambiguity. Its manifestation was revealed in the implementation of the White Australia Policy and also evidenced in Australia's militaristic history that supported either Britain or the US through distant forays and through its implementation of 'Empire cooperation' in 1946, 'forward defence' and later its 'defence in depth' policies. For Australia

---

18 For an analysis from the left see Joseph A. Camilleri, *Australian–US Relations: The Web of Dependence*, Macmillan, South Melbourne, 1980, and the right in Coral Bell, *Dependent Ally: A Study in Australian Foreign Policy*, second edition, Allen and Unwin in association with the Department of International Relations, RSPAS, ANU, Canberra, 1988.

19 Gough Whitlam, 'Australia – Base or Bridge?', Evatt Memorial Lecture, Sydney University, Sydney, 1966.

its historical ties and cultural click with Britain and then its connections with the US as an English-speaking Western democracy, were synonymous with the world's hegemonic powers in both the nineteenth and twentieth centuries. So intimate was this relationship at the conclusion of World War Two that the military intelligence relationship was formalised with other settler states of Anglo origin in the UKUSA agreement in 1948.[20]

Structural determinants of great power status and demise, however, were integral to Britain's inability to remain a willing and effective ally for Australia. So, crucial to Australia's motivations in seeking US support in the 1940s was US power in balancing against the Japanese in the Pacific theatre. Curtin's famous entreaty to the US in 1941 that Australia was 'looking to America' was born out of Australia's understanding that only the US possessed the capability to assist in Australia's defence. With the establishment of the ANZUS Alliance at a later time, Australia felt that it had secured the greater likelihood of its ally's response should it be involved in military conflict. For Percy Spender, Menzies' foreign minister who drove the ANZUS pact, the treaty:

> has been and remains the essential pillar of Australia's security. It is a treaty which accords while it endures the protective shield of the mightiest power in the world against any armed attack upon our country no matter from what nation any armed attack may come.[21]

Nevertheless, this agreement has given rise to much debate. It has exacerbated the pressure for Australia to manage the security-autonomy trade-off. In the past, poor management of any alliance may have also forced members to countenance either of the twin ruins of abandonment or entrapment,[22] Australia's fears of abandonment have precipitated a sustained effort to demonstrate allegiance and succour for its benefactors' grander strategies: a campaign designed to ensure that Australia's sponsors remain willing allies. Hence Australia assiduously pursued policy to aid both Britain initially, then the US, in military adventures with a concurrent public campaign to link Australia's interests with those of its benefactor. While for Australia and the US the operations throughout Asia and further afield were a realisation of the policies of mutual reliance and forward defence, military integration was further entrenched with the establishment of the US intelligence collection bases, (later termed the 'Joint Facilities'), at Pine Gap, Northwest Cape and Nurrungar. Although the latter two are now defunct, Pine Gap retains a crucial role in the US global strategic system.

This is only part of the story, however. If Australia was interested in a pact with the US, the United States was also advantaged by the opportunity to impose security architecture on the Pacific with itself at its centre. The San Francisco security treaty system of formal alliances signed in 1951 declared US Pacific security arrangements and ensured that smaller powers did not adopt a posture of neutrality in the

---

20 Jeffrey T. Richelson and Desmond Ball, *The Ties that Bind: Intelligence Cooperation Between the UKUSA Countries*, second edition, Allen and Unwin, North Sydney, 1990.

21 Percy Spender, *Exercises in Diplomacy*, Sydney University Press, Sydney, 1969, p. 185.

22 Glenn H. Snyder, 1997, pp. 180–85.

bigger superpower contest. The leverage to be executed by the US in the bilateral relationships was greater than could be achieved through any multilateral system. As individuals kept on separate terms, the allies were unable to match the power of the US in negotiations. Moreover, once these security conduits were established, then the trade relationships could slot propitiously into the grooves. With the US recording significant trade deficits with many other East Asian countries, a US trade policy in the latter part of the twentieth century of aggressive unilateralism utilised the entrenched bilateral channels in the attempt to redress this imbalance.

Central to the dependent ally thesis too is the maintenance of the ally's support in the absence of an alternative. A state's dependence on the alliance turns on 'the opportunity cost of terminating it'. Thus, the fewer the alternatives in either external or internal replacement sources, the more likely an ally will be dependent. In arguing from a rational choice perspective, it can be contended that weak states may be prepared to sacrifice autonomy for security and that more powerful states can utilise alliances to shape the behaviour of allies. [23]

Despite the dependent ally need to maintain continuity, there have also been counter-cyclical deviations.[24] And these deviations suggest the inadequacies of the dependent ally thesis as a sole explanation for the Howard government's emphasis on the US. These included: US suspicions of Australia's protection of Soviet spies in the early part of the Cold War, SEATO's collapse after the crisis in Laos, the US disinterest in consulting or advising Canberra of revisions to its policy in Vietnam, Kennedy's rejection of Australia's calls for assistance over West New Guinea, Whitlam's disagreements with the bombing of Cambodia, following Nixon's Guam Doctrine. Minister for External Affairs, Gordon Freeth's subsequent and supposed 'experiment' with a review of security in Asia, Malcolm Fraser's protracted attempts to extend the application of ANZUS to the Indian Ocean in 1977, suggestions of agitations in intelligence relations in November 1975, and New Zealand's ANZUS crisis added to the countervailing events. Hawke's refusal to allow the US permission to test the MX missiles, the establishment of the Treaty of Raratonga in 1985 to form a nuclear free zone in the Pacific, the Pacific Fisheries Treaty in 1986, and Gareth Evans' proposals for a regional security forum, all created some angst in the Canberra–Washington alliance.

If economic issues, such as the size of the trade deficit, the implementation of subsidies for US farmers through a series of Farm Bills, US competitive behaviour in third country markets, US contrary negotiation practices in GATT/WTO trade rounds, the exclusionary nature of NAFTA, aggressive unilateralism in Asia, were ever to create discord within Australia, the predominant response of successive governments has been to attempt to subjugate them to the defence priorities. Not only was it US public practice to separate defence and trade issues in either ANZUS, or later, AUSMIN discussions, this also reflected Australian government interests.

---

23 As argued in Robert O. Keohane, 'The Big Influence of Small Allies', *Foreign Policy*, no. 2, Spring, 1971.

24 Richard Leaver, 'Patterns of dependence in post-war Australian foreign policy', in Richard Leaver and Dave Cox (eds), *Middling, Meddling, Muddling: Issues in Australian Foreign Policy*, Allen and Unwin, 1997, pp. 69–90.

This practice has not always been successful, however; witness the eruptions of the Australian rural lobby in publicising the inequities of their position, including demonstrations during the George H. Bush visit in the early 1990s.

While the legacy of the dependent ally which prefaces entrapment over abandonment has often been the story of Australia–US relations, it is incomplete without a basis in the material assessments as discussed. The historical analysis may provide a partial account for the strategic importance of the US for Australia and Australia's historical dependence upon a greater power, but it does not offer motivations for change. It has not accounted for the counter-cyclical pattern in post-war Australia–US relations. All variations in behaviour are lost under the umbrella of dependence. There are, however, other factors that need to be incorporated into a comprehensive explanation of the Howard government's interest in this asymmetrical alliance.

Ideas of Culture and Identity in Alliance Construction and Survival

At the opening of the Asian Leaders' Forum in Beijing in April 2000, Foreign Minister Alexander Downer indicated that leaders should consider the relevance of both practical or economic regionalism and cultural regionalism to Australia. Cultural regionalism, for the Foreign Minister, was 'a regionalism which is built on common ties of history, of mutual cultural identity. One might broadly describe them as emotional links.'[25] Clearly by making this distinction here, Downer implied that while Australia may connect in practical ways with Asia, it was culturally remote. This view, then, would inform the government's thinking on how it could relate to its regional neighbours. Juxtaposed against the flavour of this perception stands the language of Australia's relationship with the United States. Certainly, this language has been consistently awash with the 'shared' nature of the relationship. Speaking to the Asia Society in Sydney in the late 1990s, Madeleine Albright affirmed that in the Asia–Pacific region, 'there is no better example of cooperation built on shared values and interests than the relationship between the United States and Australia'.[26]

Clearly, the inclusion of identity and culture assists in any understanding of why Howard chose to pursue the US relationship with such vigour. Over the past two decades, some scholars have endeavoured to add culture to the understanding of the origins and sustainability of alliance structures. A number of the realists studying alliances acknowledged but did not explore the relevance and importance of cultural or ideological components. Glenn Snyder accepted that anxieties in relation to the outcomes of abandonment or entrapment were dependent upon 'statesmen's perceptions'. Moreover, Snyder claimed that although alignment choice was theoretically indeterminate, it was still possible that this could be mediated by historical 'interests, conflicts and affinities and the domestic political composition of

25 Alexander Downer, *Opening Speech at the Asian Leaders' Forum*, Beijing, 23 April 2000.

26 Madeleine Albright, 'US–Australia ties built on shared values, interests', Address to the Australasia Centre of the Asia Society, Sydney Opera House, US Department of State transcript, 1998.

states'.[27] For Thomas Risse-Kappen, however, this failure in exploration amounted to the indeterminacy of realism in explaining the origins of alliances. Both Risse-Kappen and Michael Barnett endeavoured to add to the bank of knowledge explaining how alliances could operate. Risse-Kappen judged that threat perceptions did not result solely from power structure assessments. Actors were able to make deductions about the behaviour of others through analysis of identity. Given that the deployment of material force was regarded as illegitimate, reference to the constraints of domestic politics and institutions was commonplace in negotiations between allies.[28] In this model, the inter-ally decision-making process was largely informed by the norms of democracy and the identity of the state actors involved. Despite Barnett's claims that 'cultural capital' not 'military capability' was predominant in interstate relations in the Middle East, he nevertheless asserted his intention not to claim the primacy of identity politics, but instead to state that each assumes a different causal weight at different times in history.[29] This body of scholarly literature, then, advances the role of ideas in alliance formation.

Taking the failure of international relations theory to predict the demise of the Cold War as his point of departure, Peter Katzenstein argued that neorealism and rationalism, in their ultimate acceptance of the exogenous factors and the given nature of states' interests, obviated any opportunity for prediction in the state system. Thus an endogenous examination of social determinants, both the cultural-institutional context of the state and its collective identity, were essential to the understanding of national security. As such, Katzenstein's research departed from Walt's efforts to establish which material factors predominated in the quest for national security, to an analysis of the influence of culture in actors' definitions of their interests.[30] This in itself is an interesting departure from Katzenstein's earlier work – in particular, his writing on the behaviour of small states in world markets was essentially a state-focused materialist foray.[31]

Australia sought to institutionalise its relationship with the US in the post war ANZUS alliance. Extensive bureaucratic networks constructed to oversee military planning and procurement, in addition to the Track II Australia–American Dialogue discussions, establish and entrench personal networks that can serve to preserve the relationship. William Tow and Henry Albinski argue that this serves a normative role in preserving the relationship and further that that institutions can act to overcome a state's *ad hoc* responses to threat and thus temper regional instability resultant from reactive behaviour. Yet Tow and Albinski too, qualified their commentary on the

27 Glenn H. Snyder, 'The Security Dilemma in Alliance Politics', pp. 308 and 466.

28 Thomas Risse-Kappen, 'Collective Identity in a Democratic Community', in Peter J. Katzenstein (ed.), *The Culture of National Security: Norms and Identity in World Politics*, Columbia University Press, New York, 1996, pp. 367–69.

29 Michael N. Barnett, 'Identity and Alliances in the Middle East', in Peter J. Katzenstein (ed.), *The Culture of National Security: Norms and Identity in World Politics*, pp. 400–32.

30 Peter J. Katzenstein, 'Introduction: Alternative Perspectives on National Security', Peter J. Katzenstein (ed.), *The Culture of National Security: Norms and Identity in World Politics*, pp. 1–32.

31 Peter J. Katzenstein, *Small States in World Markets: Industrial Policy in Europe*, Cornell Studies in Political Economy, Ithaca, reprinted edition, 1997.

normative role for the ANZUS alliance by writing that even though the institution can act to shape the nature of the relationship, '(w)hat both Australia and America do as international security actors is driven by their own calculations of self-interest.'[32]

There is no doubt that the Anglo-Western cultural and ideological connection with the US has entrenched relations with Australia. However, while it can be argued that the role of pluralist liberal norms may reinforce Australia's relationship with the US, it could not be said that this argument of the role of pluralistic liberal democracies and collective identities can be applicable to the broader US alliance system in the Pacific. Even though the Japan–US security arrangements are particularly institutionalised, the sense of shared identities is inapplicable. This is also relevant for other US bilateral alliances in the Pacific.

Despite the cultural and ideological connections, the US departed company from Australia in the West New Guinea crisis in the 1960s. Percy Spender, Minister for External Affairs, expressed his concerns in 1950 that after the Dutch departure, the Indonesians were organising to assume control of West New Guinea despite their racial separateness.[33] Spender was also vitally concerned that a stable New Guinea was crucial to Australia's security and was fearful both of the Sukarno regime and communist control of territory to Australia's north. President Kennedy refused Menzies' requests for US support to confront the Indonesians in West New Guinea in 1962–63. US and Australian interests clearly diverged on this issue. Menzies was persuaded that Indonesia, a crucial geostrategic state to the US, should be allowed to pursue its foreign policy aims in West New Guinea even though they were contrary to Australia's. The question remains then of the application of these arguments outside arenas of geostrategic import.

Instrumental in its evolution to relations between states was Alexander Wendt's system level argument that social structures played an integral role in shaping both identities and interests in addition to behaviour. Taking the middle ground, Wendt consequently stated that:

> international politics is in part about acting on material incentives in given anarchic worlds. However, it is also about the reproduction and transformation – intersubjective dynamics at both the domestic and systemic levels – of the identities and interests through which those incentives and world are created.[34]

In the international system, Wendt endeavoured to explain that these social structures comprised shared knowledge, material capability and practice. Worth pursuing in the context of this argument is his concept of shared knowledge as a digest of past relations with other states. Previous relations of both cooperation and conflict are influential in determining a state's relations with others. For example, Wendt asks

---

32 William Tow and Henry Albinski, 'ANZUS – Alive and Well after Fifty Years,' *Australian Journal of Politics and History*, vol. 48, no. 2, 2002, pp. 171–72.

33 Percy Spender, Minister for External Affairs, The Hague statement, 29 August 1950, in Neville Meaney, *Australia and the World: A Documentary History from the 1870s to the 1970s*, Longman Cheshire, Melbourne, 1988, pp. 639–40.

34 Alexander Wendt, 'Collective Identity Formation and the International State', *American Political Science Review*, vol. 88, no. 2, June 1994, pp. 384–96.

why the small arsenal of North Korean nuclear weapons was more threatening to the US than the hundreds of UK missiles. A shared past of pacific relations between the US and UK functioned to ensure that the other's material capability was not perceived in a menacing fashion. Wendt argued then that past relations were clearly determinants of both threat perception and alliance relations. Furthermore, Wendt argued that this process became self-fulfilling as policy makers implemented the beliefs held by the community. Social structures, then, were often regenerative.[35] In the Australian context, the historical legacy discussed in the dependent ally section of this chapter has moulded the current social structures.

These past relations have been significant in the formation of a strategic culture in Australia. In a discerning documentation of the development of Australia's strategic culture, Graeme Cheeseman argued, however, that association with Britain, then the US, was not just a sustained ploy to ensure the hegemon's loyalty. It was also simultaneously an attempt by Australian defence and foreign policy makers to prefer to operate within larger structures. Affirmation of Australia's sense of 'place' in the international system then becomes part of this. Moreover, this has been compounded historically at times by Australia's inflated sense of its importance to its great and powerful friends.[36]

From 1996 on, it was clear that the Australian government was interested in utilising both its inherited and strategic culture to realise its objectives not only on the security agenda, but also in the trade relationship. Wendt had argued that past relations were determinants of threat perception, mediated alliance behaviour and predisposed allies to patience and restraint. This may be so, but the question for Australia remained whether it would actively deliver on the outcomes so consciously sought and stated by the Coalition. More specifically, though it was clear that the old security culture was undergoing a resurgence in Australia, how would this renewal interact with trade and industry issues, and could the Coalition's expectations of reciprocity be met?

A consideration of culture in any examination of threat perception, subsequent alliance construction and eventual bargaining in the relationship is vital. However, it is clear that this must be constructed upon a study of the material and strategic factors in the relationship.

Domestic Concerns

The final factor for consideration in any explanation of the government's preferences was that of its domestic concerns. Writing in the late 1990s, Graeme Cheeseman saw that the possibilities for cooperative, inclusive policy-making would be dependent upon the ability of the government and population to cast aside the pervasive dominant

35 Alexander Wendt, 'Constructing International Politics', *International Security*, vol. 20, no. 1, Summer 1995, pp. 71–74.

36 As David Day argues in, *The Great Betrayal: Britain, Australia & the Onset of the Pacific War 1939–42*, Angus and Robertson, North Ryde, 1988, p.16. Humphrey McQueen, *A New Britannia: An Agreement Concerning the Social Origins of Australian Radicalism and Nationalism*, Penguin, Melbourne, 1970, p. 21.

culture and pursue elements of a more uniquely independent and internationalist posture than has occasionally been evident.[37] It is thus clear that at the national level the opportunity existed for evolution despite Australia's historical and cultural constraints. Yet two caveats existed. First, Australia's suit to the region in security community terms must be reciprocated, about which there remain qualifications. Second, and importantly in the context of this book, although this analysis contended Australia had made incipient moves to relocate within the region (and this was still evident in official statements), that in any practical analysis, the Howard government was still oriented to an Anglo-American security culture.[38] In crafting the argument to upgrade the US alliance, the Coalition prepared the ground by stating:

> Australia and the United States are natural friends. We share the same fundamental cultural, social and political values and have long historical ties which bind us together.[39]

This assessment intimated that Wendt's social regeneration and constitutive processes can be utilised by actors to allay domestic threats and that his intersubjective dynamics were powerful tools in the making of foreign policy in Australia between 1996 and 2007.

When John Howard was elected in 1996, it was not only after thirteen years of Labor dominance in domestic governance, it was also after an extended period of ambiguity regarding his ability to lead the Coalition. It was thus primarily incumbent upon Howard to ensure his and the Coalition's survival. The Coalition acted to manage the perception of risks in the construction of foreign policy that originated not only from above but also from below. Des Ball has reiterated that alliances are also the product of 'irrational' factors, for instance, the vagaries of domestic politics. And in the Australian context this is premised upon a 'threat mentality' that is an ingredient of the national character.[40] However, for governments, the management of this threat mentality can be a highly rational behaviour.

Both Australia's historical legacy and its cultural identity would shape the way these risks were perceived and presented. In ensuring his survival and that of the Coalition, Howard determined that the previous government had threatened 'mainstream conceptions of identity'.[41] Economic modernisation had been linked inextricably to Asian hubs. Howard sensed, however, that along with the economic reconstruction that had altered the nature of employment for many Australians, the efforts to redefine not only the workplace but cultural identity were overwhelming. Constructing an identity for Australia within a region from which security threats

---

37 Graeme Cheeseman, 1999, pp. 73–74.

38 Richard Higgott and Kim Richard Nossal, 1998, pp. 265–88.

39 Federal Coalition, 'A Confident Australia: Coalition Foreign Affairs Policy', p. 21.

40 Desmond Ball, 'The US–Australian Alliance: History and Prospects', *SDSC Working Paper no. 330*, ANU, Canberra, January 1999, p. 19.

41 Carol Johnson, 'John Howard and the Revenge of the Mainstream: Some Implications for Concepts of Identity', in George Crowder, Haydon Manning, David Mathieson, Andrew Parkin and Leonard Seabrooke (eds), *Proceedings of the 1997 Australasian Political Studies Association Conference*, vol. 2, Flinders University, Adelaide, September–October 1997, p. 413.

emanated required a great leap of faith for some. Simultaneous economic and cultural change were challenging for the electorate.

If, in the mid-1990s, the Prime Minister's 'crisis' was one of post-Cold War uncertainty, regional place and a failure of emphasis of the US alliance, by 2002 there was much greater potency and immediacy in the threats. Through this period, the terrorist attacks in Bali, the East Timor conflict, the supposed 'contest' of Australia's sovereignty by Middle East refugees, confirmed the dangers for Australia. In 2002, Howard stated: '(n)ot since the early 1960s have we faced a more complex and uncertain region'.[42]

Thus, a return to the traditional notions of both culture and hence, security, could offer succour to the primary anxieties of middle Australia. Pauline Hanson's fears of the deconstruction of the Australian settlement and her specific anxieties of the continued feting of the region to Australia's north were informally acknowledged in the Coalition's foreign policy. Resuscitation of Australia's relationship with its powerful patron was pronounced. National pursuits would be tested against 'the national interest'. The path then returned to those traditional tracks of security and culture.[43]

Survey material of public attitudes to the US Alliance also provided a powerful impetus for the government to continue to foster relations. As both Ian McAllister and John Ravenhill recorded in 1998, while public views on closer integration with Asia was soft, support for upgraded security relations with the US was 'strong and increasing'. In addition, they confirmed that Australians felt that their country was not well able to defend itself. And despite the demise of the Cold War, the public viewed their environment as hostile.[44]

McAllister's research in 2004 further clarified the nature of the public views on the alliance. He documented that 'in 2000, 46 per cent said ANZUS was "very important" and a further 42 per cent regarded it as "fairly important"; in 2001 the same figures were 58 per cent and 32 per cent.' However, McAllister argued that while Australians consistently supported the alliance over time; they were more reserved about their belief in US preparedness to provide security assistance. (See Table 1.1 and Figure 1.1). To some significant extent then the Howard government's policies resonated on the public interest in the security relationship with the US.

42 John Howard, 'Strategic Leadership for Australia: Policy Directions in a Complex World', speech transcript, Committee for Economic Development of Australia (CEDA), 20 November 2002.

43 Michael Wesley and Tony Warren, 'Wild Colonial Ploys? Currents of thought in Australian foreign policy', *Australian Journal of Political Science*, March 2000, pp. 9–26.

44 Ian McAllister and John Ravenhill, 'Australian Attitudes Towards Closer Engagement with Asia', *Pacific Review*, vol. 11, no. 1, 1998, pp. 119–41. McAllister and Ravenhill also argued that attitudes to Asia were generationally connected.

Table 1.1 Attitudes towards the role of the United States in the region, 2000

US improves Asia–Pacific security		Trust in US to defend Australia	
Strongly agree	14	Great deal	22
Agree	62	Fair amount	50
Disagree	21	Not very much	24
Strongly disagree	3	None at all	4
Total	100		100
(N)	(1,111)		(1,176)

'I will now read out a list of statements. Please tell me whether you strongly agree, agree, disagree or strongly disagree with each of them. ... The United States helps to improve security in the Asia Pacific region?' 'If Australia's security were threatened by some other country, how much trust do you feel Australia can have in the United States to come to Australia's defence?'

Source: Ian McAllister, 'Attitude Matters: Public Opinion in Australia Towards Defence and Security', APSI, Canberra, August 2004, p. 28.

In 2000, opportunity for the Coalition to further develop the relationship was enhanced by the election of Republican President George W. Bush. Much publicised was the personal affinity between the two leaders. This was underlined by Howard's stay at the Bush ranch in Crawford Texas, 2003 – a Presidential welcome afforded to only few leaders. Consolidation of this association was evident in Bush's compliments for Howard during the US President's visit to Australia in October of that year. Of significance too was the unusually forthcoming nature of US Ambassador Schieffer's remarks on the ALP's difficulties in supporting the US administration through 2003–2004. So it was then that after 2000 the Howard government was able to continually remind the public of its intimacy with the US and play upon Australia's ongoing support for the US alliance.

Politicisation of the foreign policy process also was partner to these developments. Surveys conducted of 242 DFAT policy officers in December 2001 by Alan Gyngell and Michael Wesley, revealed bureaucratic perceptions not only of the increasing politicisation of policy considerations but also the significant role of the Prime Minister in influencing a serious bilateral issue.[45] Though so many Australian bureaucrats have adeptly provided independent advice to the government, the onerous nature of this task in an increasingly politicised environment should not be underestimated.

As the Howard government was also motivated by domestic concerns in addition to international factors it is worthwhile considering the interactive process between domestic and international politics. Contrary to some other analyses of global economic governance, Mark Beeson and Ann Capling argue that 'the interplay between the domestic and external spheres is a good deal more complex

45 Allan Gyngell and Michael Wesley, *Making Australian Foreign Policy*, pp. 277 and 275.

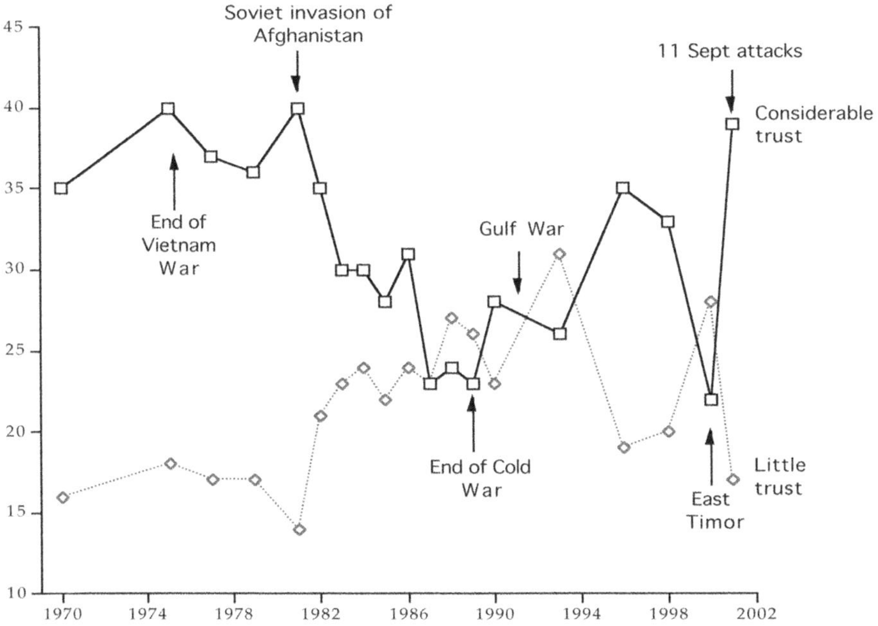

Figure 1.1 Trust in the US to defend Australia, 1970–2001 (per cent)

'If Australia's security were threatened by some other country, how much trust do you feel Australia can have in the United States to come to Australia's defence?' Exact question wordings and codings vary between surveys

Source: Ian McAllister, 'Attitude Matters: Public Opinion in Australia Towards Defence and Security', APSI, Canberra, August 2004, p. 29.

and reciprocal.'[46] It is clearly evident that governments utilise both the international and domestic spaces in responding to challenges. This has been particularly so in the economic arena where the state can purposefully utilise its domestic policies to ameliorate issues of international adjustment.[47] Further, the claim that governments can attempt to utilise exterior danger to profit from the unifying domestic climate they create is apposite.[48]

An interactive two-level game approach is relevant to both economic and security issues where there exists a synergy of international/domestic strategies rather than a primacy of international factors.[49] However, in this approach, the state leader is

46 Mark Beeson and Ann Capling, 'Australia in the World Economy', in Stephen Bell (ed.), *Economic Governance & Institutional Dynamics*, Oxford University Press, South Melbourne, 2002, p. 303.

47 John Ikenberry, 'The State and Strategies of International Adjustment', *World Politics*, vol. 39, no. 1, October 1986, pp. 53–77.

48 Klaus Knorr (ed.), 1976, p. 114.

49 Peter B. Evans, Harold K. Jacobson and Robert D. Putnam (eds), *Double-Edged Diplomacy: International Bargaining and Domestic Politics*, University of California Press, Berkeley, 1993.

central to the bargaining process, in which both domestic constraints and the actor's personal goals feature in the bargaining process.[50]

The government's choices of upgrading the US alliance were thus orientated by its material perceptions, in addition to historical, cultural and domestic considerations. Strangely enough, however, while the government was conscious of both the material and cultural inputs into the alliance relationship, it endeavoured to implement a trade policy that was based upon cultural bargaining. If its policies were simply informed by power politics it would not explain its choice to upgrade its bilateral economic policy with the US.

Practical Bilateralism?

States pursue bilateralism where they consider that 'the combination of their security interests, their relative capabilities and the systemic context in which they operate is such that dyadic relationships will be most effective.'[51] As I argued in the introduction, while bilateralism has not been the only mode of diplomacy pursued by the Howard government, it has nonetheless been its preferred brand of interaction. Opportunity, as the Coalition sensed in the trade arena, was located initially in the arena of 'aggressive bilateralism' and then 'practical bilateralism', particularly as it was acknowledged that there was room to pursue market opening and access strategies in conjunction with industry.[52] Moving into this gap in 1996 for the Coalition would entail an assault on trade promotion by a conscientious Minister for Trade, Tim Fischer. It was coupled, nonetheless, with the grander construct of invigorated security relations with an asymmetrical bilateral partner, the US.

Structural constraints do limit the appropriateness of bilateral diplomacy for Australia. Consequent lack of leverage in negotiations with greater powers suggested that Australia is aided by its own promotion of multilateralism. In the trade arena, where this argument is most commonly advanced, Richard Snape, Jan Adams and David Morgan, 'endorse(d) the common view that Australia's interests are best served by promoting the continuation and expansion of an open multilateral trading system.'[53]

---

50 Andrew Moravcsik, 'Introduction: Integrating International and Domestic Theories of International Bargaining', in Peter B. Evans, Harold K. Jacobson and Robert D. Putnam (eds), 1993, p. 16.

51 Brian L. Job, 'Multilateralism in the Asia–Pacific', in William Tow, Russell Trood and Toshiya Hoshino (eds), *Bilateralism in a Multilateral Era: The Future of the San Francisco System in the Asia–Pacific*, The Japan Institute of International Affairs and the Centre for the Study of Australia–Asia Relations, Griffith University, 1997, p. 161.

52 Geoff Stokes, 'Towards a national trade strategy: recovering bilateral trade strategies in trade promotion', *Australian Quarterly*, Autumn 1994, pp. 74 and 91.

53 Richard Snape, Jan Adams and David Morgan, *Regional Trade Agreements: Implications and Options for Australia*, Department of Foreign Affairs and Trade, AGPS, Canberra, 1993, p. 187. See also, David Robertson, 'Reciprocity and Protectionism in Australia's Trade Policy', *Agenda*, vol. 4, no. 2, 1997, pp. 138–40.

Assessing the possibilities of a specific trade arrangement with the US, Richard Snape again advised that where possible larger arrangements were preferable. Ann Capling concluded that the multilateral system gave:

> small countries a greater opportunity to pursue and protect their trade interests than would otherwise be the case. Of central importance here were the 'rules' for multilateral trade which give small states some protection against discrimination by large powers... the multilateral system with its norms of non-discrimination...and the Uruguay Round precedent of comprehensive negotiations across many different sectors, affords small countries more opportunities for improved market access than they would otherwise be able to negotiate bilaterally.[54]

Capling has also recorded that the significance of the multilateral, rules based system is 'no longer very well understood in Australia',[55] and where Australia had successfully negotiated market access with the US this has been achieved through multilateral negotiations. This track also provided the opportunity for smaller countries to construct coalitions that can counter any potentially exploitative power of the larger partner.

Of the US preference for the bilateral system of alliances in the Asia–Pacific, experienced international analyst, Coral Bell, explained that:

> bilateralism provided considerable advantages (at least during the Cold War years) for American policy makers. It enabled them to control the separate agendas of each relationship without too many arguments. In Europe, by comparison, where multilateralism had been firmly secured by the Europeans (who knew a thing or two about diplomacy) from the earliest days of the formation of NATO (1948–49), there was scope for occasional 'ganging up' by the allies against Washington when they did not like a particular policy.[56]

Robert Cox observed these states who built coalitions had a 'commitment to orderliness and security in interstate relations and the facilitation of orderly change in the world system'. This would enhance the possibilities of the 'environment within which their own interests and those of their populations could be pursued.'[57] If this was the orthodoxy of the times, then the preference of a bilateralist approach for Australia speaks to the potency of the integrated threat perception explanation.

---

54 Ann Capling, *Australia and the Global Trade System: From Havana to Seattle*, Cambridge University Press, 2001, p. 9.

55 Ann Capling, 'Democratic Deficit, the Global Trade System and 11 September', *Australian Journal of Politics and History*, vol. 49, no. 3, pp. 371–79.

56 Coral Bell, 'The Future of American Policy in the Pacific', in Gary Klintworth (ed.), *Asia–Pacific Security: Less Uncertainty, New Opportunities?*, Addison Wesley Longman, Melbourne, 1996, p. 31.

57 Robert W. Cox, 'Middlepowermanship, Japan, and the Future World Order', *International Journal*, vol. 44, no. 4, Autumn 1989, p. 826.

Integrated Threat Perception and International Bargaining

Given that the Howard government chose to upgrade relations with the US and to plot trade along the security axis, what could we expect from these policies in terms of trade negotiations between the two states? Literature on international bargaining has provided scant analysis of asymmetrical trade relations. What is known, however, is that small states possess the ability to prevail in prescribing the parameters of the bargaining process and thus increase their leverage. Factors such as the choice of terrain, skills and resources of the negotiators and government department are influential in determining the outcome.[58] Issue specifics are important, although it remains that should the issue be of significant interest to both parties, then the larger power has at hand the command of greater resources and leverage to mobilise.

Consistent with this, in spring 1971 Robert Keohane published a study that revealed that small allies could indeed exert considerable influence over their great power allies. He contended that these small allies were most effective where: they possessed the ability to manoeuvre broadly within their domestic politics, the US pursued an activist foreign policy, its relationships ensured a mutual dependence with US government agencies, and it was able to construct intimate ties with organised groups within the US.[59] So, why not Australia? As he and Joseph Nye later observed, Australian governments lacked the ability to manoeuvre because of their perception that US security protection was paramount.[60] Clearly then, a hierarchical structure was imposed on Australia's quest for security, wealth and knowledge. However, as the Howard government endeavoured to utilise its perceived 'shared' relationship with the US to achieve better outcomes (as in both the lamb and Howe leather disputes) they were still rebuffed.

As long-time alliance analyst William Tow observed, special relations are 'generally not applicable in the contemporary and increasingly open international trading system.'[61] Similarly, after investigation of Australia–US trade policy in the 1980s, Russell Solomon concluded that, the quality of the political relationship was disconnected to the trading relationship.'[62] By inverting the Keohane and Nye

58 William Mark Habeeb, *Power and Tactics in International Negotiation: How Weak Nations Bargain with Strong Nations*, Johns Hopkins University Press, Baltimore, 1988, pp. 134–35. William Zartman, *The Politics of Trade Negotiations between Africa and the European Economic Community: The Weak Confront the Strong*, Princeton University Press, Princeton, 1971, pp. 224–29. John Zysman, *Government, Market and Growth*, Cornell University Press, Ithaca, 1983, p. 297.

59 Keohane analysed the actions of Pakistan, Israel, Spain, the Philippines, nationalist China and Iran in the 1950s and 1960s, in Robert O. Keohane, 'The Big Influence of Small Allies', *Foreign Policy*, no. 2, Spring 1971, p. 167.

60 Robert O. Keohane and Joseph S. Nye, *Power and Interdependence*, second edition, Scott, Foresman and Company, Glenview, Illinois, 1989, pp. 175–212.

61 William T. Tow, 'Australia and the United States', in James Cotton and John Ravenhill (eds), *The National Interest in a Global Era: Australia in World Affairs 1996–2000*, Oxford University Press, South Melbourne, p. 184.

62 Russell Solomon, 'Political Economy of Australia's Trade Policy – Making Towards the United States', unpublished Ph.D thesis, University of Sydney, Sydney 1993.

argument, it is also evident that while Australians sought protection from the UK and the US, because of their geographic and cultural isolation, Australia's non-strategic location has also lessened the likelihood of great power commitment in the relationship. While small states in the Middle East or in Northeast Asia may have been crucial to UK or US grand strategic plans or vital to their economic hegemony, Australia's remote location and small population has denied it leverage on either geostrategic or economic grounds. Thus, when confronted by domestic US lobbying, insufficient leverage could be exerted. And even if Australia were to link trade with security, it was unlikely that this attempted construction of advantage would be enough.

In the course of this book another issue is also relevant in addition to the domestic bargaining considerations of the preceding section. This is the role of the bargaining process in transactions conducted below state level. Susan Strange would contend that bargaining between non-state actors is just as crucial in understanding relations in the international arena.[63] Save the East Timor case study, all other studies in this book consider the role of non-state actors and their influence in alliance relations. In these studies, the role of state and either domestic non-state actors or transnational actors are analysed. Achievement of outcomes for the Coalition was thus dependent upon the coincidence of success at the sub-state level, in addition to the interests of the US government. And as also evident, state power becomes significant when spread through commercial participants. Throughout the sectoral studies I have conducted in this book, US state power is also shown as enhanced via coordination of both state and sub-state actors.

Conclusion: Increased Expectations and Reciprocity Demands

The Howard's government's thinking about its interstate relations has been shaped by its interpretation of both material and cultural factors in the effort to mediate between international and domestic threats. In the process, it has prioritised bilateralism with the US. Three of the products of this process have been: first, to focus its international trade, business and security relationships even more tightly upon the US; second, to adopt the US model in its policy approach; and third, to expect US reciprocation in the relationship.

Despite the expectations, the results have not always been those desired. Reciprocity for Australia depends upon the coincidence of these expectations with US material preferences. Because of the constraints of power and the asymmetry in the Australia–US relationship, any attempt to model policy upon US aggressive unilateralism was inherently restricted in its ability to deliver outcomes. Australia's location and population does not render it vital to US strategic interests. The US too, has been inclined to transfer the imperatives for structural adjustment to its trading partners. Moreover, in any international bargaining with the US, the Administration's preferences are but one factor in the construction of policy. Congress and thus the

63 Susan Strange, '*Cave! Hic Dragones*: a critique of regime analysis', in Stephen Krasner, *International Regimes*, Cornell University Press, Ithaca, pp. 353–54.

electoral cycle, US law, producer interests and lobby groups are integral in the fall of the decisions, and as revealed in some of the following case studies, the current US debt issues loom as a significant threat to future policy preferences. While the Howard government waged its policy on the cultural relationship with the US, the results have varied upon a range of domestic and international interests, both governmental and non-governmental, that are specific to the time, and less dependent upon the cultural preferences of the greater power.

Chapter 2

Cultural Cachet? Lambs and Leather

> In launching the Coalition's trade policy for Australia in January 1996, Tim Fischer heralded a second coming for the bilateralist approach. When asked what weapons were at Australia's disposal in prevailing against US might, he was unable to identify any. The launch was duly proclaimed a success.[1]

Early in its incumbency, the Howard government discovered the persuasiveness of domestic stakeholders in US trade policy. Australia's early attempts at threat mediation to sway US trade decisions through its personal and cultural attachments to the US were smartly rejected. As both the Howe leather and lamb tariff disputes revealed, the US domestic automotive and rural producers utilising US trade law, together with their Congressional representatives, were decisive in prevailing upon the Administration's decision-making. Australia's calls to the Clinton Administration to salvage a better outcome for both its rural producer and urban worker constituencies mattered little when confronted with such powerful US domestic interests.

Australia's trade relationship with Washington provides a platform to understand the extent of the Howard government's trade dilemma with the US and the difficulties it experienced in achieving successful outcomes in its trade relationship. Australia has often shared similar general economic principles with the US and has been the beneficiary of US leadership in past multilateral negotiations, yet the more immediate bilateral negotiations have at times been contentious.[2] These assume a greater significance because of the presence of the US in Australia's trading relations. Australia's $16.3 billion trade deficit in 2006 with the US, up from $12.7 billion in 2002, was easily its most significant bilateral deficit with any trading partner, and remained the sole deficit within the group of Australia's top five trading partners. This deficit exists principally because of the parallel nature of the two economies, in particular the low level of complementarity between Australian exports and US import needs. More compatible are US exports and Australian import requirements, most often in the importation of capital and high technology equipment. Table 2.1 shows the features of Australia–US trade and investment.

---

1 Christine Wallace, 'The Fischer king? Not likely', *Financial Review*, 29 January 1996, p. 21.

2 Stuart Harris, 'International Economic Orientations: Australia', in Richard W. Baker and Gary R. Hawke (eds), *ANZUS Economics: Economic Trends and Relations Among Australia, New Zealand, and the United States*, Praeger, Westport, 1992, pp. 73–90.

Table 2.1 Australia–US Trade and Investment: selected indicators

	1984	1990	1995	2000	2002	2006
Merchandise Trade:						
Australian Exports	3.0	5.8	4.6	11.0	11.5	10.1
Australian Imports	5.6	11.9	16.7	23.1	23.1	24.4
Balance	-2.6	-6.1	-12.1	-12.1	-11.6	-14.3
Services Trade:*						
Australian Exports	0.8	1.8	2.3	5.8	4.8	5.5
Australian Imports	1.2	3.0	2.9	6.3	5.9	7.5
Balance	-0.4	-1.2	-0.6	-0.5	-1.1	-2.0
Direct Investment**						
Australian FDI in US***	1.3	8.1	18.4	90.5	73.7	116.0
US FDI in Australia	11.5	25.0	39.8	66.9	57.6	73.6

* all figures in $ billions.

** year ended 30 June.

*** FDI after 1990 calculated from the Balance of Payments Manual (BPM) no. 5. FDI calculated on calendar year in 2006.

Source: Various ABS publications and Statistical Services Section, DFAT.

As a direct trading partner Australia has fared badly. However, in 1997–98 Australia's exports to the US increased by 41 per cent, largely due to the depreciation in the Australian dollar and strong domestic growth within the US. Yet, it was not enough to alter a damaging trade balance ratio, which in 1997–98 still stood at 2.5:1 in favour of the US. Recent high growth areas include alcoholic beverages, crude petroleum, chemicals, steel, motor vehicle components and film production. The services industry, including transport, travel and insurance services have also experienced growth, with the professional sector in accounting, law, engineering and architecture looking to expand activity.[3] In the 1995 Department of Foreign Affairs and Trade (DFAT) report on the bilateral relationship, the services domain appeared as one of the few positives in the relationship.[4]

Although relatively liberal in its overall trading policy, the US restricts or denies Australian access to its markets in several key sectors. Prior to the Free Trade Agreement, the constraints placed on the access of efficient local agricultural producers to US markets have limited the opportunities for Australia to reduce the bilateral trade deficit. Australian agriculture has been the notable and public victim

3 Department of Foreign Affairs and Trade, *Trade Outcomes and Objectives Statement*, Canberra, February 1999, pp. 161–63.

4 Department of Foreign Affairs and Trade, *Australia–US Trade and Investment Review: A Partnership in Transition*, Canberra, 1996.

of US protectionism, in particular, sugar, wheat, beef, dairy and lamb products. Industrially, Textile, Clothing and Footwear (TCF) and motor vehicle tariffs created difficulties for Australian profitability in US markets; the Jones Act prohibits the export of fast ferries, while anti dumping regulations pose particular problems for the steel industry.[5]

This low level of direct complementarity between the Australian and US economies has meant that Australia is more often a competitor rather than a compatriot. This arrangement complicates the management choices for the government. However, the US completes the third point in the trading triangle with Australia and Asia, as it is the recipient of many of Asia's low-cost manufactured goods. And, as a significant commercial partner for Asia, the US indirectly assists in sustaining Australia's trade surpluses in the region.

In the mid-1990s, with the scale of the US bilateral deficit increasing, the Australian government sought to switch its focus to markets elsewhere. Retreating from problematic bilateral US trade, developing and expanding markets in the region was regarded as a more profitable venture for both producers and government resources. This plan was interrupted by the onset of the Asian financial crisis in 1997 which reignited the necessity to actively engage US opportunities. Fortunately, conditions were ripe for greater success than in the past, and as stated, merchandise exports to the US grew considerably in 1997–98. However, as imports maintained their steady growth pattern, assisted by the Australian dollar appreciation beginning in 1999 and rising to 88 cents/US dollar by mid-2007, and an expected drop in US growth rates, continued export expansion was more than matched by sustained imports from the US.

US Structural and Domestic Primacy

The ability of the Howard government to renegotiate its trade policy with the US continues to be affected by both US structural and domestic factors. The difficulty for the Howard government was that the Clinton, then the Bush Administrations also had domestic priorities that played upon their international relationships. One of the legacies of US budget and trade deficits in its recent history was that the US sought to transfer the costs of economic adjustment to others. Through the 1980s, as the US was faced with both a massive trade deficit and domestic perceptions of international 'free riders' milking the US economy, attempts were instigated to force others to assist in the reduction of US deficits. Notably, this was conducted through pressure on Western countries, particularly Japan and Western Europe, but also Australia, to open markets and reorient production to the US. 'Fair' trade became the domestic US catchword and economic pressure subsequently ensued upon others in the global trading system.

One of the effects of the translation of structural adjustment internationally was the employment of US economic and 'other' leverage across bilateral relationships

---

5 Department of Foreign Affairs and Trade, *Trade Outcomes and Objectives Statement*, 1999, p. 169.

and within sectoral negotiations.[6] Utilisation of any special relationship by the Coalition was negated by the power of US domestic interests. Material interests outweighed cultural preferences.

In the 1980s, Australia was exposed particularly to the resistance of the US to force structural adjustment upon its farmers, with the resultant Export Enhancement Program (EEP) one policy manifestation of this policy. It also ensured that many of Australia's rural communities, catchment areas for the Coalition's electoral support, were highly sensitised to the politics of trade policy with the US.

During the Clinton Presidency, however, Australia had made some significant gains in building its export profitability. Yet the Howard government's attempts to improve its trading profile with the US continued to rupture against the abrasiveness of the resistance to domestic structural readjustment within the US. Where US domestic interests maintained protective barriers, these significant specific problems were unable to be resolved solely by the Australian government's appeals to any cultural connection with the US. As the following automotive and agricultural case studies demonstrate, both US labour and capital resisted any foreign assault on their position. It is worth noting too that, inside the US, Bill Archer, chairman of the US House of Representatives Ways and Means Committee, considered that Clinton was under more pressure from organised labour in 1999 to restrict imports, than at any other time during his presidency.[7]

Through the latter half of the 1990s, given the interplay of these factors, the Clinton Administration's United States Trade Representative (USTR), Charlene Barshefsky, ardently implemented a policy of aggressive unilateralism. Across the Pacific, the US system of bilateral alliances provided opportune channels for the application of bilateral leverage. But as a twist to this, Stephen Krasner argued that it was sometimes evident that other states modeled themselves on the behaviour of hegemonic states even though it may not be appropriate for them.[8] Australia, under the Howard government demonstrated that it was one of these states. As part of its threat mediation strategy it attempted to adopt and implement Barshefsky's 'aggressive unilateral' trade tactics. However, these policies were always unlikely to yield anything. Oddly enough, this was a point duly acknowledged by the Trade Minister (1996–99) Tim Fischer, at its announcement.

Attempts at Leveraging on a Special Relationship

Tim Fischer had claimed to be 'fixated' by Australia's trade deficit with the US in 1996,[9] yet the Coalition looked to US trade diplomacy for answers to its problems.

---

6 Robert Gilpin, *The Political Economy of International Relations*, Princeton University Press, Princeton, 1987, p. 372.

7 Brendan Pearson, 'US denies tariff rate quota will harm lamb producers', *Australian Financial Review*, 30 March 1999, p. 7.

8 Stephen Krasner, 'State Power and the Structure of International Trade', *World Politics*, vol. 283, 1976, p. 322.

9 Tim Fischer quoted in Peter Hartcher and Colleen Ryan, 'US trade threat to car and textile industries', *Australian Financial Review*, 18 November 1996, p. 1.

Seemingly seduced by the United States Trade Representative's aggressive trade rhetoric and trade vision supposing relationships on a 'reciprocal basis', Fischer chose to anchor Australia's policy in what he perceived as delivering immediate trade outcomes, opting to avoid the intangibles of talking on the world stage. Howard's government too, tempted by the perception of the popularity of this in the domestic environment, subtly incorporated reciprocity as part of its policy.

Coalition foreign policy documents emphasised the desire to implement 'more proactive bilateral trade strategies'.[10] More upbeat versions of this approach appeared in specific trade documents; 'aggression' would now be an inherent feature of bilateral relations. Publication of the *Trade Outcomes and Objectives Statement* documented the assiduous travails of the government in securing greater market access.[11] But as it was obvious that the USTR threats were made credible by US might, it was unusual then that Fischer should seek to deploy it. Not only was the bilateral track to be utilised to improve market access for Australian exporters, it was also to be used directly in the resolution of the plethora of Australia's trade problems with the US. These included US export subsidies, dumping of subsidised agricultural commodities in Asia (thus threatening Australia's markets) and Australia's US trade deficit.[12] Structurally, the parallel nature of the two economies created inherent difficulties for Australian exporters to the US, and in competitive third markets.

A study of the two cases, Howe leather and lamb tariffs, reveals the Coalition's misplaced faith in Australia's belief in the US alliance over US local stakeholders and the capacity of an aggressive bilateralism to operate successfully for the smaller partner within an asymmetrical relationship. Both studies resonate with the government's flawed reliance on its cultural ally to assist in the resolution of economic threat.

The Howe Leather Dispute

According to the US, Melbourne's Howe and Company (hereafter Howe) supplier of leather upholstery for passenger motor vehicles, was allegedly in receipt of government export subsidies that disadvantaged local US suppliers in the North American market. As such, in 1996, the US threatened to pursue WTO action against Australia unless the assistance was terminated. In response the Coalition sought to divert US action through personal appeals to the Administration. It was an opportunity to implement its culturally conceived bilateralist trade strategy. The Coalition would act on behalf of its domestic constituency to alleviate international risk.

As assisted principally by the Import Credit Scheme (ICS), Howe succeeded (in less than a decade) in remaking the company from being nationally oriented, to one exporting 90 per cent of its production. Together with some assistance from

10 Federal Coalition, 'A Confident Australia', 10 February 1996, p. 4.

11 See the Department of Foreign Affairs and Trade, *Trade Outcomes and Objectives Statement*, Years 1997–1998, Canberra.

12 Federal Coalition, 'Meeting the Challenges: The New Global Economy', Liberal and National Party Strategies for the Future, 1996, p. 3.

the Export Facilitation Scheme (EFS) Howe had managed to expand dramatically its export profile from 7 per cent of production in 1988 to 90 per cent by 1996. Part of this export reorientation included securing a contract with Lear USA to supply GM in Detroit. By winning three per cent of the US market, it displaced two US tanneries: Michigan's Eagle Ottawa Company and Pennsylvanian Garden State Tanning. However, the Australian government contended that because the assistance schemes belonged to a broader package that enabled increased imports through the credit system that it could sustain a WTO challenge. It also believed that the bigger picture of Australian trade liberalisation was impressive, if not unassailable.

This plan did not acknowledge the pressing need to transfer the costs of structural adjustment present in the US, nor the Clinton Administration's quest to reduce budget deficits through assiduous attention to both market opening measures and protection of local industries. Aware of the persuasive politics of both issues in the US environment, the two US companies petitioned action from the USTR.

The Inadequacies of Cultural Bargaining

What transpired from this juncture offered an opportunity to scrutinise the effectiveness of the government's culturally bound trade bargaining. Repeated pleas to the US Administration were made by a succession of government ministers to arrest the USTR's investigation into Howe's assistance.[13] These entreaties would appeal to the strength of alliance relations.

Attempting to halt the US process, then Industry Minister, John Moore, together with former Trade Minister Tim Fischer, argued adamantly that the US should reject the local litigants and conclude in favour of their long-time ally. Fischer conversed with USTR, Charlene Barshefsky, and Commerce Secretary, Mickey Kantor, in an effort to persuade them. After the AUSMIN talks in 1996 concluded in Sydney in June, Fischer pursued the issue the following month at the APEC Trade Ministers' summit. Nonetheless, US negotiators were resolute that if they were to rebuff any claims from the US tanneries then Howe needed to be excised from the ICS. Fischer resisted these requests and banked on the potency of the Australian position.

As Australia remained intransigent the two tanneries turned litigants. A Section 301 investigation under US trade law was approved as it was argued that Howe's receipt of subsidies was illegal under the WTO Agreement on Subsidies and Countervailing Measures.[14] Australian leverage was assisted temporarily at this point by Clinton's stay in Australia later in the year and consequent need to preserve the friendly nature of relations. Unsurprisingly then, the US continued their discussions with their counterparts. Eventually the Coalition registered the futility of its approach in complete resistance. Moreover, by the APEC Trade Ministers' Meeting prior to

13 The Deputy Prime Minister and Minister for Trade, and The Minister for Industry, Science and Tourism, 'Australia disappointed at US Super 301 Action, Determined to defend Australian Interests', *Joint Media Release*, Parliament House, Canberra, 2 October 1996.

14 Section 301 allows the US to impose trade sanctions on a foreign country where it deems that country has constrained US commerce.

the Subic Bay Heads of Government Meeting in November 1996, a restructuring of Howe's assistance was agreed: or at least thought to be agreed.

Despite US interest in locating an appropriate out-of-court settlement, the Coalition was intent on demonstrating to its own domestic constituency that it would protect them against *dirigiste* US aggression. The ironic point, of course, was that it had modeled this aggressive bilateralism upon US superpower trade behaviour and was endeavouring to deploy this strategy against the US itself.

Barshefsky soon discovered, however, that the substitution of one subsidy by another was equally untenable for the US tanneries, which had quickly become organised politically. The Coalition's recompense for Howe was granted in the form of a $25 million loan with a deferred five-year repayment period and grant money linked to a maximum of five per cent of sales projections. However, as this support appeared to the US producers and their lobby group as a replacement subsidy, the US duly pursued its WTO claims. The US producers also quickly realised that although Howe's subsidies had been restructured to apply to production, 90 per cent of this production was exported. US jobs were thus staked against foreign raiders. As usual, the tanneries' advocates were also keen to press the need for the USTR to address the unsavoury aspects of this infiltration in order to model US preparedness to address illegal subsidies.

The litigants in this dispute were also savvy manipulators of the political environment. By positioning the complaints to intersect with the US Presidential elections the litigants maximised their chances of executing a proper result. In this 1996 election, the Democrats were under pressure to exhibit their trade enforcement credentials in addition to their protection of a labour constituency. Moreover, it was not only Clinton who was campaigning. Acting USTR Barshefsky too was seeking election for a permanent position. Consequently, both Clinton and Barshefsky were acutely conscious of the demands of local capital and labour. As Barshefsky declared: '(o)ur willingness to enforce trade laws and existing agreements is crucial to our support at home and our credibility abroad.'[15]

Yet both Howard and John Moore remained convinced that the US would not proceed against Australia. Both were persuaded of the extent to which the US friendship would insulate Australia from litigation. Moore also contended that it was the US as recipient of some considerable benefits from the ICS through increased exports into Australia that it would comprehend the entirety of the trade picture. Furthermore, for Tim Fischer, this larger canvas also included the dramatic nature of US subsidies and trade barriers that precluded Australian exports to the US and sustained the $12.1 billion bilateral trade surplus for the US.[16] The Coalition rightly understood the need to be defenders of Australian industry *per se* and they also recognised the need to be strident in their defence. However, the culturally bound nature of the request ensured that Australia's supplication was to no avail.

---

15 Charlene Barshefsky, Statement before the Senate, 1997, p. 4.

16 Deputy Prime Minister and Minister for Trade, Tim Fischer, and the Minister for Industry, Science and Tourism, John Moore, 'Australian Leather Exports to the US', *Joint Media Release*, Parliament House, Canberra, 20 August 1996.

More extraordinary in the Coalition's tactics to court the US was Fischer's proposal to the USTR in early October. After Cabinet discussions on the issue, he communicated to the USTR that Australia would drop its plan to allow parallel CD imports, which posed a threat to the US music and software industries, if the US was willing to retract its actions against Howe. The 1996 regulations had allowed only for holders of music copyright to import sound recordings. Australia's plan to lift its restrictions on these imports, thereby hoping to offer reduced prices to the consumer, had provoked US ire. Fischer had been advised that the US would proceed with action if Australia lifted its restrictions on CD imports. Cabinet's plan here was seen to be an opportunity to eliminate two trade confrontations.

But Barshefsky was in no mood for compromise. The US flatly rejected the deal. And by late October, the USTR announced her disaffection with Australia. Not only was she 'deeply troubled' by Australia's decision to eliminate protection for sound recordings but was 'gravely concerned' about the bilateral relationship.[17] At the end of January 1998, the Coalition's nostalgia for the special bilateral relationship had been wounded by the USTR's angst over both Howe and CD imports. Howe would now be examined by a WTO panel fast tracked to resolve the issue after the bilateral talks failed.

Protection of US domestic constituencies and the procedural nature of the US trade law process were integral in the Administration's rejection of Australia's pleas, whatever its ally's claims. Not only was the government unable to prevent the Section 301 investigation from proceeding, neither was it able to arrest the WTO activation. After the Section 301 investigation, the USTR invoked WTO dispute settlement on the basis that the ICS contravened the WTO Agreement on Subsidies and Countervailing Measures. This pursuit marked the first time the US had confronted Australia with a WTO dispute settlement action. This action, of course not only threatened to respond to the specific Howe issue, but the US suit also encircled the textile, clothing and car industries as they were recipients of the export schemes. Further, the US threatened retaliation against the wine industry and other successful Australian exporters.

That the Minister for Trade, Fischer, sought to resolve the matter through a phone deal that would see the US jettison the Howe case if Australia banned the parallel imports of CDs, highlighted the Coalition's inexperience with US trade law and practice.[18] It also highlighted the inadequacies of an approach that not only failed to factor in the primacy of US domestic politics and material reward, but misunderstood the inequities of power.

In this instance the government's choice to resolve disputes – the prioritisation of its cultural relationship with the US – clearly failed. Subsequently, after a protracted WTO process, and threatened US retaliation through a range of sectors (including risks to wine exports) the WTO panel ruled in 2000 that Howe repay $7.2 million of the

---

17 USTR, 'USTR Barshefsky announces results of Special 301 "out-of-cycle" reviews', *Press Release* 93–97, Washington, 27 October 1997, p. 30.

18 Peter Hartcher, 'Bum note: how the US refused Cabinet's CD deal', *Australian Financial Review*, 9 October 1997.

original loan money to the government.[19] This was also the first instance whereby the panel had actioned a private company to restore government funds. The concluding comments from the government acknowledged the difficulties of negotiating US aggression and the necessity for the proper functioning of the multilateral forums. Industry, Science and Resources Minister, Senator Nick Minchin responded:

> (a)lthough disappointed with the outcome of the WTO Panel Finding, Howe has accepted the terms of the understanding, which will now bring to an end the harassment inflicted on the company over the past four years.[20]

Mark Vaile concluded:

> (w)e have never been happy with the way the US has pursued this globally successful Australian company, while at the same time handing out billions of dollars in assistance to its own agricultural producers. It highlights the real inequities in WTO rules between manufacturers and agriculture which is why the Government strongly supports a new WTO round to rectify the situation.[21]

The importance of a rules-based multilateral system was again revealed through the US imposition of tariffs on Australasian lamb meat imports.

Lamb Tariffs

Notwithstanding that the US was preparing to host the Seattle WTO Round of Multilateral Trade Negotiations, seemingly with a view to extend the realm of free trade, in 1999 the Clinton Administration chose to protect its lamb industry from the 'onslaught' of Australian and New Zealand imports. While at the time this tactic might have seemed to embody some incongruity, it was, nonetheless, a pointer to Clinton's retreat in Seattle and an acknowledgment of the perennial potency of US domestic pressures, especially pertinent in advance of a Presidential election. Any efforts by Australia to influence the US decision through a process of cultural bargaining would be rendered impotent by US attention to its local concerns.

In 1998, at various US Congress Committee Hearings, the American Sheep Industry (ASI) began a vociferous campaign to highlight their plight. In February, Steve Raftopoulos for the ASI announced that the direct competition of Australian and New Zealand lamb was creating havoc for US producers. Further, he also denied the claim that the foreign producers had created a niche market and thus were irrelevant

---

19 Howe was also removed from the Textile, Clothing and Footwear (Strategic Investment Program) Scheme and the Automotive Competitiveness and Investment Scheme. Minister for Trade, Mark Vaile and the Minister for Industry, Science and Resources, Nick Minchin, 'Settlement reached with US on Howe leather dispute', *Joint Media Release*, MVT64/2000, 21 June 2000.

20 Minister for Trade, Mark Vaile and the Minister for Industry, Science and Resources, Nick Minchin, 21 June 2000.

21 Minister for Trade, Mark Vaile and the Minister for Industry, Science and Resources, Nick Minchin, 21 June 2000.

to the local producers' troubles.[22] By 1998, approximately one third of lamb supplies in the US originated from Australia and New Zealand. Imports were all too regularly reported to be 'flooding' the market. And 98.3 per cent of this tsunami originated in Australasia.[23] To add salt to the wounds these Antipodean exports dominated the Mexican market. Together with Chile, they had routed American exports to Mexico, such that US live sheep exports had dropped from 830,000 in 1993, to 280,000 by 1997.[24]

These overseas exports were roundly aided by the Asian currency crisis in 1997/8. During this period, the Australasian exports became 10 per cent less expensive while the Asian market itself became a much less attractive market for imports. (By December, the Australian dollar had fallen against the greenback by about 6 cents since the start of the year.) At the same time, the European Union (EU), true to form, steadfastly maintained strict quotas, thus preventing any respite for the US producers. Exacerbating the problem for the US, the ASI claimed the EU provided government subsidies to producers in excess of US$2 billion annually. The US market then was one of the few significant attractions left for Australian lamb exporters.[25]

To compensate an industry beset by an efficient foreign opposition and a marked volatility in the market, the ASI was vocal in requesting assistance from the government. The US Department of Agriculture had responded to the deluge of imports by purchasing $US 8 million of lamb. But this was not enough for a beleaguered Industry. A phalanx of US producers turned to the US International Trade Commission (ITC).

By February 1999, the six ITC commissioners had determined unanimously that the US domestic industry was threatened by increased imports of meat from Australia and New Zealand.[26] Ultimately, however, it was for Clinton, with final authority over Section 201 of US Trade Law, to decide whether to impose restrictions on foreign lamb, and if so, also to determine the severity of the measures. It was expected that he would deliver a verdict by 4 June 1999. And so the lobbying began…

Believing that they had worked assiduously to overcome difficult times through the investment of ideas and capital to create the US opportunities, Australian farmers were rightly frustrated by the possibility of constraints. Half of their total lamb meat exports were produced for the US market. Farm lobby groups mobilised to respond. Direct action was taken to publicise the farmers' plight. Staff at the US Embassy in Canberra were met with a much televised lamb barbeque to protest the US

---

22 Steve Raftopoulos, Testimony on behalf of the ASI, *The Subcommittee on Livestock, Dairy and Poultry Committee on Agriculture transcript, US House of Representatives*, Washington, DC, 26 February 1998, p. 1.

23 United States International Trade Commission, Lamb Meat, Investigation No. TA-201-68, Determination and Views of the Commission, *USITC Publication No. 3176*, April 1999, pp. I–5.

24 Testimony of Lorin Moensch, Jr., *US Senate Committee Hearing*, pp. 1–4.

25 For details of Australian lamb exports to major destinations in 2000 see, Warren Truss, Minister for Agriculture, Fisheries and Forestry, 'Lamb levy relief to continue following US decision', *Media Release*, September 2001, p. 2.

26 USITC, 'ITC says increased imports of lamb meat threaten US industry', *News Release*, 99–022, 9 February 1999.

restrictions when they opened their doors one evening. More emotion was vented at the 10 June meeting in Harden, southern NSW. At the Harden Sheep Abattoir, a joint US/Australian lamb export facility, Deputy PM, Tim Fischer addressed a community that was anticipating a loss of approximately $60,000 per week in direct and associated revenue.[27]

Australian lamb producers were infuriated by the prospect of restrictions and took their protest to Washington. Acting to protect their hard won $108 million industry, these farmers pursued all available options. Fuelled by reports that the White House was considering even more stringent measures than those recommended by the ITC, the Australian farmers sought to argue their case visibly and vocally. Most galling for them was that the US product was considered to be inferior. Poor farming techniques coupled with inadequate business strategies left the US beleaguered by low demand. US farmers did indeed have a problem with a poor quality product and were suffering as a result. Structural decline was clearly evident, with 90 per cent of US farms reduced to holding less than 100 sheep.[28] While this had been recognised in the past, assistance offered by the US government in previous years had not been utilised. Congress had already established the ineffective National Sheep Industry Improvement Centre in 1996 and allocated US$20 million to improve the quality of the attendant processes and product. This money remained at the table however, as the Secretary of Agriculture had not received any plans for its utilisation.[29]

Importantly, Commissioner Carol Crawford also recorded that '(t)here is no allegation of any unfair trade practices by the foreign producers.'[30] This notion was restated at the Trade and Investment Framework Meeting conducted in Washington in May where Tim Fischer attempted to counter the momentum generated by the ITC decision.

In attempting to salve the wounds of the American sheep ranchers, their Australian and New Zealand counterparts had also offered $1.5 million over four years to improve product demand through a high-level marketing campaign within the US. But, in signaling their focus on internal assistance, the ASI rejected comprehensively both the offer and its suggestion of an outward looking expansive solution. Contrary to the Australasian producers, in difficult times the US producers had chosen to sequester themselves from the global trading environment.

In attempting to broaden the Australian argument, the National Farmers' Federation endeavoured to broadcast the hypocrisy of the US free trade rhetoric. NFF President, Ian Donges, claimed US policy for Seattle would invariably be singed by this dispute

---

27 National Farmers' Federation, 'Aussie lamb producers have an impact in The White House', *News Release*, NR 72/99, 10 June 1999.

28 Minister for Trade, Mark Vaile, 'Background: WTO Dispute Settlement – US Lamb', *Media Release*, 2 May 2001.

29 USITC Report, 'Lamb Meat: Investigation No. TA-201-68, Determination and Views of the Commission', p. I–57.

30 See Commissioner Carol T. Crawford's assessment in the USITC Report, 'Lamb Meat: Investigation No. TA-201-68, Determination and Views of the Commission', p. I 34. See also Additional Statement by Commissioner Carol T. Crawford on Remedy Investigation No. TA-201-68 Lamb Meat, 26 March 1999.

should Clinton retreat to domestic protectionism.[31] Dean Kleckner, President of the American Farm Bureau Federation also admitted that should Clinton restrict foreign producers' entry into the US market, US free trade credentials would be damaged. While indicating his opposition to the move, nonetheless, he was concerned for US farmers suffering in difficult times.[32]

As the Howard government had promoted its intended alliance relations as a feature of its 1996 electoral campaign, it was keen to demonstrate its effectiveness to its constituency. Howard had written to Clinton on 22 May detailing the government's concerns regarding its prospective protectionist approach to its sheep meat industry. He had followed up on this with phone calls to Clinton, and Alexander Downer had met with Barshefsky in Washington.[33] Andrew Peacock, Australian Ambassador to the United States, was dispatched to the ITC to present evidence at the hearings and Fischer ran hard with the issue in his visit to the US in May.[34] In order to sway the US decision, an Australian government delegation gambled on the offers to American sheep producers and increased the assistance offer to $6 million. Fischer met with Deputy US Trade Representative Richard Fisher, Trade Ambassador Susan Esserman and Assistant US Trade Representative, Donald Phillips to discuss the issue. 'LAMBPLAN', the Australian quality assurance programme, whereby the size of lambs was increased and leaner meat produced to suit the American market, was also offered to the Americans.[35] However, as Fischer had stated at Harden, the Australian government was willing to pursue this matter in the WTO should the US isolate their market.[36]

Although the government intended to use the APEC forum to further its arguments in an environment claiming credentials in lowering trade barriers, it would find little solace. Ian Donges' plans to continue discussions with Barshefsky at the Trade Ministers' conference were thwarted by her timely absence from the meeting altogether. Moreover, APEC's malaise in committing to reductions in trade barriers was becoming problematic. Liberalising commitments to the Early Voluntary Sectoral Liberalisation (EVSL) as decided upon in Kuala Lumpur (1998) and Auckland (1999) were eventually referred to the WTO because of the intransigence in progression and delivery. Despite much talk of sheep at APEC then, peer group pressure was decidedly ineffective in affecting the US decision. Certainly, the US was not one to be co-opted by the ruminations of its trans-Pacific allies.

---

31 National Farmers' Federation, 'Bad News on Lamb', *News Release*, NR 71/99, 8 June 1999.

32 Dean Kleckner, 'Recent Developments in US Trade Policy – Implications for the Next WTO Round', *Speech at the National Press Club*, Canberra, 16 April 1999.

33 The Hon. Alexander Downer, MP, Australia's Minister for Foreign Affairs, Washington D.C., *Transcript of Door Stop Interview*, 16 June 1999, p. 1.

34 John Howard, MP, PM (Bennelong), 'Trade: Lamb Exports to the United States of America', *Commonwealth Parliamentary Debates, House of Representatives, Hansard*, Question without notice, 3 June 1999, p. 5989.

35 National Farmers' Federation, 'It's Official! – White House torn Over Lamb Tariffs', *News Release*, NR 90/99, 29 June 1999.

36 Tim Fischer, MP (Farrer), 'Trade: Lamb Exports', *Commonwealth Parliamentary Debates, House of Representatives, Hansard*, Question without notice, 24 June 1999, p. 7451.

US Trade Law

If Australian farmers may have found some solace in Clinton's delay in decision-making, they had underestimated the potency of domestic politics within the US. And for an indication of the final decision, Australian sheep farmers needed to have looked no further than Barshefsky's understanding of how US trade law operated.

To be sure, the USTR had already foreshadowed the hard-line response that Clinton would eventually choose. At US Senate hearings, Barshefsky had explained how the internal trade law process operated. It is worth quoting at length as it clearly enunciates the primacy of US constituents over allies and the use of US trade law to defend domestic interests:

> ...on the one hand, there's no question that Australia and New Zealand are critical allies of the United States, and there is no question that the United States policy these past six and a half years has been one substantially favoring free trade over any forms of import protection. But in this case, where domestic industry has decisively won the case that it brought...then I think it is incumbent on the administration to think carefully through the remedy options and to look out for the interests of American producers, particularly inasmuch as our trade laws don't contemplate public interest or national security waivers but instead are concerned with the health and vitality of our domestic industries.[37]

Any Australian question as to the priorities of the Clinton Administration was explicitly answered by Barshefsky's testimony.

If the US trade law juggernaut was suggesting assistance for the US farmers, then Clinton's domestic political environment was also inexorably oriented to support their cause. Al Gore's Democrat presidential campaign was reliant on the support of trade unions focused on the immediate security of US workers and industries.[38]

More intimately, Clinton was acutely aware of the particular demands of two influential Democrat senators. South Dakotan Tom Daschle and Max Baucus of Montana both represented ailing lamb farming states and were urging Clinton for assistance. As Daschle had been crucial in sustaining Democrat senate support for Clinton during the impeachment trial, Clinton's options for denying support for the lamb industry were considerably weakened. Thus, the Clinton Administration remained untouched by Howard's assessment that '(a)ny restraint on imports would be a damaging step in the bilateral trade relationship between Australia and the United States'.[39]

---

37 US Congressional Hearings, Hearing of the House Agriculture Committee, '1999 WTO Ministerial in Seattle Washington', 23 June 1999, Washington D.C., accessed from *Federal Information Systems Corporation*, p. 21.

38 Informed Australian politicians from both political parties, and negotiators, had always acknowledged the potency of the AFL-CIO union group in influencing decision-making in the US.

39 John Howard, MP, PM (Bennelong), 'Trade: Lamb Exports to the United States', *Commonwealth Parliamentary Debates, House of Representatives, Hansard*, Question without Notice, 3 June 1999, p. 5989.

Crisis for Australian Lamb Producers

Unmoved by any connection with Australia, Clinton imposed a temporary quantitative limitation on the imports of lamb from Australia and New Zealand in order to safeguard the US industry. This amounted to a tariff rate quota and increased duties on the foreign lamb.

Although the US Embassy in Canberra claimed that Washington was sensitive to Australian concerns and had considered its ally in its decision-making,[40] Clinton's impositions were more restrictive than the ITC recommendations. Canberra's lack of influence was then further exposed when Howard visited Washington the following week. Andrew Peacock had prearranged an array of luminaries such as Albright, Greenspan, Wolfensohn, Nasser and Korth to fete the PM at the Embassy barbeque, but Clinton remained unresponsive. Clinton instead, regarded the lamb dispute in anti-dumping terms and was more interested in the US producers and employment issues than in Australia or its laments.

Eventually the dispute was resolved not through any particular influence exercised through bilateral channels. Only after the Australian challenge in the WTO was the US forced to revoke its restrictions. However, by the time of the eventual resolution, US producers had enjoyed two years of assistance. Eventually, after a US appeal against the original decision, the WTO Appellate Body upheld the panel's initial findings that, although the temporary institution of safeguard measures is allowable under WTO guidelines, their necessity remained unproven in this dispute and thus was inappropriately applied. The Bush Administration, newly elected in 2000, rescinded the tariff-rate quotas effective 15 November 2001 (after the June deadline for retraction had passed). Not to be constrained by the international body, however, the new USTR, Robert Zoellick, announced that the US lamb industry would receive up to US$42.7 million through the financial year 2003, to continue its adjustments to import competition.[41]

Even though the Australian government had made no impact on the US decision, they had demonstrated their ardent and vociferous support for the lamb producers. Important to the individual farmers though it was, the effects of the US tariffs probably amounted to a loss of $10–15 million. With government support, the industry received compensation in the form of payments equivalent to half the transaction levy for all lambs sold within Australia, monies estimated to be approximately $6–7 million. Establishment of the lamb industry development plan was also made available to producers and processors.

Yet much was made of this $10–15 million issue as the government had been quite intent on elevating the dispute with the US beyond its immediate powers to implement a resolution. Two factors explain the government's motivations; first, a local agricultural industry was threatened and second, one sector of the Coalition's constituency was rural voters. To be sure, as a farmer himself, Tim Fischer was

---

40 US Embassy Canberra, 'Decision on US Lamb Imports', *Press Release*, Canberra, 8 July 1999.

41 USTR, 'Bush Administration Settles Lamb Safeguard Issue with Australia and New Zealand', *Press Release*, Washington, 31 August 2001.

readily able to empathise, acknowledge the endeavours and plight of Australian agricultural producers, and thus dash to defend the sheep producers' interests. Through necessity, many Australian agricultural producers had become efficient producers and exporters. Self-preservation against the assailing and ongoing decline in world commodity prices and the exigencies of farming in a small country unable to match the agricultural subsidies of the major players, particularly the EU, Japan, and the US, meant that the many farmers who had survived had become highly proficient practitioners. Australia's farming heritage was also etched indelibly on the white Australian psyche. So although agriculture only comprised three per cent of the Australian economy (higher as an export component) sustaining the farming community for its multifunction role also had relevance in Australia. It was not just a preserve of the European or Japanese societies.

It should also be noted that the farmers were well organised and vocal through bodies such as the National Farmers' Federation. Through their activism in the Cairns Group, the NFF were highly conversant with the WTO rules on agriculture. As such, they were often effective in working with DFAT and lobbying for government action. Some Australian farmers also looked cynically on US agricultural trade practice while others had previously been affected directly by the restrictive nature of US Farm Bills and EEP restrictions in the 1980s and early 1990s. When George H. Bush visited Australia in 1991, wheat farmers were quite prepared to vent their frustrations publicly. In this dispute then, farmers were no less infuriated, nor active. Lamb farmer Sue Morrison interviewed by the ABC laid it bare: '(m)ore of the same. Kick in the pants from America. I mean they've done it before and they'll keep doing it I guess.'[42] Any agricultural *shadenfreude* was not about to be assuaged by ineffective political rhetoric. NFF President Donges had declared:

> (w)e expect the PM to transmit our fury to the President Clinton when he meets next week. Without a doubt, that meeting will be extremely important and Australian lamb producers will be watching for the outcome of that meeting.[43]

Politically, however, no goading was necessary for the Coalition government to respond to the farmers' plight. Smarting from One Nation's plunder of the Coalition's rural vote in recent elections, here was an opportunity to resurrect their credentials. As Pauline Hanson's One Nation was a direct competitor with the Liberals and the Nationals, the latter moved to the right to maintain its voter base.[44] Given that Fischer had noted in parliament that the prime lamb industry was particularly prevalent in the electorates of Wannon, Mallee, Ballarat, and other Victorian seats,[45] here was an

42 Sue Morrison interviewed by Barrie Cassidy, 7.30 Report transcript, 'America's free trade credibility on the line after closing door on lamb', *ABC Television*, 8 July 2001.

43 Ian Donges, NFF, interviewed by Barrie Cassidy, 7.30 Report transcript, 'America's free trade credibility on the line after closing door on lamb', *ABC Television*, 8 July 2001.

44 Rick DeAngelis, 'Pauline Hanson's One Nation Party: xenophobic populism compared', *Policy, Organisation and Society*, 16 Winter 1998, p. 12.

45 Tim Fischer, MP (Farrer), 'Trade: Lamb Exports', *Commonwealth Parliamentary Debates*, House of Representatives, Hansard, Question without notice, 29 March 1999, p. 4563.

opportunity for the Coalition to bolster its support in crucial Victorian electorates. After the Victorian state election, where the Coalition had lost support in rural areas, this was an opportunity for the Coalition to be vigorous in its defence.

And vigorous it was: but so much so that it concluded with the government hand overplayed. While governmental fervour may have whipped up a storm in the Australian media, given the exigencies of the US political environment, little could be done to alter the trajectory of the dispute. Even the visit to the US by Howard was futile in swaying the Administration's decision. Where Australian Prime Ministers have had productive exchanges with US Presidents, these discussions have been in their interpretations of the region. Yet Howard, to that point, had sparse experience in regional affairs. That the lamb dispute took precedence over the precariousness of the East Timorese scenario was further testimony to the intensity of Howard's focus on immediate domestic claims. While Howard had discussed the lamb dispute with Clinton for a cursory twenty minutes in private, the deteriorating situation in East Timor was hardly touched.

So, intended as astute domestic politics, the government's tactics were found wanting internationally. By the time the Administration was embarking upon the decision-making process it was too late for Australia. Both Bruce Wolpe and Paul Kelly had observed that, glamorous barbeques notwithstanding, Australia had not done enough to forward Australia's free trade arguments against the disintegration of the 'craven' political environment in Washington.[46] Not only was the media not utilised effectively but there also appeared to be little employment of effective lobbyists and lawyers to advance Australia's case. Moreover, these immediate inadequacies were exacerbated at that time by the more disturbing reductions in the Australian Embassy's Congressional liaison staff. Any small opportunity Australia may have had to affect the decision-making process had been forfeited.

Further, the government had made much of the need for greater intimacy in the bilateral relationship with the United States. On this issue Howard made much of his government's lobbying of the Administration and of his expression of dissatisfaction to the President: to no avail. Having raised expectations so much within Australia, the downside was exacerbated. Furthermore, it was illogical that Howard should comment that '(t)he decision is all the more disappointing because Australia is a close ally and friend.'[47] US trade law and politics are wholly separate entities from the Alliance. That the two should be connected at that time was a misinterpretation. This was a misperception that was subtly reinforced by the language of various AUSMIN meetings in its implications to the public: that cultural connections were of great significance and potency. Disappointment and resentment against the US, especially in the agricultural community would eventually be a product of such rhetoric. Why is it that even though the EU is such a great protectionist force, the US arouses greater public ire? In part, it is this shaped expectation of reciprocity that

46 Bruce Wolpe, 'Australia and America: Renewal and Reinvention', *Australian Journal of International Affairs*, vol. 54, no. 1, March 2000, p. 11, also Paul Kelly, 'We'll be losers in a lamb war', *The Australian*, 14 July 1999, p. 13.

47 John Howard, Prime Minister, 'US restrictions on Australian Lamb Exports', *Media Release*, Tokyo, 8 July 1999, p. 2.

amplifies the public disappointment. Ultimately, too, this will be counterproductive in any campaign to maintain and/or upgrade relations.

This dispute highlights the difficulties farmers and governments encounter in terms of efficiencies and multifunctionality on both sides of the Pacific. Yet even if farmers embrace new efficiency demands there is no guarantee, especially for those in smaller countries, that the *modus operandi* of world trade as it currently stands will reward their efforts. Farmers still await equity with manufactured goods in the trading arena. Although the WTO did eventually recognise the rights of the Australian producers to trade, a resolution was two years in the making. Ian Donges reflected in 2001 that:

> Australian farmers acknowledge that the WTO was the only process that would allow us to have a fair right of appeal under the international trading rules, but the time frame to achieve an outcome is obviously an area that needs reform when a new WTO round is launched – hopefully in November this year.[48]

Mark Vaile conveyed this message to the meeting of key trade ministers in Mexico in September 2001 in preparation for the Doha WTO talks, where Australia continued to press for another trade round to eliminate 'unfair agricultural rules'.[49]

These solutions, however apposite, have little to say about the saliency of domestic politics in both countries. Clinton, believing that Al Gore's election prospects would be assisted by a protectionist decision and under pressure to respond in similar fashion from party powerbrokers, was impelled to restrict the Australasian imports. Howard, too, saw opportunity in a striking reaction in the dispute. Despite having little effect on the outcome, Howard's public stance worked to enhance his broad political appeal, even if the agricultural producers themselves were too experienced and wily to be beguiled by political rhetoric.

Conclusion: Cultural Capital Flaws

Both of the trade disputes have provided an ideal opportunity to consider the Coalition's threat mediation strategy and deployment of bilateral policy-making in its early years in office. They display the Coalition's attentiveness to its domestic constituency in the quest for better international economic outcomes. They reveal the Coalition's attempts to employ culturally bound bargaining within the bilateral trade relationship with the US. While the government was keen to demonstrate the strength of its relationship with its American partner, it was unable to exercise the leverage persuasively enough to exact a suitable response. Conscious that Australia's trade position needed to be continually attended Australia attempted to trade on its alliance relations to effect results. However, cultural capital was an ineffective tool in countering US domestic interests' recourse to US trade law. Thus, any expectation that alliance relations of

48 National Farmers Federation, Ian Donges, in 'Spring finally back in Aussie lamb producers' steps', *NFF Media Release*, NR 107/2001, 1 September 2001.

49 Department of Foreign Affairs and Trade, Mark Vaile, Minister for Trade, 'US to Remove Lamb Tariffs on 15 November', *Media Release*, 1 September 2001, MVT119/2001.

themselves would suffice was inflated. In the asymmetric bilateral relationship with its traditional ally, this choice of diplomacy reliant on an intangible amity proved for the most part ineffective. Multilateral dispute resolution processes were the eventual catalyst for resolutions in both the lamb and leather disputes.

These disputes also indicated to the Australian government the relevance of the mediation process to US policy choices. Not only was the Howard government conscious of threat from both above and below but so too was the US. That the US should consider retaliation across different sectors was also indicative of the strength of the domestic dynamic in US trade policy. Trade policy choices made across the Pacific were highly responsive to the domestic sector and the Administration's interest in electoral survival. It was clear, then, in the trade arena that unless material interests were compatible or fungible, then negotiating a bargain was a difficult task. This issue was clearly evident in these two trade disputes: the next chapter takes up the need for convergence in security situations.

Chapter 3

Australia, the United States and East Timor: The Importance of Convergent Interests

When Sandy Berger, the former United States National Security Adviser, was asked about the importance of addressing the carnage in East Timor in September 1999, he likened it to the questionable need to direct his teenage daughter to clean up her room.[1] While this, of course, was a diplomatic slip hastily repented, it does suggest some of the difficulties for Australia as a smaller country, geographically and economically remote, in creating greater presence in alliance relations. The teenage metaphor itself is also an apt one for Australia in the context of the East Timor crisis. One of the consequences of a slew of Australian political and diplomatic failures prior to its International Force East Timor (INTERFET) successes was the precipitation of tension in the alliance at the margins, and the more significant ultimate reliance on US power. As such, one of the legacies of East Timor has been the re-emphasis on Australia's need for a potent ally.

As the initial foray into trade policy revealed, trade outcomes in alliance relations required more than reference to cultural associations. This too was evident in the security realm through the East Timor crisis. Despite the Coalition's upgrading of alliance relations in their term in office, their pattern of decision-making through East Timor's transition to independence served, temporarily, to exacerbate problems that power asymmetry and distance may precipitate. By implementing a defensive foreign policy derived from a set of internal preoccupations while simultaneously saddled with the sophisticated task of managing a complex set of special external relationships, the Coalition struggled, initially, to preside over good threat management policy. This dispute indicates the complexities of threat mediation and the sophistication needed to enact successful foreign policy management.

At the onset of the East Timor crisis, the familiar complexions of the alliance were seemingly altered. Australia rejected US interest in a more assertive role in the impending crisis in February 1999, refused US requests for Australian intelligence material (albeit small), and was denied direct US military involvement. Yet, despite the Coalition's public protestations of lack of US support during the crisis, the US provided the leverage whereby Indonesia would consent to outside intervention and Australia could partly extricate itself from a crisis.

---

1 Lincoln Wright, 'US adviser apologises for stupid metaphor', *Canberra Times*, 20 September 2000, p. 5.

The East Timor crisis constituted a learning experience for the Howard government in its relationship with the US. It is also clear, once again, that US interests need to be engaged for a bargain to be enacted. Cultural affinity would not suffice in determining US action, especially in the commitment of US combat personnel. This was particularly the case after a period where the deaths of US troops in Somalia had been so widely publicised. Yet, here, the Australian government also realised that without adept multilateral diplomacy skills or potent leverage of its own, the US was indeed a valuable ally to have in a crisis.

Waiting for the Sky to Fall and the Penny to Drop

As 1998 concluded, expectations within East Timor for a resolution with Indonesia over sovereignty issues became heightened. So too did those of the international community. Although in the air a whiff of greater independence was apparent, on the ground the potential for conflict was increasing. On 19 December 1998, Prime Minister Howard wrote to President Habibie explaining his proposal for East Timor's autonomy. And as Howard regarded the isolation of the East Timorese from the United Nations' autonomy process itself as detrimental to a lasting solution, he proposed that they be included. Although the Prime Minister believed that it was in each party's interests that East Timor remained part of Indonesia, Howard argued that elevated expectations in East Timor for a more democratic process could be met via the incorporation of a Matignon-style review mechanism within the autonomy package. In this way, both domestic East Timorese desires, together with pressures arising from the international community, could be assuaged. For Howard, a lengthy autonomy process, culminating in an offering of self-determination, would avoid any possibility that the Australian Defence Force (ADF) would confront the Indonesian military (ABRI). Not one for Matignon, however, Habibie fast tracked the process on 27 January 1999.

Captive of the 'historic shift',[2] the Australian Government now had the possibility of an immediate solution to its East Timor problem and a correspondent opportunity to brandish its regional credentials. And yet, despite Howard's claim that '[w]e played no small role' in the Habibie decision, he did not 'want to commit the Australian Government in advance to any particular role' in East Timor.[3]

Thus, when in Washington in February, US Assistant Secretary for East Asia, Stanley Roth, met with senior Australian diplomats Ashton Calvert and Peter Varghese to discuss East Timor, he discovered he was also meeting with resistance. Although Roth and his Indonesian advisor, Karen Brookes, had a collection of considerations in their presentation, Roth differed from the Australians in that he personally considered the possibility of a solution to the determination issue in much more proactive terms. It was evident that underlying his thoughts was a clear and considerable analysis of the security situation and a plan to achieve reconciliation.

---

2 Alexander Downer, Minister for Foreign Affairs, 'Australian Government Historic Shift On East Timor', *Media Release*, 12 January 1999.

3 Paul Daley, 'Howard unwilling on peace force for Timor', *The Age*, 30 January 2000, p. 1.

As stated in his testimony to the US Senate Foreign Relations Committee, the East Timor process had to be observed closely, as the prospect for violence was real.[4] Eventually, as the State Department viewed the situation as unacceptable, Secretary of State Madeleine Albright delivered a speech in Jakarta which sought to remedy a declining security situation. The four prongs of her message involved: ABRI's immediate disarmament of the factions; the proposed 'Peace and Stability Council' be given serious consideration; encouragement of ABRI to begin a 'draw down'; and the implementation of 'confidence building measures' which included the reduction in troop numbers and an 'international presence to reduce the prospects for future violence'.[5]

As to the process by which the East Timorese would be consulted, Roth and Brookes thought that a consultative council was the best option. Aware that unity in Indonesia was a primary concern, they considered a referendum in East Timor would raise the stakes for Indonesia in managing its sovereignty dilemmas in other provinces. As a consequence, it was vital that both Congress and the UN be persuaded that this was necessary. This Council would build on the UN's conceptualisation of a 'friends' group that would help to construct and preserve international interest and support for a peacekeeping operation.

The Australians, however, were reticent to respond to Roth's proposals. Instead, Australia presumed that Jakarta could be persuaded to consider its international reputation more carefully and that the East Timorese should understand that UN assistance would not necessarily be forthcoming, because it was up to them to 'sort themselves out'. At the time the Australian government was making this statement, it had been in receipt of intelligence material that had stated ABRI's role since the end of 1998 in arming local militias and subcontracting out its security intentions.[6]

DFAT has argued since that Australian policy did not stand in 'opposition' to Roth's proposals. It maintains that Roth understood Australian policy-makers to be cognisant of the potential for a worst-case situation developing. It was also clear that Australia needed to encourage the international community to insist that the Indonesians and East Timorese cooperate on a peaceful solution.[7]

Since the Australian diplomats presented a view that 'adept diplomacy' would render a military option unnecessary, and that troops would not be sent into a bloodbath, a proactive rather than a passive diplomacy was necessary. Most certainly, the management of conflicting Indonesian territorial and East Timorese sovereignty claims needed a sophisticated diplomatic act that understood the necessity for a multilateral response. However, Howard's inability to elevate the standing of the East Timor issue in formal talks with President Clinton in May in Washington – instead

---

4 US Congressional Hearings, US Senate Foreign Relations Committee, *Hearing of the East Asian and Pacific Affairs Subcommittee, Indonesia and the Countdown to Elections*, Washington, 18 March 1999, p. 3.

5 Secretary of State, Madeleine K. Albright, 'Indonesia, the United States and Democracy', Remarks at the Borobodur Intercontinental Hotel, Jakarta, 5 March 1999, p. 5.

6 Desmond Ball, 'Silent witness: Australian Intelligence and East Timor', *The Pacific Review*, special edition, vol. 14, no. 1, 2001, pp. 43–50.

7 DFAT, *East Timor in Transition 1998–2000: An Australian Policy Challenge*, Canberra, 2001, p. 52.

of choosing to focus on the lamb dispute – was demonstrative of the government's mood.

In response to a parliamentary question shortly after, Downer outlined the government's thinking on the issue of peacekeeping. He stated that 'it has been widely agreed that discussion of peacekeeping (was) premature' because there was no peace to keep. Furthermore, he contended that: (a) it often undermined the processes of conflict resolution by removing direct responsibility from the participants and; (b) there was an absence of broad UN support for further action. Crucially for Downer, as East Timor remained under Indonesian sovereignty, Indonesia's assent was essential to any intervention.[8] But the peace to keep was diminishing. In April 1999, at least twenty-five East Timorese civilians were slaughtered by the Red and White Iron militia in Liquicia, followed by the massacre of twenty civilians in Dili on the 'Invade Dili' day organised by the local militias. Meanwhile, the Howard government had organised the Bali bilateral summit on 27 April in the attempt to stem the violence by simultaneously exerting pressure on Indonesia to act responsibly in East Timor and to seek peaceful solutions among the East Timorese. Indonesian international adviser Dewi Fortuna Anwar recalls that Howard asked Habibie to accept an international peacekeeping force, but was rebuffed. So, while Australia continued to exercise its belief that it could influence Indonesian policy (and numbers of UN civilian police were increased by 200–300),[9] the militia destruction continued.

While the UN pushed ahead with the 5 May tripartite arrangements whereby the people of East Timor would have the opportunity to accept or reject special autonomy within the Republic of Indonesia,[10] the US State Department was so concerned over the violence being perpetrated in East Timor that it requested Australian intelligence material to assist in its assessment of Indonesian military involvement. If it could be ascertained that it was not just rogue elements of the military implicated but an orchestration conducted by senior ABRI personnel, then the ability to sway both the US Congress and the UN for more forceful action would be enhanced. Grasping the Australian government's reluctance to pursue the matter, the US would also be able to discuss it directly with the Indonesians. If, however, it was uncertain who was responsible and the links in the chain of command were unable to be established, then the case for external international action was untenable. The Australian government, at the time of the initial request in March, had clearly placed its faith in the Indonesians to arrest the violence and in its own ability to address the problems at a diplomatic level. As a consequence intelligence material was denied to the US on the grounds that it would compromise Australian sources within Indonesia.[11]

---

8 Alexander Downer, response to question on notice, no. 459, 'East Timor: Peacekeeping Forces', *CPD, House Hansard*, 8 March 1999, p. 5104.

9 DFAT, *East Timor in Transition 1998–2000: An Australian Policy Challenge*, Canberra, 2001, p. 80.

10 United Nations, 'Appendix: Constitutional framework for a special autonomy', 5 May 1999.

11 Marian Wilkinson, 'Why we kept Timor secrets from the US', *Sydney Morning Herald*, 13 August 1999, p. 3.

The requests for information, however, also continued at a bureaucratic level within the intelligence organisations themselves. Intelligence expert, Desmond Ball, stated that under recent secret agreements between Australia, the United States, the United Kingdom and Canada, Australia had new responsibilities for intelligence collection in Southeast Asia. As a result, the Central Intelligence Agency (CIA) was pushing Australia's Defence Intelligence Organisation (DIO) for access to selected material. However, the Office of National Assessment (ONA) asserted that DIO's links with the CIA should be channelled through its arrangements. Consequently, the DIO liaison officer in the Washington Embassy, Merv Jenkins, was then placed in a difficult situation in the conflict between the three intelligence agencies. Jenkins committed suicide shortly after documenting the pressure he felt through this dilemma.[12] Clearly, the new intelligence sharing arrangements had presumed a policy consensus that was unable to be met in this instance.

It was during this period, however, that the Howard government was gradually overwhelmed by the information insinuating the ABRI's involvement. (The Indonesian military was renamed as the TNI.) Australian intelligence organisations continued to report on the links in the chain of command which culminated with TNI's Commander in Chief, General Wiranto. The Australian Secret Intelligence Service (ASIS) had been assisted in its investigations by the defection of Tomas Goncalves, a former senior ranking militia leader. His information was damning.[13] In addition to the direct reports received through intelligence agencies, non-government organisations and Australian Federal Police (AFP) workers also contributed commentary on the violence. Wayne Sievers, with the AFP, provided an array of detailed logistical information, together with command structures, that once again confirmed the militia–TNI links. As for the violence that erupted after the ballot, Sievers expressed his dark expectation as: 'it was like waiting for the sky to fall in on you'.[14]

Darkness in Timor: Dawn in Australia

At this point the government made some attempt to act upon the intensity of this evidence and endeavoured to revisit discussions with its 'special relationship' partners: Indonesia and the US. Even though they aimed to persuade the Indonesians to arrest the violence, the government was still focused upon the conduct of the ballot. If any intervention was to be contemplated, it would be done with a post-ballot result in mind. Still assured of its ability to influence the Indonesians, the government chose Vice CDF Marshal Riding to discuss the evidence with TNI senior officers, including Lieutenant General Bambang Yudhoyono, the second most senior

12 Desmond Ball, 'Silent witness: Australian Intelligence and East Timor', *The Pacific Review*, special edition, vol. 14, no. 1, 2001, pp. 52–53.

13 Tomas Goncalves, interviewed in, 'The Ties That Bind', Four Corners, *ABC Television*, 14 February 2000.

14 Lincoln Wright, 'Secret Defence Papers Show "conspiracy" at Highest Level', *Canberra Times*, 24 November 1999, p. 1.

army officer. This approach was received with some hostility and was dismissed by the TNI.

Nearly three weeks after Riding's meeting with the TNI, the Australian Embassy in Washington was instructed to brief the US Department of Defense on TNI–militia links. Fearing that the US was preoccupied by Kosovo and not engaged with East Timor, Australia moved to speak frankly with the US. By this stage, however, both US and Australian defence forces had been contemplating possible involvement. Air Vice Marshal Treloar, Commander of the Australian Theatre, had already been briefed by US Pacific Command (PACOM) on their *preplanning* should the US administration decide either a peacekeeping or peace enforcement operation was necessary. Although they were aware of the Howard government's attitude, they still sought Australian assistance and the use of Darwin from which to stage an operation. Australia and the Marine Forces Pacific had already been working collaboratively on possibilities for a peacekeeping operation with the Third Marine Expeditionary Force in Okinawa as the task force for further activity.

Australian and US officials met again in Washington on 16–17 August where there was joint concern for the security situation. Two days later, however, DFAT had instructed personnel in regional Australian diplomatic posts to seek the earliest deployment of civilian police and military liaison officers in the period immediately post-ballot but prior to the ratification of the vote by the Indonesian Parliament which would allow for the UN-administered transition to independence.

After the ballot on 30 August, 78.5 per cent of registered voters in East Timor rejected the proposed autonomy proposition and voted for independence. However, widespread violence ensued following the ballot. Further, Australia's confidence in its ability to influence Indonesia and its presumption of authority borne from years of building the bilateral relationship was shattered when President Habibie and General Wiranto ceased to communicate with their Australian counterparts. At this time, the US was reporting on their aggressive and consistent public and diplomatic efforts in tackling the Indonesians. Stanley Roth, who had maintained an acute awareness of the potential for collapse since the alteration of the process of autonomy, held the TNI 'accountable for incidents that take place in the capital city and...around the UN compound'.[15] Moreover, he suggested that as Indonesia had not kept its tripartite commitments as it agreed, then it risked international intervention in the province.

This message was reinforced repeatedly by the US over the following ten days. In her discussions with Ali Alatas, on 7 September, Secretary of State Madeleine Albright responded to Indonesia's implementation of a 'state of military emergency' by suggesting that Indonesia 'did not have much time, that they had to deal with this, otherwise it was essential for the international community to take care of this'.[16] Albright had also conveyed US concerns to Habibie and Wiranto. US Ambassador to Indonesia Stapleton Roy continued to reinforce Roth's message, and Defense Secretary Cohen had communicated in writing to Wiranto. Clinton had communicated

15 Stanley Roth interviewed by Kerry O'Brien, 7.30 Report, 'World losing patience with violence in East Timor', *ABC Television*, 2 September 1999.

16 Secretary of State, Madeleine K. Albright, *Transcript of 'East Timor Crisis: US others consider "variety of options" re Timor terror'*, 7 September 1999, US Department of State.

US views directly to Habibie.[17] It was, however, Joint Chief of Staff General Henry Shelton's telephone call to General Wiranto, conveying a message from Clinton that the carnage was 'unacceptable', that was believed to be most persuasive. By 9 September, Admiral Denis Blair, Commander in Chief, Pacific Area Command, informed Wiranto that the US had suspended operational military contact with Indonesia. Congress warned that further International Monetary Fund (IMF), World Bank and Asian Development Bank aid funding was also jeopardised.

The regional Asia–Pacific Economic Cooperation (APEC) meeting in Auckland presented as an opportune time for Clinton both to conclude this series of public threats seeking to elicit a response from Indonesia and to galvanise international support for a UN response to the crisis. However, the APEC Heads of Government summit in New Zealand was fortuitous, as those countries that would be most likely to react to the crisis were those attending the APEC summit. With US pressure propelling Indonesia toward the acceptance of external assistance, Clinton thus entreated his counterparts to assist.[18]

Acknowledgment, in part, of the effect of aggressive US diplomacy came later that day with Habibie's eventual invitation for a UN peacekeeping force to join the Indonesians in establishing and maintaining security. This was taken up by the UN Security Council which, under Resolution 1264, approved of a multinational force, to restore peace and security in East Timor and to protect and support United Nations Assistance Mission East Timor (UNAMET). This force was authorised to do whatever necessary to ensure success. By 6 September, Annan had requested that Australia direct a multinational force. If the US had exuded strength and clarity in its efforts to persuade Indonesia to accede to assistance, confirming its role in the provision of UN personnel was much more elusive.

With the opportunity now provided for UN peace enforcers, and a public overwhelmingly supportive of Australian military involvement, the Australian Government was frantic to secure significant assistance from other governments. Reportedly, Australia's request for up to 15,000 US Marines was denied.[19] With the reluctance of both the US and the Association of South-East Asian Nations (ASEAN) to commit forces, the Australian Government was struggling to enhance both its operational and political authority. Although Downer had informed parliament in early August of US reluctance to participate with ground troops, at least prior to any UN force structure,[20] many in the Australian public had assumed support from their traditional ally. By 7 September, however, it seemed that in Howard's discussions with Clinton it was decided that because the US had heavy peacekeeping

---

17 Statement by Thomas R. Pickering, Undersecretary of State for Political Affairs Indonesia, *Testimony on East Timor Crisis*, 9 September 1999.

18 President Bill Clinton, *Transcript of Remarks at CEO Summit Breakfast*, 'The eyes of the world today...are on East Timor', 12 September 1999.

19 Leon T. Harder, 'East Timor and the "Slippery Slope" Problem', *CATO Institute, Foreign Policy Briefing*, no. 55, 20 December 1999, p. 6. Also, Rod Lyon and William T. Tow, 'The Future of the Australian–US Security Relationship', *Strategic Studies Institute, US Army War College*, Carlisle, December 2003, p. 7.

20 Alexander Downer, 'East Timor: Peacekeeping', *House of Representatives Hansard*, 10 August 1999, p. 8246.

commitments elsewhere in the world, it would not be committing combat troops.[21] This was stated categorically the following day by Defense Secretary William Cohen when he outlined what would be US unwillingness to deploy combat troops. Here, he pre-empted Sandy Berger's reluctance to involve the US:

> The United States cannot be and should not be viewed as the policeman of the world... We act where it's in our national interests to act ... But we have to be selective where we commit our forces, and under the circumstances, this is not an area that we're prepared to commit our forces to.[22]

Acting both on Cohen's recommendation and on the advice of the national security team, as well as consultations with Congress and the Australian Government, Clinton chose to contribute to the UN force in restricted fashion. This included approximately 200 personnel as well as resources to assist in communications, logistics, intelligence and air lift operations.

This was, however, in addition to the intelligence assistance already provided in 1999. Temporary realignments of one of the Pine Gap satellites had been agreed to by the US to assist in the collection of super high-frequency materials. The US Navy flew airborne reconnaissance aircraft on numerous missions gathering communications data. It also tapped underwater cables and anchored US Navy ships offshore for the same purpose. Furthermore, the US had updated Australian intelligence technological resources for more sophisticated processing, integration and dissemination.

Australian and US Interests

Nonetheless, for the Howard government, which had sought to further its ties with its traditional allies, the absence of US 'boots on the ground' came as a disappointment.[23] Howard had recounted to parliament that he had discussed this issue with Clinton on three occasions, the first of which took place on 6 September, and that Defence Minister Moore had also explored direct US involvement with Cohen. Both received the same negative response. As a consequence, the Prime Minister reflected in parliament that no *formal* request was made: 'You do not formally request something which you know from earlier discussions, for a combination of reasons, is simply not going to be available.'[24] The informal Australian request had been rejected; Clinton had advised that the US already had 14,000 troops in Kosovo and a Congress that was unsympathetic. Although the Prime Minister had indicated to Clinton that

21 Tim Fischer, 'Good, bad and ugly of US–Australia relations', *The Australian*, 5 June 2000, p. 13.

22 Defense Secretary, William Cohen, *Transcript: Cohen Remarks on Situation in East Timor* (Says there is no plan to send US peacekeepers), Pentagon, 9 September 1999.

23 PM John Howard, Response to a question without notice from Stephen Martin, *CPD, House Hansard*, 30 September 1999, p. 11088, and Response to a question without notice from Kim Beazley, *CPD, House Hansard*, 29 September 1999, p. 10899.

24 Prime Minister, John Howard, *CPD, House of Representatives Hansard*, Questions Without Notice, 'East Timor: United States Forces', 29 September 1999, pp. 102899–900.

both 'the Australian government and the Australian people expected an American involvement',[25] the US had fleshed out its own expectations by stating that Australia 'must take the lead on this' and considered that it should be assisted by ASEAN contributions.[26]

Since it had stated its stretched capacity, the US then allocated 260 personnel to provide airborne reconnaissance, intelligence capability and secure telecommunications to assist INTERFET. This also included a coordination centre integrating both the military and humanitarian operations. The cruiser USS *Mobile Bay* monitored the Timor Sea and offered a mid-ocean landing pad for pilots between Darwin and Dili if necessary, while destroyer USS *O'Brien* and ammunition ship USNS *Kilauea* were also on assignment in the area as part of the Crocodile 99 Australia–US combined exercises.[27]

When Operation Stabilise commenced on 20 September, by far the majority of the INTERFET troops landing at Komoro Airport in Dili were Australian. Major General Peter Cosgrove commanded a force of around 2,800 troops, 2,000 of whom were Australian. The initial naval contingent included frigates HMAS *Anzac*, *Adelaide*, *Darwin*, the heavy lift HMAS *Tobruk*, catamaran HMAS *Jervis Bay*, the replenishment ship HMAS *Success* and two Heavy Landing Craft. Firm commitments of troops also came from Singapore, Thailand, Italy, The Philippines, France, Canada, Ireland, New Zealand, United Kingdom, Malaysia and Brazil.[28] INTERFET was ultimately composed of over 9,000 troops from sixteen countries, 6,000 of which were Australian. Japan's contribution, of approximately US$100 million to the UN Trust Fund to support INTERFET, assisted developing countries to participate in the multinational force. Although US Brigadier-General John Castellaw, who was attached to INTERFET, based in Darwin, flew into East Timor with Cosgrove, at that time only nine Americans were deployed for duty in Dili.

If it appeared that the Australian public opinion and the Howard government were experiencing some ill feelings in the relationship, they were reputedly not alone in their discontent. *The Australian* newspaper's banner headline on 17 September wailed 'US fury at our "failings"'. Journalist Dennis Shanahan reported a raft of US senior officials' criticisms over Australia's role in the East Timor crisis. These were:

> a) Australia did not pass on full intelligence regarding the influx of refugees to West Timor, b) Failed to explain the dangers of the independence ballot during May talks with President Clinton, c) Underestimated the number of refugees needing aid, d) Poor contingency planning, e) Defence Minister John Moore's handling of the logistics of the

---

25 Prime Minister, John Howard, *CPD, House of Representatives Hansard*, p. 102900.

26 William Cohen, 'Countries in region must do their part for peace', *The Today Show*, Channel 9 Television, 29 September 1999.

27 Jim Garamone, 'Clinton Says US Would Aid Aussie Peacekeepers in Timor', *American Forces Information Service News Articles*, DefenseLink, US Department of Defense, 10 September 1999.

28 The Hon. John Moore, Minister for Defence, 'East Timor and Australia's Security', *Speech by minister for Defence*, House of Representatives, Media Release, 284/99, 21 September 1999.

> peace force criticised, f) John Howard's public call for US Army 'boots on the ground' in East Timor resented, g) US believes Canberra did not fully realise the depth of the crisis until early last week.[29]

Sensing the potential for adverse drama, the US State Department and US Embassy in Australia issued a press statement on the same day declaring the collaborative and intimate workings of both governments. In moving quickly to avert any diplomatic or public flak, it asserted the falsity of any suggestion that contested the cooperative nature of the Australia–US relationship over a lengthy period.[30]

Acting to communicate a message to the TNI as well as shoring up Australia–US relationship perceptions after these and further comments that Australia's precise demands for US logistical assistance were initially uncertain, Cohen, on 30 September, announced a further increase in US assistance for the INTERFET force. USS *Belleau Wood*, a carrier-like amphibious assault ship, complete with sophisticated target-tracking equipment and a 300-bed hospital, was despatched from Sasebo in Japan and was operational off Dili on 6 October. Nine-hundred marines from the 31st Marine Expeditionary Unit constituted part of the ship's complement. The *Belleau Wood* also allowed four CH-53E *Sea Stallion* helicopters to lift heavy equipment into East Timor. In addition, 130 personnel were deployed from Arizona to set up and operate a sophisticated high-capacity voice and data communications network and a small number of military planners were sent to assist the multinational force.[31]

Significantly, US diplomatic and political pressure was maintained at a crucial time for the ADF. As the INTERFET force had arrived in Timor in a volatile environment where the potential for force fatalities was high, Cohen maintained pressure on the TNI. The US Defense Secretary considered that the TNI had arrived at the Rubicon, and conveyed this message to Wiranto. With the Indonesia Parliament about to be convened, Cohen 'saw' a crucial role for the military in both the restoration of peace and order in East Timor, in its role in Indonesia's broader transformation to democracy and in the ultimate acceptance of the civilian control of the military. The US stated it would not restore military ties with the TNI until it had undergone a reformation.[32]

With the appointment of Indonesian President Abdurraman Wahid's new cabinet, its acceptance of the East Timor ballot through the Indonesian Parliament and restatement of civilian control, the promise of greater stability heralded an opportunity for some return to order in Timor. This, together with INTERFET's success in restoring order, paved the way for the UN establishment of the United

29 Dennis Shanahan, 'US fury at our failings', *The Australian*, 17 September 1999, p. 1.

30 US Department of State, *Statement by James B. Foley*, Deputy Spokesman, 'East Timor – US–Australian Cooperation', 16 September 1999.

31 Douglas J. Gillert, 'US Support Increases to East Timor "Operation Warden"', *American Forces Information Service, News Articles*, DefenseLink, US Department of Defense, 29 September 1999.

32 Statement by US Defense Secretary William S Cohen after meeting with General Wiranto, 30 September 1999, <http://usinfo.state.gov/regional/ea/timor/cohen930.htm>. Accessed July 2000.

Nations Transitional Administration in East Timor (UNTAET). UNTAET's main role was to ensure security, coordinate and deliver humanitarian aid, support the transition to self-government, and assist with sustainable development.

Australia has regularly experienced tension in its relations with the US arising from the asymmetry in size and power, from US distant interest in Australia's specific regional affairs, and a related preoccupation with the Americas and transatlantic affairs. At times the US has been subject to criticism for engaging in foreign policy overstretch borne of an ideological predisposition. Complicating relations for Australia, too, were the number of actors within the US political scene with whom Australia needed to negotiate. Ironically, however, despite sectional disinterest, the US could offer Australia objectivity in analysing the crisis in February 1999 and might to aid in its resolution in September.

In this instance it was underpinned by geographic distance and distant histories, and as engineered by the Asia–Pacific expertise and acuity of State Department personnel and resources. While it appeared that in the meeting in February the Australians were hamstrung by a set of political constraints, the US brought a more independent view.

Albeit untested in the early parts of the crisis, the US also possessed inherent financial power to wield both in its bilateral relations with Indonesia and in international forums. As Cohen and Pickering stated, the US would consider all means in its repertoire to persuade Indonesia to consider a peaceful resolution to the crisis and conveyed this successfully. The US had the power and the preparedness to use it.

It presumed unparalleled military prowess effective both on the ground and as threat. Although the US did not provide combat troops, its intelligence, communications, transportation assistance and funding arrangements were a significant force multiplier initially for the ADF and later INTERFET.[33] US intelligence worked adeptly to prevent clashes between the INTERFET forces and any renegade Indonesian troops. The US decision to increase its commitment in Timor by anchoring *Belleau Wood*, with its complement of 900 marines, offshore from Dili, was designed as a highly visible statement of US presence. As Brigadier-General Castellaw observed: '[w]e meant for it to send a signal'.[34] No doubt the US was also aware that should the situation deteriorate further, where INTERFET were engaged in physical combat with the TNI, then pressure on the US to intervene more dramatically would be increased. Prevention here was not only paramount but successful in reducing militia activity in East Timor, at least.

The US, however, was also circumspect in outlining its concerns for the bigger picture in Indonesia. Indonesia's future, as the world's fourth most populous nation and largest Muslim population, was of concern to the US. As the US contemplated the regional panorama, Indonesia's significance was evident. Positioned with a population of 212 million people, spread over 17,000 islands, it was guardian of

---

33 DFAT, *East Timor in Transition 1998–2000: An Australian Policy Challenge*, Canberra, 2001, p. 144.

34 Marian Wilkinson, 'Timor: The Quest for Justice', *Sydney Morning Herald*, 29 January 2000, p. 35.

access to two-fifths of the world's sea lanes. Along these sea routes, oil was carried from the Gulf to Japan and US ships accessed the Middle East. Indonesia assumed a key geopolitical role in the region: a region of significant US economic and strategic interests. Disorder in Indonesia had the potential to aggravate a series of transnational issues and swamp its regional neighbours. Not only was Indonesia a decisive player in ASEAN, and thus the ASEAN Regional Forum (ARF), but it was also instrumental in the formation of APEC. And in the US post-Cold War China consciousness, Southeast Asia's strategic importance was emphasised.

With Indonesian elections in 1999 and the civil unrest circling Suharto's departure, the US had two principal concerns both within Indonesia and for regional stability: the practice of more radical Islamic politics and the advancement of the armed forces' dual function as police and army. Clinton drew attention to Indonesia's plight in its transition to civilian democracy while simultaneously pursuing a recovery from the financial crisis. The US provided assistance to Indonesia for the administration of the elections. In this respect, the US offered both reward and punishment for Indonesia's actions. Carrots of economic assistance and international support and sticks of financial and military isolation, together with military threats, were the tools of negotiation. More broadly, in the administration's reluctance to allocate ground forces was a consciousness of the anti-US sentiment that prevailed in some quarters in Indonesia. Over the previous decade, Indonesian–US relations had been strained. Disputes over human rights, including Indonesian brutality in East Timor, had influenced US decisions to terminate the supply of US fighter planes earlier in the decade. After the 1991 Santa Cruz massacre in Dili, US Congressional pressure moderated the tolerance of US military support for Indonesia. In 1992, Congress voted to cut military training aid and pressed the executive to co-sponsor a UN Human Rights Commission resolution critical of Indonesian human rights abuses in East Timor.[35]

The photograph of Michael Camdessus (former IMF Managing Director), with arms folded, standing over President Suharto as he signed the economic assistance pact in 1998, was also etched indelibly into the Indonesian psyche. Symbolic of the power the US could wield and a reminder of the damage of restrictive economic prescriptions hatched by US Treasury, the photograph ensured that the Indonesians were not predisposed to further US incursions on their sovereignty. With the Indonesians already threatened by economic crisis, a military incursion would be untenable.

For Australia, in seeking assistance to intervene in East Timor, two factors further added to US reluctance to respond with the commitment of a ground force. These were, the number of actors within the policy-making community with which Australia needed to strike a consensus, and the public debate questioning Clinton's foreign policy of external interventions. The interest of the former group and the sensitivity of the latter were exacerbated by the onset of the US electoral cycle.

First, while Stanley Roth was clearly prepared to address the issue in its early stages, his section of the State Department constituted only a small component of

35 Alan Nairn, 'US Complicity in Timor', *The Nation*, 27 September 1999, <http://www.thenation.com/doc/19990927/nairn>.

the policy-making community. As was commensurate with their role, US Pacific Command was preparing and planning for intervention should they be required to do so. But as evidenced by both Sandy Berger's initial comments and Cohen's reluctance to engage in all conflicts, a unified approach took some time in coming. US Defense, too, had other preoccupations within Northeast Asia. China and Taiwan's sovereignty dispute continued to focus their attention, as did their ongoing management of both North and South Korea. Additionally, Japanese and Taiwanese interest in the missile shield development programme was contentious in the region. While some saw US preoccupation with Europe and a neglect of Southeast Asia as limiting the appropriateness of US responses, others were much more wary of US involvement. Until then, deployment of ground forces was premature. Amid this, too, stood the concern over the implications for security as a result of the financial crisis. Thus, East Timor did not rate highly as a priority in the decision-making echelons. As Clinton remarked in his statement on US involvement, it was on the advice of both Defense and National Security that he determined the nature of the force. After foreign policy forays and troop commitments that had previously bypassed Congress, the administration was politically compelled to consider Capitol Hill. The notable absence in the Clinton statement was any mention of the State Department.[36]

Second, an ongoing, broad and topical debate scrutinised the Clinton Administration's propensity to commit US involvement in external crises and peace operations. Influential academics contributed to the debate and reflected the spectrum of US opinion in the foreign policy discussion that many considered long overdue and contributed to the views held on Capitol Hill. Australia's September requests for assistance in the UN force would abrase against some obdurate views on peace operations and US participation.

In Congress, Democrat Senator Tom Harkin, who had led a small delegation to Timor, voiced support for a US presence. The trend, however, after the Congressional summer recess, was to initiate and support the implementation of a range of diplomatic and financial measures as a priority over specific military intervention. As it was a Congress that had sliced the international affairs budget and withheld UN payments and a public that offered less support for military spending, foreign aid and international institutions than any other in recent history, it was perhaps unusual that East Timor elicited the reaction it did. Others in Congress saw parallels in a lack of early awareness and action in responding to human rights abuses as precipitating the need for more drastic responses later in both Kosovo and East Timor.

Donald Emmerson, long time Indonesian analyst, although writing after UNTAET's establishment in October, claims that Australia's preparedness to act also precipitated his more optimistic analysis of peace operations. Even if the moralpolitik/realpolitik pendulum continued to swing at varying tempos in different countries, once Australia acted it demonstrated that a future remained for

36 President Bill Clinton Statement on East Timor, 'US Role in East Timor Peacekeeping Force', Office of the Press Secretary, The White House, 16 September 1999.

humanitarian intervention. What is more, he suggests there was 'almost audible relief' in Washington once Australia assumed its active intervention role.[37]

As has been argued, if a conflict really mattered to the US, then the Clinton Administration, despite the rhetoric, would have no hesitation in the unilateral demonstration of power. So, even though the US was not a shoe in with 'boots on the ground', it appears that in the longer term the preferable support was that which was provided. And even though the government was wont to focus on 'Australia's' INTERFET success, both in its inception and its operational success, without US political and diplomatic initiatives and strength, Australian relations with Indonesia may still be tenuous.

Managing International Threats: Indonesian Intimacy

It remains hypothetical, nevertheless, as to what may have eventuated should Roth have been supported by the Australians early in 1999. Whether he may have been able to mobilise US interest at that point without the brutal denial of formal democratic processes, as evidenced in August, is now a moot point. His departmental secretary, Madeleine Albright, was not renowned for her interest in Asia. Not only was she criticised for her absorption by matters European but subject also to speculation regarding the diminution of her power in Washington. In Australia, John Dauth claimed, in Australia's Senate inquiry that it was 'absurd' to suppose that an international force may have been able to intervene in April.[38] It was impossible to contravene Indonesia's sovereignty. Yet the US, as demonstrated, held considerable power to exercise. While the Administration, Pentagon and National Security advisors would have baulked in a similar fashion at the deployment of troops, more adept and aggressive diplomacy on Australia's part may have ensured that US power could have been exercised earlier than was utilised: power, that when requested, was shown to be incredibly effective. If US threats could be so persuasive, why then did Australia not consider the opportunity to either entertain the possibilities they embodied, or utilise them? In failing to assist the Americans, Australia effectively delayed US involvement and tacitly conveyed approval to the Indonesians. Only when the Coalition was drenched by information did they seek to brief the Pentagon and contact regional missions.

Why did Australia act in the way it did? Australia had a foreign policy problem of its own making. Its ability to create an effective foreign policy, to enact an adept diplomacy and to work with the US was confused by the incompatibility of a weight of ingredients. These were: the intent of Australian policy-makers to ensure good relations with Australia's nearest, largest neighbour, Indonesia; East Timor's particular significance in the Australian consciousness and public press; the coalition government's employment of a 'defensive' foreign policy; a stated foreign

37 Donald Emmerson, 'Moralpolitik: The Timor Test', *The National Interest*, no. 58, 1999, pp. 63–69.

38 John Dauth, *Senate Foreign Affairs, Defence and Trade References Committee Hansard*, 'Economic social and political conditions in East Timor', Canberra, 6 December 1999, p. 1004.

and trade policy that declared the importance of a cartel of special relations; and a set of specific bureaucratic problems evident in 1999. In short, during this period the Coalition was weighing up its international and domestic pressures and deciding how best to manage them. While it was keen to establish its own foreign policy credentials and conscious of the need to manage a domestic constituency supportive of the East Timorese, it was also learning about how the US ensured its preferences would be maintained in international relations.

If Paul Keating had declared the importance of Indonesia for Australia in his statement that 'no country is more important to Australia than Indonesia',[39] John Howard, too, had acknowledged its significance in his statement that '[o]ne can hardly overstate the importance of Indonesia to Australia'.[40] Both Keating and Howard were avowing the centrality of Indonesia in both Australia's regional strategic and political concerns. Indonesia was crucially positioned in the sea–air gap and a key link in the 'arc of stability/instability' (depending on the times) to Australia's north. As a core participant in Southeast Asian politics, Indonesia was crucial to the establishment of APEC and the ARF: two of the cornerstones of Australia's foreign and trade policy in the region. Arguably, it had also played a counterweight to Malaysian intransigence against Australian engagement in the region. For some policy thinkers, Australia's efforts at closer engagement with Indonesia have dissipated the perception of external threat from the south within Indonesia. Australia's relocation of the ADF to Darwin and the upgrade of the submarine force could be executed without antagonising Indonesia. Furthermore, this argument suggests that it has held in check Indonesian defence spending by averting Indonesia's need to counter both a more sophisticated Australian defence force and a defence force oriented to external threat, unlike the Indonesian force structure. INTERFET Commander Peter Cosgrove also acknowledged the importance of the links between the ADF and TNI as vital in the relatively peaceful transition to INTERFET control.

Much had been done by sections of both the Departments of Defence and Foreign Affairs and Trade to shore up the relationship. Maintaining sound relations with Indonesia had been an integral part of Australian foreign policy. But, as Ali Alatas surveyed the relationship, 'the pebble in the shoe' remained East Timor. By 1995, however, Evans characterised the pebble as 'fast becoming the rock in the path'. And by 1999: a landslide. Since the 1975 Indonesian annexation of East Timor, attempts to ameliorate relations had been hampered by the differences in thinking on Timor. Australia did, nonetheless, attempt to work with its neighbour. Although US policy was re-routed after the Santa Cruz massacre in 1991, Australia, together with Japan, vetoed the United Nations criticism of Indonesia for human rights abuses. While Australia reviewed this position in 1992, its efforts were concentrated on securing its relationship with Indonesia. Keating's initiative, the Agreement to Maintain Security, evidenced Australia's enthusiasm for building closer relations and formalising trust. Arguably, Australia was successful in these efforts to improve the Indonesian relationship. In 1986, the David Jenkins article in the *Sydney Morning Herald* criticising the Suharto family almost precipitated the collapse of the relationship.

39 Paul Keating, *Engagement: Australia faces the Asia–Pacific*, Macmillan, 2000, p. 136.
40 John Howard, *The Sunday Telegraph*, 21 June 1992.

But, by 1991, Hawke's condemnation of the Santa Cruz massacre, followed by the Mantiri affair, while offensive in Jakarta, did not spark the wider deluge across the broader relationship.

Throughout, however, it appears that Australia was unsuccessful in navigating a path that both fostered relations with Indonesia and assisted the East Timorese. Ultimately, this was manifested in the destruction wrought in East Timor, a misplaced trust of the TNI to peacefully resolve the crisis in 1999, and a severed relationship with Indonesia from September 1999 onwards. Australia failed to appreciate the significant difficulties of transition to democracy and the implications of formal relinquishment of military control.[41] And while it is relevant to consider the effect within the TNI of Australia's 'containment' of US interests early in 1999, it is also pertinent to deliberate on what Australia may have conveyed implicitly to the TNI over many years, culminating with a possibility that the violence in Timor in 1999 may be ignored. More profoundly, for Australia, it appeared that the level of intimacy in the relationship obscured objectivity and the ability to articulate forcefully its concerns. Ultimately, Australia's *hamartia* may not have lurked within its policies of greater engagement but in its trust and expectations of what its policies could deliver.

Managing Domestic Demands: East Timor Sovereignty

The Howard government continued to be highly attuned to its domestic constituency. In the electorate there existed a strong pro-East Timor lobby. Howard was conscious that East Timor, more than almost any other of the islands in the Indonesian archipelago, was prominent in the Australian psyche. Principally, security, economic and humanitarian issues were Australian's concerns. Since East Timor is only 500 kilometres from Darwin, Australia has been conscious of the linked security issues. For most of the past century, Australia has feared hostile control of East Timor. Initially, it was the Japanese threat of occupation, culminating in its World War II attack, which preoccupied Australia. However, by the late 1960s, it was the fear of the spread of communist forces or communist-aligned regimes throughout Southeast Asia that concerned Australia. By 1998, it was the corruption of the Indonesian archipelagic unity with its consequent military and refugee problems that was prominent in the minds of Australian policy-makers.

Australian economic interests have been sharpened by the presence of the Timor Gap oil and gas reserves. Although it was in 1989 that the Timor Gap treaty was signed, as early as 1901 Australians had interests in oil reserves in the province. It was, nonetheless, the humanitarian concerns that have remained at the forefront as issues mobilising significant domestic support. Some, aware of the deaths of 60,000 East Timorese assisting the two companies of Australians stationed in the province to repel Japanese invasion between 1941–43, and others, troubled by the deaths of the Timorese and cultural repression since Indonesian annexation of the territory in

41 S. Wiryono, former Indonesian Ambassador to Australia, 'Goodwill should be our mission', *The Australian*, 1 October 1999, p. 15.

1975, have formed part of a public opinion that was ripe to persuade the government that Australia needed to react vigorously in organising and committing Australian troops to INTERFET. Both the media, encumbered with the legacy of the deaths of five journalists in Balibo in 1975, and an active Timor lobby, which included the East Timorese diaspora, the Catholic Church, unions and the Communist Party of Australia, were catalysts in the formation and sustenance of public opinion. It was, however, the militia violence in response to the ballot result that galvanised opinion and drowned even the notorious Australian predilection for apathy. Such was the overwhelming Australian reaction to intervene in the post-ballot destruction, that Paul Dibb and Peter Prince were wont to surmise that: 'No Australian government could have survived if it stood by and did nothing.'[42] Domestic threats needed to be allayed and quickly. Howard needed to act.

Assuaging guilt, however, was not the only motivating factor in the Coalition's change of policy. The government's new-found confidence, bred during Australia's survival of the Asian Financial Crisis, precipitated a greater proclivity to regional intervention than would otherwise have been with a conservative government. The security of successful financial management proffered the opportunity to engage with regional elites, albeit in a confined fashion. Nevertheless, it did flag the ground for further forays. And even though the government had criticised both Keating and Evans for their 'regional preoccupation', one of the political legacies bequeathed to the Coalition was a necessity to establish their Asian credentials. Presented here was an attractive opportunity because it had the potential to become a cachet in the Coalition's diplomatic bag, whereas the Australian Labor Party (ALP) was decidedly bare on this issue. Until Laurie Brereton, Shadow Minister for Foreign Affairs, had redefined policy, Labor had failed deeply on the issue. However, in domestic Australian politics, Brereton, in arguing for greater intervention, effectively closed out Howard's options.[43] Moreover, Indonesian Ambassador Wiryono's letter to Brereton that claimed the new ALP policy would precipitate an Australian–Indonesian collision also sounded a cautionary note.

Fine Tuning Australia's Special Relationships

In the design and implementation of policy, public opinion can be led by well crafted government strategies. However, symptomatic of recent times has been the inclination of both parties to fall prey to following the pack. As an experienced politician, John Howard recognised that one of the political failures of the Keating–Evans era in foreign policy was the inability of the Labor government to ensure broad public support for their regional policies. Howard did not intend to risk the same fate. One of the casualties, then, since 1996, was regional foreign policy, which became essentially defensive in nature. As enunciated in the Foreign and Trade Policy White Paper, policy was to have a pragmatic focus and retreat from the

42 Paul Dibb and Peter Prince, 'Southeast Asia Needs Indonesia and Australia to Make Up', *International Herald Tribune*, 27 October 1999, p. 8.

43 Richard Leaver, 'The meanings, origins and implications of the "Howard Doctrine"', *The Pacific Review*, special edition, vol. 14, no. 1, 2001, pp. 15–34.

grand statement, especially in Asia. If the Labor government was perceived to suffer from overstretch and a consequent inability to effectively lead public opinion, the Coalition's response was to retreat. Explained as a rejection of the politically correct and as attentive to the perceived needs of middle Australia, government engagement with the region primarily manifested itself through the trading relationship. In this, the government failed to dissociate from Hanson's views on race, particularly her anti-immigration and Indigenous people's statements. The government seemed only to engage with the region from positions of perceived strength. Moreover, Howard not only spoke to the region from the pulpit of financial strength but also reiterated the presence of Australia as a country with links to powerful Western interests.

In the midst of the crisis, Howard was aware that domestically the electorate would have an expectation of US assistance in INTERFET. Even if the alliance obligations did not prescribe direct US participation in this type of operation, after Australian assistance in US initiatives in the Gulf, the Australian public would consider reciprocal US support appropriate. Realising the symbolism of combat troops, Howard chose then to publicly call for US troop involvement. Whatever fealty the Coalition espoused for the US, it was fleetingly swamped in the reaction to East Timor.

For the most part in the US, Howard's prognostications were met with expert insouciance. But intuitively, too, this also presented the opportunity for the US to emphasise Australia's independence in the region and US interest in Australia's role in the region in future. In this respect it carries with it the possibility of a return to haunt Australia. Appreciative, however, of some minor possibilities that the Howard remarks could create unfavourable publicity for the US and thus jeopardise US interests in the region, Defense Minister Cohen was quick to dismiss US association and thus reiterate Australia's independent strength.[44] This is not to argue, however, that the US was unwelcome in Asia. Although the US maintained a security presence in Asia, it was regarded, at least implicitly by the ASEAN governments and more explicitly by Japan and South Korea, as having a strategic balancing role against China. Moreover, unlike Australia, the US could make comment upon human rights issues because of its leverage – as it did in East Timor. Australia's critical commentary was derided within Indonesia as alone it lacked the power to act. And, as is sometimes the case, anger at the more powerful can be transferred to the smaller, weaker country. As Alatas recounts, Habibie was irate at the original autonomy proposal: '(i)t made Pak Habibie mad, it made Pak Habibie angry, because it came from Australia. Why should Australia become involved?'[45]

Part of Australia's conflict in dealing with both the demands of the Indonesian and the US relationship was the problem of negotiating a number of special relationships simultaneously. In the spring of 1999, Howard recognised that too many special relationships were blurring the clarity of Australia's foreign policy approach. Howard was right. But it was, nevertheless, a view circumscribed by the

44 William Cohen and John Moore, *Joint Press Briefing*, Darwin, US Embassy in Australia, 29 September 1999.

45 No author supplied, 'Ali Alatas looks back on 11 years of Indonesia's foreign policy', *Jakarta Post*, 2 November 1999, p. 5.

immediate East Timor experience and contained by a perspective on the topical issue of Australia's engagement on Asian sovereignty. It commented upon Australia's inability to convey its displeasure on human rights in Asia and it spoke to a domestic audience perceived to desire a message of strength in locating Australia within the Asian region. It confined itself to the spheres of security and values. The problem, it seemed, was not just the quantity of special relationships but also what the 'special' intimated. Although Howard was concerned that the 'special relationship' in Asia was suppressing the espousal of Australian values in the region, relationships being constructed with China, and later, India, seemed more explicitly focused on trade issues alone. Indeed, two years prior, the foreign and trade policy White Paper, with its mercantilist basis, had highlighted the importance of economic issues with countries in the region. Moreover, bilateralism was the foundation of the White Paper's approach. Heading the paper's nominated list of substantial interests in the Asia Pacific was the United States, followed by Japan and China as 'the region's three major powers and largest economies', and Indonesia, 'our largest neighbour'.[46]

All countries must manage a range of relations with others, both near and far. But the difficulties for Australia were broad-ranging and problematic. Australia endeavoured to negotiate its past and present security, economic and cultural ties across the Pacific. The East Timor crisis exposed some of the conflicts inherent in Australia's position. It was Indonesia's presence as an integral facet of Australia's immediate security environment that temporarily clouded Australia's alliance relations. Australia risked some disruption to the US alliance, as it regarded its understandings (albeit judged later as misplaced) with the Indonesians in the initial stages of the situation as a priority. Later, in September, the government publicly added to the tension by declaring that it expected US combat troops to assist in the multinational force. From Australia's perspective the testing ground for the alliance would always be its performance in the region closest to Australia.

Contributing to the difficulties of policy at different levels through the crisis had been the politicisation of the bureaucracy and resource cuts to the public service. It has been suggested that affected here were both the increasing hesitation of the bureaucracy to offer independent advice and the disturbance of the process from the assessment of raw data to its translation into government policy. Resource reductions and personnel changes within DFAT over the past decade have hampered this process. However, Des Ball has been open in his analysis of the foreign policy public service performance in 1999. He contended that, as intelligence bureaucrats have become more conscious of the domestic political climate and aware that advice that conflicts with party policy threatens not just informational but also personal irrelevancy, the difficulties in providing frank advice have increased. This is despite the 'very capable' talents of the public service.[47]

Exacerbating the problems in the advice provided by the Defence Department, and the government's interpretation of it in 1999, was the ongoing tension between

46 Department of Foreign Affairs and Trade, 'In the National Interest: Australia's Foreign and Trade Policy White Paper', Canberra, 1997, p. iv.

47 Des Ball interview with Fran Kelly, 'Academic discusses the relevance of intelligence assessments', transcript, *Radio National*, 21 September 1999.

the minister, John Moore, and Paul Barrett, then Departmental Secretary. By 1 September relations had deteriorated to the point where Barrett departed and Hugh White (Deputy Secretary, Strategy and Intelligence) was appointed acting secretary, until his replacement by Allan Hawke in the following year.

Conclusion: Australia's US and Regional Relations

The East Timor crisis revealed much about Australia and the US. Since Kim Beazley's term as Defence Minister in the Hawke government, Australia has characterised its defence posture as one of 'self-reliance within alliance'. This accepted the exigencies of size but also presupposed a maturity on Australia's part and the ability to manage its affairs in a sophisticated fashion. It also acknowledged the US expectation of Australia's self-reliance. However, Australia's role in the East Timor crisis over many years revealed a sequence of diplomatic difficulties. This marked lack of self-reliance precipitated a dependence on US diplomatic and military assistance in 1999 to avert a disaster for Australia, and Indonesia, and further destruction in East Timor.

There was much to learn about alliance relations from this crisis for the Howard government. While identity may have an orientating role in directing behaviour between the alliance partners, the US would still pursue its material preferences as domestically motivated, regardless of any cultural relationship with its long-time ally. The American interest was primary. It was for Australia to deduce how these might coincide if it desired US assistance. Through this crisis Australia was also reminded of the potency of US power to exact outcomes in international affairs. If it was to access this power, however, it needed to make choices about its allegiance. Equivocation was hardly suitable for a dependent ally.

What of the wash in specific alliance relations? Prior to the East Timor crisis, Australia sometimes touted the importance of its 'expertise' on Indonesia to the Americans. This was particularly evident in the public domain in Australia's attempts to ameliorate international financial institutions' assistance to Indonesia in the financial crisis, although, arguably, Australia was communicating to the recently converted. Nevertheless, Australia regarded its familiarity in Asia as of value to the alliance. Some questions now remain as to the validity of these claims. However, INTERFET's success, brokered on the professionalism and efficiency of the ADF, generated respect within the US. It has also sighed relief. In some quarters, too, it has reinforced the desirability of the 'regional allies as leaders' model in future peacekeeping operations where direct US interests are not threatened. The deputy sheriff notion may well have latent appeal. Yet a preference for the delegation model should emphasise to elite policy-makers in Australia the need to seek regional solutions to the spate of existing and potential state and human security dilemmas. Human rights, environmental issues, transmigration and the narcotics trade require a cooperative multilateralism that thus far has been absent in Asia–Pacific politics.

Aware of the significance of US assistance in East Timor, Australian policy-makers perhaps felt compelled to fortify ties with the US. Pressure possibly emanated from within Australia and from the US as both policy-making groups realised the significance of the US assistance to Australia. Would the US have acted with the same strength had Australia not been involved? While it would have responded in some way to the domestic pressure within the US, it is debatable whether it would have responded with the same strength. Richard Armitage used this to advantage when he made the timely suggestion in November 1999 that Australia needed to consider its role should the US enter into a conflict involving China and Taiwan. More generally, this was part of a specific group of US policy thinkers counselling Australia to review its defence capacity so as to increase the potential contribution it could offer as an ally. Mindful that a significant proportion of Australia's equipment was becoming obsolescent, they advised a consideration of its defence capability with regard to the alliance.

Two further events comment upon Australia's association with the US since the East Timor crisis. First, in the following July, Australia signed the defence principles statement that was designed to enhance cooperative efforts in the region and provide Australian access to US technology. It also offered qualified approval for the development of the Theatre Missile Defence programme—although the seriousness of Australia's support at this time lay more in the political support it proffered to the US. This becomes more critical in the impetus the programme gives to the arms race, and, in particular for Australia, how it manages the three-way political interaction with China given its vehement opposition to the project and its advice that Australia should do what was right for Australia.[48] Second, in 2000 also, Australia ratified the ten-year extension of the Pine Gap treaty.

Under the new rationalisation of intelligence-sharing responsibilities, it could be assumed that the countries involved had understood the need for greater reliance upon allies. Nonetheless, Australia's refusal to submit all information from Indonesia created some mistrust in that process. Moreover, as Australia had criticised the US in the past for its failure to disclose information, it had now loosened its grip on the force of its future claims.

For Australia, the problems of asymmetry in the alliance are inherently difficult without exacerbating its weaknesses. In this ongoing crisis, Australia's initial diplomacy was found wanting. In Australia's enduring quest for middle power status and independence, its actions initially betrayed its desires. As a consequence, in the necessary resort to crisis management, the choices for Australia in mediation were circumscribed, and ultimately it was dependent on the US for assistance. It was also reliant on the coincidence of US interests in enabling it to produce a desirable result. From an analysis of the events of the crisis in East Timor in 1999, it is apparent, once again, that for the US to be engaged in Australian concerns there needs to be a compatibility of interests. The irony, however, is that the East Timor crisis may have unintentionally strengthened the Coalition's need to upgrade the alliance, in ways it could not foresee in 1999.

48 Zhou Wenzhong, the Chinese Ambassador, interviewed on the 7.30 Report, 'China warns against going all the way with the USA', *ABC Television*, 25 July 2000.

Chapter 4

Establishing an Australian Culture? Managing Biotechnology and Pharmaceuticals

Alliance relations are played out over an array of tracks and through a multiplicity of sectors. In various sectors, the US relationship has been used by the Australian government to mediate between threats from above and below. My concern in this chapter is to examine one of these sectors: that of biotechnology and pharmaceuticals. For the Howard government, like its immediate predecessors, this was a sector that, if managed well, could not only assist in delivering the health needs of the population but also add much to the health of the Australian economy. Previous ALP governments' international economic diplomacy and 'clever country' agenda was a recognition, too, of the need to reposition Australia in the international system and allay threats in the international environment.

The US loomed large in this equation. Through the availability of capital and markets, the US presented significant opportunity to develop and commercialise local research. Yet, the potency of the US interests, both state and commercial, required adept management on Australia's part in order to preserve the benefit to Australia. So, for this the Howard government, with its preference for upgrading the US relationship, the skill would be to develop and strengthen domestic industry together with US participation, and simultaneously sponsor an international diplomacy that both secured Australian sovereignty and encouraged the US to support a 'rules-based' global trade system. Many biotechnology companies exist mostly in nascent form in Australia and look to the US model to commercialise. Moreover, the US draws Australian companies toward it with the lure of more freely available capital and a massive market for superior goods. Opportunities for the development of new products also abound as the giant US pharmaceutical companies endeavour to secure their profits as their traditional base is eroded. Although at the company level these factors sometimes blur the national boundaries, issues of national sovereignty resonate through both the development and operation of the biotechnology and pharmaceutical industries. This desire to construct a vibrant industry, develop an export market and preserve the character of the related health environment poses a number of challenges for Australian government and industry. Further, if border issues have been the topical component of bilateral trade negotiations in Australia–US relations in the past, more recently attention has also been focused on relations and governance in areas such as industry development, intellectual property rights, regulatory systems, investment environment, monitoring transnational firms' practice and partnership potential. These governance issues have also been reflected in the incorporation of the Agreement on Trade Related Aspects of Intellectual Property (TRIPs), Trade Related Investment Measures (TRIMs) and the General Agreement on Trade in Services (GATS), in the multilateral negotiations of the WTO. Thus, the Australian government's threat management policies in this sector can be considered over a range of levels.

Just as computer technology and semi-conductors were wealth creators in the past, biotechnology has that capacity in the future. If states do not become involved in the biotech revolution, they will be in the position of having to purchase the technology from others. Australia found itself in this position in the IT sector as it was unable to maximise the opportunities in computer technology development of the past two decades. Although Australia utilises this technology in large numbers, it is unable to produce the technology at commensurate levels. One facet of this may be seen in Australia's need to import high levels of computers and computer parts from the United States. Imports of this technology alter the trade balance markedly in the US favour. Given this problem, Australia must avoid similar errors and provide both scientific and commercial infrastructure to exploit possible opportunities. Promotion of this sector then can offer the government the opportunity to prioritise the domestic health needs of the population together with the opportunity to reposition Australia in the international economic environment and thus allay international economic threat.

Put simply, biotechnology is 'the application of science and technology to living organisms as well as parts, products or models thereof, to alter living or non living materials for the production of knowledge, goods and services'.[1] The Australian government expects that biotech could be a critical driver of growth and employment in the next decades with this growth evident particularly in the agricultural, medical and pharmaceutical sectors.

There is, however, a critical difference between the innovations in the computer industries and the developing biological technology – and that is the issue of biosafety. Although biotechnology can be utilised in the treatment and prevention of disease and with many applications in improving quality of life, including environmental regeneration, waste treatment, reduction of greenhouse emissions, restoration of polluted sites and reduction of waste production, it remains that biotechnology has inherent safety questions that require a cautionary approach. The safety of genetically modified crops presents concerns to consumers that have not been fully unanswered.

In Australia in 2005, there were approximately 420 biotechnology companies, placing Australia in sixth position globally. By 2006, 72 core biotech companies were listed on the Australian Stock Exchange (ASX). Market capitalisation for these companies was $16.74 billion (the majority of which was contributed by CSL). 33 per cent of these companies listed over the past three years. Over 6,000 people were employed in the industry with human therapeutics as its largest sub-sector. The strengths of the Australian industry were situated in the depth of its research in particular areas of medical technology. Included in this sector was research in

1 OECD definition of biotechnology cited in the Department of Industry, Tourism and Resources, 'Global Partners: Australian Biotechnology', Canberra, 2004, p. 7.

immunology, reproductive medicine, hypertension, genetics, molecular biology, cancer research and delivery agents.[2] Further afield, 460 biotechnology related companies exist in medical and biomedical devices production, diagnostics, agri-food and environmental products. More broadly, Australia's pharmaceuticals industry (consisting of manufacturers, research institutions, biomedical research and development firms and associated services sectors) turned over $17 billion in 2005–06, employed approximately 34,000 people, and was the second largest exporter of manufactured goods in Australia after the automobile industry.[3]

The US Pharmaceutical Industry and the Embrace of Biotechnology

US structural power is both an attraction and a source of concern. Any relationship with the US in this sector requires careful management: and threat mediation is sometimes problematic. Undoubtedly, the US pharmaceutical companies are not only potent forces in the global commercial environment, but also effective lobbyists within the US political system. With a US market that represents 40 per cent of the global market in pharmaceuticals, the US companies and their industry association, Pharmaceutical Research and Manufacturers of America (PhRMA) wield enormous power. The US too is at the forefront of the biotech industry. Whereas many Europeans have hesitated to embrace biotechnology (particularly Northern Europe and Germany), the US has responded more enthusiastically.

In addition to speculation on specific socio-cultural factors[4] that may have influenced the evolution of the US biotechnology industry, there were five historical and financial explanations that have assisted policy formation and industry regulation in the US. These were: i) the establishment of 69 land grant universities through the Morrill Act of the 1860s. The Act effectively allowed for the development of agricultural colleges with a focus on agricultural and scientific research.[5] ii) The university system was uniquely placed to foster and develop plant and animal biotechnology innovation and was aided by the intellectual input of European refugees

2 Commonwealth of Australia, Ernst and Young and Freehills, 'Australian Biotechnology Report 2001', Canberra, p. 13.

3 Department of Industry, Tourism and Resources (ITR), 'Australian Pharmaceuticals Industry Fact Sheet', Canberra, 2007 and Department of Industry, Tourism and Resources, (ITR), 'Pharmaceuticals Industry Action Agenda: Local Priority: Global Partner', Canberra, 2002, p. vii.

4 Gerald Gaull argued that the biotechnology industry in the US has flourished because of specific socio-cultural factors. He suggested that as the US society had its philosophical origins in the Enlightenment, coupled with a Protestant-Christian heritage that society's emphasis was predisposed to science and progress. An 'imperial' relationship with nature was struck. The particular 'deep ecology' resistance to biotechnology as espoused in Europe and established through an organised socialist voice was denied to the same extent in the US. Gerald F. Gaull, 'Biotechnology Regulation in America and Europe: Viewed in a Cultural Framework', *Institute of Economic Affairs*, London, 1 August 1998, pp. 4–5.

5 US Department of State, 'Basic readings in US Democracy, Industrial America: Morrill Act 1862', <http://usinfo.state.gov/usa/infousa/facts/democrac/27.htm>. Accessed March 2007.

post-World War II. The universities enjoyed substantial financial assistance from the National Institutes of Health. American universities provided the basis for current US leadership in biotechnology. They also exude a culture where scientists are not discouraged from the industry commercialisation process and many of the industry hubs now are located proximal to the tertiary institutions. iii) Capital markets have allowed embryonic companies pursuing high risk research, substantial and flexible funds to design, develop, test and market their product. The NASDAQ exchange ideally offered not only a suitable arena for the successful high tech companies to list, but also an exit mechanism for the venture capitalists who had provided the backing for their development. iv) The US patent system, initiated by Thomas Jefferson and constitutionally documented, facilitates innovation by offering time and market protection to the inventor. v) The regulatory system for food and drugs embodies flexibility. It does not consider the genetic engineering process to be dangerous of itself, although the resultant product may be. It is also arguable that as Europe has few corresponding regulatory bodies, consumers are more wary of new products or those resulting from new scientific processes. vi) The biotechnology industry is also aided by a potent lobby group in Washington.

Consequently, the US welcomed both the information revolution and the commercial opportunities offered by scientific and medical research. Not only has the US embraced pharmacology, but now biotechnology. US companies are at the forefront of biotechnology research in the health and agricultural sectors. In agricultural biotechnology the US has been quick to pursue returns. Five million acres of the first transgenic crops were planted and exported from the US in 1996.[6] By 2005, 123 million acres were planted, with major cropping taking place in soybeans, corn and cotton.

Conversely, Australia grows only a small portion of biotech crops, has an emerging biotech industry and a market that represents only one per cent of the world pharmaceutical sales. While the Australian government has made some inroads into assisting the development and commercialisation of research, this industry still requires external input to increase the prospect of benefits. Clearly US financial resources can support the development of this sector in Australia. However, these opportunities require astute management.

Australian Industry: The Imperative for Funding

It is clear that governments can make innovative choices to assist in the amelioration of economic threat. Since the early 1980s governments in Australia have contemplated the prospects of this industry and boosted biotechnological and pharmaceutical funding. However, if the previous Labor governments had been concerned to promote knowledge-based industries in Australia, it was not always supported by

6 US Secretary of Agriculture, Dan Glickman, 'New Crops, New Century, New Challenges: How will Scientists, Farmers, And Consumers Learn to Love Biotechnology. And What Happens if they Don't?', *Speech to the National Press Club*, Washington D.C., 13 July 1999, p. 6. US Government Accounting Office Report, 'Concerns over biotechnology challenge US agricultural exports', 15 June 2001, p. 5.

their funding on health and medical research. Australia's per capita expenditure in this sector in 1995 was significantly less than the OECD average for developed nations.[7]

In 2000–01, $968 million in public funding was allocated to biotech research and development.[8] In 2000 the Coalition government acknowledged the role for biotechnology in the economy and announced a series of changes to funding. Also under pressure from Labor's rhetoric of extending the breadth and depth of the knowledge base in Australia, the Coalition announced their national strategy for biotechnology. As Treasurer Peter Costello restated in the 2007 budget, through its *Backing Australia's Ability-Building Our Future through Science and Innovation (2001–2011)* plan, the Coalition was instead allocating $8.3 billion over ten years to spawn ideas, expand the skill base and commercialise research.[9]

One of the specific actions from the Howard government through the Pharmaceuticals Industry Action Agenda has been the use of Invest Australia and Austrade in the promotion of increased investment and pharmaceutical products and services exports. As disclosed in the 2003–04 Federal Budget, the Pharmaceuticals Industry Investment Program was superseded by the Pharmaceuticals Partnerships Program (P3), which allocated $150 million in grant money through a five year plan. These funds would be open to both pharmaceutical and biotechnology companies.[10] Prior to this the government had allocated funding for research centres in proteomics, genomics, biodiversity, neuroscience, nanotechnology, stem cell and synchrotron research. States' funding too, has endeavoured to court biotechnology companies, with Victoria and Queensland leading the way.

Government funding has been designed to avoid the difficulties past researchers encountered in commercialising their work. Early indications that this was a difficult process for Australia were evidenced in the overseas commercialisation of the Australian discovery of Colony Stimulating Factors (CSFs). These hormones, responsible for stimulating blood cell growth in the human body, were identified by two Australian scientists, Don Metcalf and Ray Bradley. However, the US, EU and Japan pursued the commercialisation process of two of the hormones that have been utilised clinically in the treatment and management of cancer. Annual global sales for these drugs as early as 1993 were in excess of $500 million. Australia must now pay for their importation.[11] Similarly, CSIRO's research work with the gene shears technique, a technology designed to protect the cell against virus attack, was commercialised by overseas companies, although on this occasion the licensing agreement struck more profitable terms.

---

7 Commonwealth of Australia, Health and Medical Research Strategic Review Discussion Paper, December 1998, p. 12.

8 Department of Industry, Tourism and Resources, 'Biotech Business Indicators', Canberra, February 2005.

9 Commonwealth of Australia, DEST Portfolio, Budget Statement 2007–08, Outcome 5, Canberra, May 2007.

10 Department of Industry, Tourism and Resources, Pharmaceutical Industry Action Agenda Newsletter, Bulletin No. 10, May 2003.

11 Australian Science and Technology Council, 'Gene technology: Issues for Australia', *Occasional Paper No. 27*, August 1993, APGS, Canberra, p. 21.

In this sector when Australia considers how to best manage its international threats and improve its international economic situation it has often looked to the US as a model of industry development and as a source of funding. US capital is attractive as Australian capital is more risk averse than its US counterparts, principally because of its inexperience in the sector. In Australia, where the field is new and the investment markets remain still quite unsophisticated, the limited numbers of institutional investors are wary of the high risk, long-term nature of the investment. Valuations for investors also present difficulties with greater subjectivity evident in the analysis for a lengthy project. As a consequence of few attractive commercial biotech opportunities in the past and even fewer with visible returns in Australia, there has been little development of the specialist biotech venture capital sector. In this respect it is a disappointment that Biota's flu drug Relenza was not more successful in its initial stages.

For venture capital investors, a three to four year investment period is considered lengthy. *Fin de siècle* experiences in the IT industry had sharpened the profit recovery environment for the venture capital investors. Returns became expected in more dynamic time frames. Yet the discovery-to-market journey in biotech can be convoluted and lengthy. Of concern too is that the immature venture capital industry in Australia occasionally adopts the worst traits of its US counterparts. Pursuits of fast ramp ups, stagging and quick Initial Public Offerings (IPO) are sometimes noxious to sustainable business.

One of the significant differences here is that of scale. Usually in the US an IPO can only be conducted after a company achieves a market capitalisation of US$300 million or more. Most are multiples of that. As supported by venture capital these companies are then able to achieve analyst recognition which enables both financial and product momentum. In the past, Australian listed companies such as BresaGen, despite their technical capabilities, are often too small in market capitalisation to attract the necessary attention.

Taxation, pricing and reimbursement have been regarded as the most significant issues in determining the direction of investment. Australia has favoured a competitive industry environment over the past two decades. Its corporate tax strategy has been to deny the opportunity to pick winners federally and refrain from allocating tax-based incentives. In 1999 foreign capital, often in the form of American pension funds, were subject to Capital Gains Tax (CGT) at the exit point of their investment in Australia. Although they may have encountered no similar taxation in the US, CGT amounted to 36 per cent for companies and 48.5 per cent for individuals. Relative to the US, this marked a considerable disincentive to investment in the Australian biotechnology industry.[12] Despite concessions in the CGT treatment by 2003 and some allowances for non-residents, companies within Australia feel that this has had little impact on the overall tax environment. Compounding the difficulties for these companies had been the weakness of the Australian dollar. Australian companies

12 Keith Hardy, Tax Partner, Ernst and Young, Commonwealth of Australia, Industry Science and Resources, Ernst and Young, 'Australian Biotechnology Report 1999', Canberra, p. 46. AusBiotech, 'Growing Australia's biotech through improved access to people and capital: updated recognition for changes to taxation', February 2003.

were increasingly vulnerable and came cheaply for interested US investors in the late 1990s up until the latter half of 2003. However, by 2004 the Australian dollar's rise altered this situation significantly.

Intellectual Property Protection

Intellectual Property (IP) protection is an area in which the government has clear responsibilities both to conserve and to maximise the research conducted in Australia. In addition, it has a unique role to foster the opportunities for local manufacturers in domestic and regional markets. This is an important and highly specific area for threat mediation by the government. While it must encourage involvement from the US companies, it also must be prepared to protect the intellectual property of the local inventors and producers. That the US pharmaceutical companies wield such effective power and that intellectual property is such an emerging issue in intergovernmental relations demands that the Howard government devote sufficient resources to its effective management.

In the few years prior to 2001 Australian biotechnology patents taken out in the US increased 250 per cent. This was over double the rate of increase from the rest of the world.[13] Seventy Australian inventors were granted US biotech patents in the period March 2003 – March 2004. However, intellectual property issues are complex. Some licences have been gained by overseas companies at the expense of the Australian researchers. This may have reflected the inexperience or disinterest of the biotechnology scientists or managers. Alternately, it may have reflected the lack of clout on behalf of small Australian firms when negotiating with US companies.

In the US, some major firms have acquired broad patents covering genes with wide application. For Australian companies to utilise these they must endure high access costs and restricted access. This has occurred particularly in the agricultural industry. The US has continually issued patents that apply to entire plant lines, for example herbicide-resistant rice. Agracetus, a US company recently acquired by agricultural giant Monsanto, owns patents that, if valid; cover all transgenic cotton and soybeans. Recent trends in agricultural biotechnology evidence the move by five predominant companies to acquire smaller biotech firms. In doing so, Monsanto, DuPont, Dow Chemical, Syngenta and Aventis not only have acquired the companies' technologies but also their respective patents.[14]

Australian firms attempting to break into the US market encounter a range of national treatment obstacles. Apart from the initial temporary relocation costs of personnel, US law awards patent protection to the first to invent, not the first to file.[15] US law awards the patent where 'the invention was known or used' in the first

13 Department of Industry, Science and Resources, 'Biotechnology in Australia: International Reputation and Growth', Canberra, 2001, p. 2.

14 John H. Barton and Peter Berger, 'Patenting Agriculture', *Issues in Science and Technology*, vol. 17, no. 4, 1 July 2001, pp. 43–47.

15 See John R. Thomas, 'An Examination of the Issues Surrounding Biotechnology Patenting and Its Effect Upon Entrepreneurial Companies', *CRS Report for Congress*, 31 August 2000, pp. 9–11.

instance. Understandably, this has created a system where contests are rife. However, for Australian companies it is more often the interpretation of licence agreements and patent defence after issue that has been more problematic. Protracted and complex legal battles for the establishment of invention or in the enforcement of a patent are financially exorbitant as well as costly in both time and resources.

Furthermore, the transnationals have funds at their disposal that are unavailable to the small Australian companies. Patent protection for a range of countries may cost between US$100,000–$200,000 and much more than double that figure to fight a legal challenge where the patent is contested.[16] Arguably too, national treatment in patent processing occurs. This may be because US companies are familiar with the experience and are better placed to pull an application through the process. A more cynical analysis might suggest that financial power can often ensure an appropriate result. Johnson and Johnson, and Abbott Laboratories' challenge of Australian company, Peptech's patent rights have been regarded as demonstrative of attempts by larger companies to avoid payment of royalties to smaller companies in the expectation that they cannot afford expensive legal disputes.[17]

Attraction of capital investors is usually linked to appropriate protection for the intellectual property involved. Without patent rights, a biotechnology or pharmaceutical company may be left with little of commercial value. It appears that, increasingly, investors are attracted to later stage projects with more mature data. As such, the risk is minimised as investment is more likely justifiable. Thus, the comprehension of patent law is crucial to 'expedite capital infusion and technology transfer'.[18] It becomes one consideration in reducing the risk associated with the investment. Indicative of the value attached to intellectual property are company share price losses following court rulings in patent litigations. By way of example, US Company CellPro Inc., lost 50 per cent in value after its Ceprate bone marrow transplant system was deemed to infringe a competitor's patent.[19]

Alternately, some industry analysts consider that the valuation of an infant biotech company arises not so much from the valuation of intellectual property but from the record and expertise of the managers and their timeframe for market availability.[20] Yet this has been considered a significant weakness in the Australian industry and conversely, part of the pull of the American industry

The US Regulatory System and Marketing Approval Constraints

Although Australia and the US have signed the memorandum of understanding to facilitate a more streamlined system of US Food and Drug Agency (FDA) approval,

16 Commonwealth of Australia, 'Developing Australia's Biotechnology Future', *Discussion Paper*, September 1999, p. 26.

17 Beth Quinlivan, 'Peptech's Happy Holiday', *Business Review Weekly*, 29 January 2004, p. 38.

18 John R. Thomas, 31 August 2000, p. 2.

19 John R. Thomas, 2000, p. 8.

20 Kiara Bechta-Metti quoted in Beth Quinlivan, 'Hype and high hopes', *BRW*, 6 April 2001, p. 69.

and the Australia–US Free Trade Agreement (AUSFTA) further eases the process, registration in Australia does not ensure automatic approval by the FDA. Australian companies endeavouring to market products in the US must begin the lengthy process virtually from the start. The FDA, responsible for examination of the applications, has been inclined to favour trials conducted via FDA protocols and thus has been open to charges of national treatment. As the wealthier Australian companies have become more astute in their understanding of the mechanisms for FDA approval they have employed US Contract Research Organisations (CROs), known to the FDA, to interpret the guidelines, construct appropriate trials in the US and advance the prospects of their applications. It remains to be seen whether US companies will continue to be favoured informally in the approval process and foreign companies subject to adverse reports.

The Lure of the US: Acquisitions and Partnerships

For Australian companies such as Biota, its $600 million market capitalisation did not register on the US radar screens nor did it have the resources to acquire a fully-fledged company in the US. Given this, Biota Holdings chose to set up its own biotech company, Biota Inc, through the acquisition of a small company, and develop it to the point where it would become more attractive to venture capital. The perception here was that Biota Inc would grow at much faster rates than an Australian company.

One of the obvious difficulties for Australian companies, even if they have successfully completed the product development process ready for the Australian Therapeutic Goods Agency (TGA) or FDA assessment, is the lack of access to major markets. For those companies that have a product to market, the US is alluring. However, breaking into this market is fraught with obstacles, including those related to costs. Moreover, costs involved in proceeding through phases II and III of the clinical trials have almost become prohibitive. In these trials where the efficacy of the drug is tested through human trials, costs become substantial. Given the costs associated with running a product in the US, Australian companies are increasingly looking to partner with the big US firms. Formation of alliances with major multinational companies is one solution. Not only does this overcome issues of geographical proximity to major markets but also offers access to the extensive networks available in the US. These US companies have both capital at their disposal and established links and goodwill with the medical community, wholesalers and huge sales forces to drive the eventual purchase of the product.

However, they are also ripe partners. Many are searching for fresh links with innovative research often born in academia or research institutions. Conscious that the tsunami of the new science is swamping their ageing investment in medicine such as antibiotics, the US leviathans are hunting for less expensive methods of linking into the prevailing science. The major pharmaceutical companies are now trying to defend themselves as their base becomes obsolete. Arguably, massive investments in personnel and facilities created for the antibiotic era have aged rapidly, ominously signaling concerns for profitability. While this may be the sunrise for Australian biotechs, it is incumbent upon them to create a compelling story for the gatekeepers of the pharmaceutical companies and drive it through the deal process. For some lacking commercial acumen, this has been too onerous.

Thus far, US global giants such as Pfizer, Bristol-Myers Squibb, Pharmacia and Johnson and Johnson have already established international alliances with Australian biotechnology companies. A number of features of the Australian environment are highly attractive for investment. Then Department of Industry, Science and Resources, boasted that Australia is one of the leading three nations in numbers of researchers, scientists and engineers engaged in R&D per capita and produced more highly qualified graduates than its competitors. Furthermore, in 2004 KPMG ranked Australia the second most cost competitive location for biomedical research after Canada.[21] Complementing these factors is Australia's established reputation for quality research supported by quality hospitals, statisticians and an English-speaking population.

Globalising processes, with company consolidation but industrial production fragmentation, offer opportunities for Australia in an industry with low volume but high value products. Industry is able to locate different parts of the supply chain in different locales. R&D may be separate from manufacturing and the location of the market. Outsourcing work may be possible even if the Australian companies are not commercially partnered with the US companies. The issue is obviously managing the US association. It is clearly better that the research can be commercialised but that it is not appropriated entirely. Having said this, where the product leverage is dramatic, that is, in meeting an unmet need, the US pharmaceutical companies are clearly interested in development. The difficulty remains of managing the ownership and profitability issues. In the endeavour to insulate against these possibilities, the government has structured some of its programmes such as the Pharmaceutical Industry Investment Programme (PIIP) to reward companies but ensure their results are delivered here. The challenge for Australia remains to increase the value adding processes conducted in Australia and to consider how it may become instrumental in the supply to developing markets in Asia (and South Asia) and its possibilities as a distribution channel for Southeast Asia.

The US offers commercial opportunities for Australia. These occur often to fill the space created by Australia's structural vulnerabilities. In this sense the US can play a role in the calming of international economic precariousness or threat for Australia. However, the profit motive of the US transnationals in this sector complicates the management task for the government. Here, then, the government must be ready to counter the threats posed by the US pharmaceutical companies both to the provision of affordable health care in Australia and also to the ability of the local manufacturers to compete internationally. While these issues have not been subject to general public debate in Australia in recent years, they have assumed a greater significance since the outcome of the Australia–US Free Trade Agreement negotiations in 2004.

---

21 Department of Industry, Tourism and Resources, 'Global Partners: Australian Biotechnology', Canberra, 2004, p. 9.

Contentious Bilaterals

While US investment in Australia is attractive in assisting in the development of research and in the promotion of Australia as a regional industry hub, the Australian government continually contends with issues of national sovereignty. If anything, the delicacy of these concerns has been exacerbated by the interest the Howard government has had in upgrading relations with the US. At the bilateral level, negotiations between Australia and the US tend to be direct and continue to be driven by industry concerns. PhRMA remains a powerful lobbyist adept at utilising the USTR process. As a result, the Special 301 process often defines the agenda for specific discussions on biotech and pharmaceutical issues. Since 1996 (and again in the Australia–US Free Trade Agreement, which is further examined in Chapter Eight), five issues have received particular attention: i) the protection of test data awaiting approval by Australian regulatory authorities, specifically the TGA; ii) Australia's use of Bolar provisions (commonly referred to as 'springboarding') whereby manufacturers can prepare for registration while the patent still applies; iii) the attempts by Australia to provide generic manufacturers the opportunity to develop drugs for market earlier to compensate for US shorter patent life; iv) the Australian Pharmaceutical Benefits Scheme (PBS); and v) Australian restrictions on imported blood plasma products.

Intellectual property rights disputes are thus prominent in bilateral negotiations across many US international relations. It has been powerful US groupings such as the pharmaceutical industry that lobbied for the use of punitive measures against countries that did not enforce IP rights.[22] Executives from Pfizer were instrumental in the Advisory Committee on Trade Policy and Negotiations in persuading Congress and the Administration to reduce flexibility in IP law and utilise sanctions against those who were seen to contravene it.[23] Congress amended Section 301 of the Trade Act of 1974 to allow the US to take action against others and in 1988 amended Section 301 of the Act, spawning 'Special 301' to fuel its retaliatory powers.

After the Doha Declaration on the TRIPs Agreement, which strengthened developing states' capacity to provide access to affordable medicines against perceptions that some developed states and their respective industry bodies were restricting access and preventing health care reforms, the US responded by tightening restrictions through FTA agreements.[24] The US aims in this sector within the Australia–US Free Trade Agreement (AUSFTA) were twofold. First, its intent

22 Michael P. Ryan, *Knowledge Diplomacy: Global Competition and the Politics of Intellectual Property,* Brookings Institution Press, Washington D.C., 1998, Chapter 4, and Susan K. Sell, *Power and Ideas: North–South Politics of Intellectual Property and Antitrust*, State University of New York Press, Albany, 1998, Chapter 4.

23 Michael P. Ryan, 1998, p. 68. Ryan notes that the pharmaceutical industry was joined by the software, chemical and entertainment industries in its quest for strengthened IP protection.

24 Frederick M. Abbott, 'Intellectual Property Provision of Bilateral and Regional Trade Agreements in Light of US Federal Law', *UNCTAD and the International Centre for Trade and Sustainable Development Project on IPRs and Sustainable Development*, Issue Paper No. 12, February 2006.

would be to insist that a developed country pay greater IP rent and thus bear more of the costs of pharmaceutical development, and second that the agreement could be used as a model for future FTAs. It is also worth noting that while the US has sought to export increasing regulation on both IP and health policy commensurate with industry ambitions, these actions may eventually also be regarded as detrimental to the US public concern for affordable health care.

a. PhRMA Demands for Test Data Exclusivity

In 1996, the USTR cited Australia in its national trade estimates for its lack of IP protection. The US claimed that the WTO TRIPs Agreement provided for the protection of test data against 'unfair commercial use'. However, Australia rejected that interpretation and provided no protection for test data. In response the USTR stated it would 'review its options' regarding the resolution of this concern.[25] By April 1998, the Australian government introduced the Therapeutics Goods Legislation Amendment Act to comply with the TRIPs agreement, providing a five-year data exclusivity protection period for registered products containing a new chemical entity. In 2000, PhRMA requested that the USTR place Australia on the 2000 Special 301 watch list for inadequate intellectual property protection. PhRMA argued that protection should be extended to ten years and cover confidential data for all chemical entities, including new uses for existing compounds.[26] This is despite the fact that the test data exclusivity period in the US exists only for five years.

Pharmaceutical companies contest that the production and provision of data is extremely expensive, reflecting an enormous investment of resources. Consequently, they argue that this data should be protected during the approval process from others such as generic manufacturers who could use the original data in the registration of their own generic drug. At the time Australia responded by stating that these laws complied with its international obligations and a further extension was unwarranted. The USTR registered PhRMA's complaint in its 2000 trade estimates, stating that the US remained concerned with Australia's minimalist approach on this issue and similarly with agricultural chemicals and veterinary medicine. The USTR stated that it has 'made its concerns known to the Australian Government on numerous occasions'.[27] Eventually the AUSFTA provided an opportunity for the US to secure an extension of test data exclusivity and to extend this exclusivity to the second use of all pharmaceuticals.

25 USTR, 'National Trade Estimates 1996: Australia', 1996, p. 6.

26 PhRMA, 'Issues Around the World, Watch Country: Australia', Washington, pp. 1–2, <http://www.phrma.org>. Accessed September 2001.

27 USTR, 'Foreign Trade Barriers: Australia 1999', 2000, p. 12, <http://www.ustr.gov/pdf/2000_australi.pdf>. Accessed September 2001.

b. Generic Pharmaceuticals

In 1997, John Moore, former Minister for Industry, Science and Tourism, announced the amendments to the Patents Act to allow for extensions of up to five years for 20 year standard pharmaceutical patents. The amendments would also allow for 'springboarding' (the preparation of generic drugs for market approval before the innovator's patent rights expired), for eligible patents. This excludes the pharmaceutical production and stockpiling manufacture. Australian generic manufacturers would be able to conduct the preparation of these drugs during the patent term of the original to be ready for marketing at the same time as patent expiry of the original. Moore stated that the government chose this path to 'maintain an internationally competitive operating environment for (Australia's) pharmaceutical industry in the 21st century'. The government's actions would respond to the two principal factors determining investment in the industry on an international basis, those being: 'the extent of price controls and the competitiveness of a country's patents regime.'[28]

In a WTO dispute in 2000, where the EU issued a complaint against Canada's patent protection of pharmaceutical products, Australia registered as a third party. While Canada may be regarded by some as having a 'weak' system in terms of its protection of patent rights, it has a long history of securing public interests in public health issues of this nature. In reporting, the dispute panel deemed it necessary for Canada to rein in its sweeping exceptions to patent rights, yet Australia welcomed the final ruling as the panel dismissed EU claims that would have affected Australia's provisions for springboarding. Although Canada was ruled to constrain some of its patent exception approvals, the dispute settlement panel deemed that the overarching aspects of Canadian law did conform to the TRIPs Agreement and allowed manufacturers to utilise a patented invention for research purposes. At that time, Trade Minister, Mark Vaile, rejoiced that:

> (t)he WTO panel findings endorse Australia's springboarding rules that provide a balance between innovations and the public interest...The outcome of this case is a timely reminder of how the WTO system is working for Australia.[29]

It should also be noted here that if the EU's 'absolute' complaint succeeded, this would have represented an astounding victory for those backing patent interests.

PhRMA, however, was not rejoicing in Australia's patent exceptions. That the US also allowed for Bolar-type extensions, or springboarding, did not deter PhRMA from reacting with opprobrium to Australia's changes to patent laws. PhRMA issued a statement requesting that Australia be placed on the USTR Watch list as it 'does not agree with the necessity of maintaining a 'springboarding' provision that basically undercuts the current value of intellectual property protection in Australia', and

---

28 The Hon. John Moore, MP, Minister for Industry, Science and Tourism, 'New Policies Promote Investment in Australia's Pharmaceutical Industry', *Media Release (87/97)*, 8 April 1997.

29 Mark Vaile, 'Good Outcome for Australia in WTO Pharmaceutical Case', Trade News, *MVT 22/2000*, 29 March 2000.

certainly does not agree that a 'springboarding provision is needed to compensate for the value of patent term restoration.'[30] PhRMA argued that Australia already had delayed market launches because of lengthy regulatory processes and that future R & D may be undercut by reduced economic returns for products currently marketed in Australia.[31] Australia did not respond to these concerns through any alteration of the patent rules and steadfastly maintained its allegiance to these health and industry policies. Furthermore, Australia referred to Article 8 of the TRIPs Agreement that allowed for 'regulatory exceptions', to sustain its position.[32]

Nevertheless, the AUSFTA negotiations reveal how the TRIPs Agreement is strengthened and flexibility eroded in the new bilateral agreements. In this area, Australia agreed that these types of generics would not enter the market during the life of a patent and further that the generic manufacturer would advise the patent holder of the specific request for approval to enter the market during the life of the patent. Australia's TGA would now need to consider extensions on the basis of IPR in addition to health and safety matters.

c. Generic Drug Manufacture for Export: Positioning for Lucrative Markets

Changes to the Australian patent laws as effective at the end of January 1999 had attempted to provide extended patent life to compensate for an extended regulatory process in Australia. These laws had an unintended side effect for some Australian generic manufacturers. As the legislation calculated the extended patent terms via the use of the first date of registration in Australia, innovator companies were advantaged over Australian generic manufacturers as their products could be developed overseas and only registered in Australia at a later date. In 2000, Australian generic manufacturers such as Faulding and Alpharm had voiced their concerns that as some US and EU patents effectively expired three or four years earlier than the 15 year patent terms in Australia, the Australian companies felt decidedly disadvantaged by their delayed start. Not only would this mean that the Australian generic manufacturers were at a disadvantage in overseas markets, but also in Australia, as overseas companies would be better placed to supply the Australian market.

By 2001, in 70 per cent of cases, these particular extended patents had expired in the US and Europe prior to those in Australia. In an industry where the 'first to market' is vital to the breadth and depth of future sales and in a market where brand name is omnipotent, these companies sought some amelioration of the situation. In 2002, ITR specifically stated that: 'Australia needs to find a solution to this problem, to better calibrate its intellectual property regime with world markets and in a way that does not impact on the rights of patent holders in Australia.'[33]

30 PhRMA, 'Issues around the World, Watch Country: Australia'.

31 PhRMA, 'Issues around the World, Watch Country: Australia'.

32 WTO, 'TRIPs and Pharmaceutical patents: Obligations and exceptions', Geneva, April 2001, p. 3, and WTO, 'Pharmaceutical patents and the TRIPs Agreement', Geneva, September 2006.

33 Department of Industry, Tourism and Resources (ITR), 'Pharmaceuticals Industry Action Agenda: Local priority – Global partner', Canberra, 2002, p. 39.

The then Department of Industry, Science and Resources had previously attempted to devise a solution whereby certain generic pharmaceuticals could be manufactured for the export market for countries where the patent expired earlier, or patent extension terms could be calculated by the first registration in approved countries. If Australia regarded this solution as consistent with its TRIPs obligations, it was rendered irrelevant by the overwhelming vehemence of US opposition. Threat of action in the WTO and opposition from international companies saw Australia recant its plans to alter patent law enabling export manufacturing. As advised by DFAT, Australia retreated. Hurt by recent losses in the WTO in the Howe leather and Tasmanian salmon disputes, DFAT assumed a reluctant disposition and offered conservative advice. Although the eventual Canadian win against the EU claim should have demonstrated the flexibility inherent in the TRIPs Agreement and buoyed the Department's *mien*, the matter was not pursued. The result, settled largely in reaction to the dominance of the US companies, allowed for no leeway for generic manufacturers and no threat to the former's profits.

The pathology of the US companies' response involved threats to relocate investment offshore. While the pharmaceutical companies' threats of plant closures reached a point of overkill in 2001, by 2003 the threats implied a cessation of new investment. Perhaps most potently, they provide a reminder that Australia is not an irreplaceable component of many international firms' global business strategies. Companies that terminated business in New Zealand because of unhelpful government business policy in New Zealand effectively transmitted a warning to the Australian government that there is a limit to disincentive.

Pertinent too, in this discord, is the necessity for Australia to manage the desirability of its investment environment. Investment promotion and the avoidance of antagonistic industry markers are important management issues for the government. The government was acutely reminded of the potential destructiveness of hostile industry hothousing in the parallel importing and copyright law wrangle. Moreover, US pressure on Australia in these issues does little to assist in the development of regional regulatory systems to protect intellectual property. Moreover, the agreements within the AUSFTA which effectively extend the time period for the production of generics has a significant impact on the generics manufacturers' ability to compete in overseas markets. It would appear that in this sector the Australian government has traded away some significant commercial advantages through its AUSFTA negotiations.

d. Preserving Accessible Medicines: The Pharmaceutical Benefits Scheme (PBS)

Australia's PBS aims to provide affordable and reliable pharmaceutical access to the community. The Howard government has been careful to be seen to acknowledge its valued place in the Australian health system. It has been cognisant of the domestic political importance of the preservation of this scheme. Yet the scheme is under constant threat from the US transnationals eager to recoup investments. Though the government claimed to quarantine the PBS from the AUSFTA negotiations, that review mechanisms were included in the final agreement suggests that a breach has been created for greater industry intervention within the PBS. Further, Chapter 17 on IPR constrains opportunities for reform of the PBS by enshrining the agreed arrangements. With an aging demographic, it is likely that future governments would seek to review the functioning of the PBS, for example by examining the prospects for parallel importing. However, the 2004 agreement made this process much more difficult. Arguably too, the delays in the production of generic pharmaceuticals would add significantly to PBS costs.[34]

From 1 February 2001, the PBS encompassed approximately 2,351 drug products. This amounted to much of the Australian market for pharmaceuticals. By 2007 the government costs amounted to over $6 billion, which accounted for approximately fifteen per cent of the health budget. Thus, the industry is supported by sales through the PBS and ultimately the PBS underwrites the demand for products. A 2001 Productivity Commission research report found that, on average, prices for pharmaceuticals on the PBS were 80–160 per cent lower than in the US and 50 per cent lower than in Canada, the UK and Sweden. Australian prices are similar to those in France, Spain and New Zealand.[35]

Although the Australian Pharmaceutical Manufacturers Association (APMA) has expressed its support for the PBS, the US PhRMA does not concur. US concerns regarding the PBS focus on its monopolistic grip on the market and the contention that any drug not on the list is effectively denied market access. Furthermore, the US perceived that there is not adequate distinction made between drugs marketed for similar ailments, despite their respective quality, effectiveness and innovatory capacity varying considerably. By grouping new drugs in the same price bracket as those already on the market, pharmaceutical companies claimed that it did not reflect the research and development costs associated in the production of the new drug.[36] Arguably for PhRMA, the process was thus also an infringement of IP. And through the therapeutic group premiums, which link the price of patented medicines to non patented medicines, IP may be seen to be devalued. In addition to these concerns, the US has also riled at the delays for approval through two systems: the TGA and the PBS. This has been compounded by their perception of a seemingly random process for approvals. US PhRMA would argue too that cross subsidisation for the rest of world depends on higher pricing being maintained in the US.

It appears that the US pursuit of the PBS has decreasing support in multilateral forums. Instead, there is global support for accessible medicines and affordable health care. It is also worth noting that, compared to a compulsory licensing regime; the PBS is much less objectionable. Given that compulsory licenses occur where

34 Peter Drahos, Thomas Faunce, Martyn Goddard and David Henry, 'The FTA and the PBS', Evatt Foundation, <http://evatt.labor.net.au/publications/papers/126.html>. Accessed March 2007.

35 Productivity Commission 2001, 'International Pharmaceutical Price Differences', Canberra, July 2001, <http://www.pc.gov.au/study/pbsprices/finalreport/pbsprices.pdf>. Accessed April 2007.

36 See USTR, 'National Trade Estimates 2003, Foreign Trade Barriers: Australia', p. 12, <http://www.ustr.gov/assets/Document_Library/Reports_Publications/2003/2003_NTE_Report/asset_upload_file835_6179.pdf>. Accessed March 2007.

a government allows for the production of a patented product without consent of the patent owner, there is much acrimonious debate about the rightful protection of interests. However, it appears that the PBS remains an ongoing matter for US interest, particularly as it was subject to discussion in the 2003 negotiations for the Australia–US Free Trade Agreement. And if, as observed in the proceeding section on multilateral negotiations, the US has encountered a strong global interest in promoting and maintaining affordable health care, then the pursuit of this agenda through the recent spate of bilateral or regional trade arrangements is an attractive alternate strategy.

While US industry groups may be dogmatic on some of these issues, the US domestic environment is by no means a pure environment. US compulsory licenses are issued regularly by US courts. The irony is that the US is a repository of legal expertise and experience in the area. In a number of these issues, the US pharmaceutical companies continue to act on the offensive. Yet, some demands are made for higher levels of protection than the US courts are prepared to allow domestically.

In the consideration of this debate, it is also worth reflecting upon the role of the pharmaceutical industry in 'generating unsustainable rises in the national drug bill.'[37] David Henry, Professor of Clinical Pharmacology at the University of Newcastle, claims that the functioning market has failed in its ability to provide affordable pharmaceutical products globally. And while the industry claims much in R&D expenditure, the pharmaceutical industry's expenditure on marketing and promotion is twice that spent on R&D. Although this may be no different from the expenditure patterns of consumer products, the pharmaceutical companies' objections to the operation of the PBS is undermined to some extent, by their own fund allocation. Those drugs, too, of national significance such as anti-cancer and anti-retroviral drugs have utilised a great deal of public funding in their production. This is not to say, however, that development funds are not crucial. Clearly, they outweigh the costs of research and research development remains vital.

e. Blood Barriers: Restricting Imports

Australia continues to reserve the primacy of local blood products. Only Australian blood plasma products used in hospitals receive government reimbursement. Moreover, before the FTA for imported products can be registered in Australia they must have attained 'clinical superiority' status.[38] The US government continued to press for alteration of these barriers to the Australian market through the FTA and in 2007, under the FTA agreement, the Australian government reviewed the supply of blood products and blood fractionation services in the supply of blood products. However, as a side letter to the FTA states that Australian States and Territories must be in accordance with the Federal government on any changes to policy, their

37 David Henry, Review of Peter Baume's Paper, 'How do decisions on the listing of pharmacueticals influence health and health services in Australia?', Australian Health Policy Institute Commissioned Paper Series, 2001/03, University of Sydney, 2001, p. 30.

38 USTR, 'National Trade Estimates 2003, Foreign Trade Barriers: Australia', pp. 12–13.

agreement was sought. The States and Territories duly exercised their authority and maintained the *status quo* on the local sourcing of blood products.

Regional Harmonisation...and Competition

The Australia–US relationship in this sector is also played out in two broader settings. As part of the East Asian region, Australia has acted to assist its neighbours to deal with the emerging IP issues. Australia's perception in the past has been that it is best served by multilateral cooperation in this sector. The US mediation choice has been to operate bilaterally. As the following analysis reveals, the two approaches are sometimes at odds.

If Australia and the US agree on harmonisation of intellectual property rights within the region, they have embarked upon achieving that goal in varying fashion. Although the US, as an APEC member, has the expertise and resources to offer valuable input into this group's activities, it has not been an active supporter of the group's operation. Choosing instead to interact bilaterally, the US maintains a greater degree of control over IP rights processes than in the more open forum of IPEG's operations.

Stuart Harris has documented previously that the US has used its influence in Asia to support varying domestic industry sectors.[39] It also appears that the US pharmaceutical industry has been the beneficiary of Congressional and Executive assistance in less than desirable circumstances. An Australian generic manufacturer intending to register its product in a range of countries within Asia was confronted by a double-edged offensive of misinformation. Australia's listing on the USTR's Special 301 watch list was used by both the US pharmaceutical competitor and the American politicians enlisted in their support, to prevent the Australian product's registration. While politicians regularly tout the strengths of their local industries when offshore, the manner in which this campaign was mounted was flawed. It is also indicative of the aggressive nature and use of the department of the USTR.

Reaching globally, too, are the pervasive networks of US educational institutions. Spin-offs are substantive for US companies as a number of executives in Asia either have studied in the US or have networked with these universities.

Global Trade Negotiations: More TRIPs

Australia has often considered that the multilateral arena has afforded it the best opportunity to manage threat in the international environment. In the global trade negotiations Australia has found itself attempting to mediate between the US and developing countries. Australia has looked to the GATT and subsequently the WTO to afford itself and those of developing countries protection against the unilateral endeavours of the major players. As Intellectual Property Rights (IPR) became a

39 Stuart Harris, 'International Economic Orientations: Australia', in Richard W. Baker and Gary R. Hawke (eds), *ANZUS Economics: Economic Trends and Relations among Australia, New Zealand, and the United States*, Praeger, Westport, 1992, p. 88.

trade-related issue through the Uruguay Round, Australia once again assumed this role. However, the suspension of the Doha Round in 2006 meant that the multilateral negotiations for both the TRIPs and Convention of Biological Diversity (CBD) agreements remained on hold. Moreover, Australia's approval of the IPR restrictions within the AUSFTA erodes its capacity to mediate in the multilateral arena.

Prior to the 2006 suspension, the big US corporations pursued unilateral means to bolster and enforce IP rights and they targeted both the Uruguay and Doha Rounds of global trade negotiations to enshrine an international code for IP protection. US policy resonated with the demands of the corporate sector. The US specifically opposed the 'Group of Ten' developing countries' efforts to maintain their sovereignty over IP law in the lead up to the Uruguay Round.[40] In the absence of adequate enforcement measures of the World Intellectual Property Organization (WIPO), the US chose to transfer the institutionalisation of IPR to the GATT. Here the US could utilise the GATT's enforcement procedures to maximise their position. The launch of the new WTO and attendant promises of a fairer multilateral system of trading would eventually become conditional for the US on the TRIPs incorporation in the agreement. Although the developing countries had acquiesced at this time in the hope that a multilateral agreement might stave off the threat of unilateral action by the bigger players, they had ultimately succumbed, nonetheless, to an agreement dictated by the US. Jagdish Bhagwati and Arvind Pangariya have argued that the TRIPs, with its focus on royalty collection and not trade, was inserted into the WTO at US insistence despite the absence of any intellectual argument for it.[41] To be sure, the tensions inherent in this arrangement surfaced immediately in the interpretation of the TRIPs. In ensuing discussions, it would be in the laboratory of biotechnology and eventually public health policy that generated the most heat.

By 2001, the WTO TRIPs Council set about a review of the Agreement's implementation. This included consideration of specific IP concerns such as the scope of biotechnology patenting and plant variety rights. Thus far, the TRIPs Council has focused on the treaty language itself; however, Australia highlighted the necessity for an examination of the varying practical options available via diverse national experiences to enhance IP protection. In particular, Australia has sought to promote an understanding of how developing countries understand patenting in biotechnology and plant variety protection, so that the WTO documents more accurately reflect its entire membership. Australia also promoted its interests through active participation in the review, in addition to safeguarding its specific interests, such as geographic indicators and biotechnology and pursuing these through bilateral, regional and multilateral forums and dispute settlement mechanisms.[42] The US bridled at this

---

40 Michael P. Ryan, 1998, pp. 107–108.

41 Jagdish Bhagwati and Arvind Panagariya, 'Bilateral trade treaties are a sham', *Financial Times*, 14 July 2003, p. 17.

42 DFAT, 'A briefing on the WTO TRIPs Agreement and related intellectual property issues', *TRIPs Update, Edition 1*, March 2001, pp. 4–5. For a more comprehensive discussion of Australia's position on Article 27.3(b), see pp. 11–13, <http://www.dfat.gov.au/ip/trips_update_index.html>. Accessed April 2007.

approach, instead favouring an ad hoc solution via individual dispute panels. It believed the TRIPs Council should refrain from involvement in this issue.[43]

Affordable access to medicines, especially by developing countries, has also stirred the TRIPs Council. In June 2001, the Council conducted a special meeting to examine access issues. Australia has attempted to mediate in an argument shaped by North–South concerns. Some developed countries had attempted to isolate the issue as a threat solely to IP rights. The USTR characterised the dispute solely in trade terms. It criticised attempts by developing countries to 'justify protectionist measures by associating these measures with the AIDs crisis when no linkage exists'.[44] Associated with this were the claims that developing countries were neglecting reform of public health infrastructure and failing in their promotion of preventative medicine. Some developing countries countered that TRIPs offered no leeway to discuss these issues; instead, TRIPs demanded a resolution of the tensions in the availability of medicines and patent protection. However, the priority for many remained the state of public health and their sovereignty over policy.

How this could be addressed was subject to discussion in Doha. In explaining the Doha Declaration, the WTO stated that 'the interpretation and implementation of the TRIPs Agreement should support "governments" rights to protect public health'. The Declaration emphasised that 'the TRIPs Agreement does not and should not prevent member governments from acting to protect public health.'[45] In August 2003, the WTO General Assembly allowed for all the flexibilities in the TRIPs Agreement to be exercised for developing and least developed countries. Thus, countries with significant HIV–AIDS problems, such as Brazil, India, Kenya and South Africa were allowed to produce some generic medicines even though they did not retain patent rights. Further clarification was also provided on the flexibility in compulsory licensing and parallel importing.

Through these discussions Australia argued that TRIPs offered a balance between IP interests to ensure the creation of innovative medicines and the opportunities for developing countries to access medicines, particularly in cases of national health emergencies. This could be achieved through compulsory licensing of pharmaceutical patents, however, through the AUSFTA Australia agreed to significant restrictions on governments' capacity to issue compulsory licences. While there remains some greater understanding by the developed countries of the necessity to address major public health concerns, the issue remains highly contentious and a number of countries fear reprisals from the US. Such is the global concern that it is subject to talks in other international forums, including the WHO and UN General Assembly, particularly in conjunction with discussions on HIV/AIDS.

43 DFAT, 'A briefing on the WTO TRIPs Agreement and related intellectual property issues', p. 14.

44 USTR, '2001 Special 301 Report', Washington D.C., p. 5.

45 WTO, 'The Doha Declaration explained: Trade-related aspects of intellectual property rights (TRIPS)' (pars 17–19), <http://www.wto.org/english/tratop_e/dda_e/dohaexplained_e.htm>, accessed 16 March 2007, and WTO, 'Implementation of paragraph 6 of the Doha Declaration on the TRIPS Agreement and public health: Decision of the General Council of 30 August 2003', 1 September 2003.

It is also problematic that the negotiations within the recent spate of regional and bilateral Free Trade Agreements, as evidenced by the AUSFTA, strengthen the hands of the major powers in preserving IP rights. Now that Australia has agreed to many of the TRIPS plus provisions within the AUSFTA, its capacity to play the mediating role in multilateral negotiations is diminished.

Australia, however, has increasingly found companionship with the US over the production of genetically modified agricultural products as international forums collide progressively with the TRIPs Council's discussions and regulations. The Convention on Biological Diversity (CBD) at the Rio Environmental Summit in 1992 outlined the protective management and trade of biological organisms. Some of the debates also centred on whether advanced forms of life may be patented. If so, the fear of the transfer from public to private ownership of biological resources was raised. While many transnational corporations wish to protect their intellectual property on genetically modified products, a number of countries are concerned to protect their biological resources. Some are concerned that sovereign resources may be plundered and captured by larger firms pursuing genetic material of native biology. Thus individual countries may lose control over the processing of native species. Furthermore, many farm groups are concerned that more comprehensive patenting will deny their free access to traditional seed varieties.

In response to the nature of these debates at the Rio Summit, the Biodiversity Convention refused to condone the application of patents for gene manipulation of plants and processes. The aim of the 1992 Convention was 'the conservation of biological diversity, the sustainable use of its components and the fair and equitable sharing of the benefits arising out of the utilization of genetic resources'.[46] The Cartagena Protocol on Biosafety, as initiated in 1992, was eventually adopted by 176 countries in January 2000 and entered into force in September 2003. It aims to protect biological diversity from organisms altered through biotechnology processes. More prominent in the discussions in recent years has been the safety of genetically modified organisms, (GMOs). The Protocol's objective is to:

> contribute to ensuring an adequate level of protection in the field of the safe transfer, handling and use of living modified organisms resulting from modern biotechnology that may have adverse effects on the conservation and sustainable use of biological diversity, taking into account risks to human health, and specifically focusing on transboundary movements.[47]

One of the concepts inherent within the Protocol has been the 'precautionary principle', whereby countries have determined that if the safety of any of these products has not been established with certainty, by valid scientific research, then a cautionary approach must be taken. The Protocol also establishes the necessity for a raft of information, both scientific and legal to accompany any trade in GMOs.

46 United Nations, Secretariat of the Convention on Biological Diversity, United Nations Environment Programme, Cartagena Protocol on Biosafety, p. 4, <http://www.biodiv.org/biosafety/faqs.asp?lg=0>. Accessed 17 March 2007.

47 United Nations, Secretariat of the Convention on Biological Diversity, United Nations Environment Programme, Cartagena Protocol on Biosafety, p. 5.

Despite being the pre-eminent leader in biotechnological development and trade, the US did not sign these agreements. Although President Clinton signed the agreements in June 1993, which indicated his support for the principles of the Treaty, the US Senate has refused to ratify the treaty and the US remains not legally bound by the articles. Thus, the US has been excluded from official proceedings, with 'observer only' status and no rights to vote.

Toward the turn of the century, explicit discussion of the US position became more pronounced. Alejandro Segurra suggested that some oppose the CBD as the US (as principal global producer and exporter) is already in a position to determine the playing field and rules in the industry. Furthermore, the 'precautionary principle', together with the demands for transparency and disclosure as documented by the Protocol, is regarded by some critics as an alternate form of protectionism and able to be utilised by other countries in the establishment of a more competitive position for their own industries.[48]

Nonetheless, the US has been active in all associated discussions and attempted to influence the course of the negotiations. As part of the Miami Group, the US joined with other principal agricultural exporters including Australia, Argentina, Canada, Chile and Uruguay to leverage their position in the discussions. In this area Australia has largely sided with the US. Australian farmers, through the NFF, had originally lobbied the government not to ratify the Protocol. They argued that if the Protocol effectively diminished any of the WTO rules and endangered the interests of Australian farmers, then it should be opposed. The NFF believed that the WTO, through the food safety and plant and animal health (sanitary and phytosanitary), and the TRIPs, allocated countries' rights to protect human, animal and plant health. It was also a concern to the Cairns Group, that as the original ratification meeting of the Cartagena Protocol was intended for February 1999, it was possible the strengthening of the environmental and trade links and an accompanying erosion of WTO norms would endanger the upcoming agricultural talks. As such, it would place formidable pressure on the WTO to incorporate environmental issues more formally into the rules. Both the US and Australia were opposed to any linkage between world trade talks and environmental and labour standards.[49]

It has also surfaced that one of the major difficulties of the tracking demands for the US grain producers, is that the US grain handling system does not differentiate between conventional and GM grain. To alter the vast network of grain handling operations would be a costly exercise for the US and provoke vehement opposition from some producers unwilling to deny their competitive advantage. Nonetheless, the dangers of this system became evident in 2000 when a biotech corn variety known as

---

48 Alejandro E. Segurra, 'Biosafety Protocol for Genetically Modified Organisms', Congressional Research Service: Report for Congress, RL 30594, 5 July 2000, pp. 1–3. Also Donna U. Vogt and Mickey Parish, 'Food Biotechnology in the United States: Science, Regulation, and Issues', *CRS Report to Congress*, 2 June 1999, p. 2.

49 Cairns Group, 'Biosafety Protocol Could Erect New Barriers to Trade', news release, undated, <http://www.cairnsgroupfarmers.org/ni/reportspapers/biosafety.htm>. Accessed March 2005.

Starlink, approved only for animal feed, was detected in processed foodstuffs in US supermarkets. It was also identified in corn shipments to Korea and Japan.[50]

While Australia and the US worked together in the Miami group in seeking to reduce the documentation accompanying agricultural biotech exports, Australia's labelling requirements in 2001 created some tension with its US partner. Together with Mexico and New Zealand, Australia required that foods are adequately labelled with any relevant GM information. ANZFA, the Australia New Zealand Food Authority, amended the Foods Standard Code which required foods produced using gene technology be labelled as such, as of 7 December 2001. US producers argued that, depending on the specifications of the labelling requirements, not only may this decrease demand for these foods but will inevitably increase the costs of the products.[51] By 2006, however, the Parties to the protocol had agreed that until 2012 conventional exports from GM commodity-producing states would not come under the scope of the Protocol. In addition, the Miami Group attempted to integrate the CBD with WTO agreements, particularly in relation to the proprieties in sanitary and phytosanitary measures affecting world trade. In bilateral negotiations, the sanitary and phytosanitary terms of the AUSFTA stated that 'each party should give positive consideration to accepting as equivalent the technical regulations of the other Party' (Article 8.5). Some Australian agricultural producers have concerns that this will eventuate in changes to GM standards that reflect US producers' interests in Australia.

As an agricultural competitor, Australia may find itself under pressure to develop biotech products in order to compete with the US in global markets. Yet it is not only the practical exigencies of production that Australia must consider but also whether the safety aspects of the trade can be ensured. Manifest in the CBD is the intersection of these issues. It is also worth considering the option that if Australia refrained from the introduction of GM cropping or production, this may confer its own competitive advantage. To date, however, Australia has no timetable for planned accession to the Protocol and remains concerned about the ability of states to retain sovereignty in decision-making. It is concerned to isolate profitable agricultural concerns. In much the same way as it has attempted to separate labour and environmental standards from WTO discussions, Australia is attempting to simplify the CBD discussions. The magnitude of this approach should not be underestimated.

Conclusion: Mediation in Medicines

Management of the US relationship within the biotech and pharmaceutical sector remains an archetypical study of how the Howard government has dealt with its international and domestic demands. While the government must respond to Australian society's needs for quality and affordable health care, a vibrant economy, and the US role in assisting in this, the government is also subject to the threats posed by its bilateral partner in all its manifestations of power.

---

50 US Government Accounting Office Report, 'Concerns over biotechnology challenge US agricultural exports', 15 June 2001, p. 5.

51 US Government Accounting Office Report, 2001, p. 3.

Acknowledgement of the sector's importance for the economy is increasing. In allocating some increases in funding for research in this area, the government has recognised the potential of the industry, including the beneficial offshoots of an innovative industry. In fostering the conditions whereby Australia can increase the value-adding component in the entire production process, the government can work to realise the industry's ability to generate wealth in Australia. In its regulatory and legislative apparatus it can provide companies with a framework for both profitable and safe practice. At the margins, the Australian government can assist in facilitating the smooth operation of business interaction with the US.

In its embrace of biotechnology, the US is sometimes touted as a model for the organisation of research and commerce. Australia now has the opportunity to consider this model. Albeit attractive, the commercialisation of research brings with it some ethical dilemmas regarding the independence of its scientific base and the narrowing of scientific inquiry to financially profitable platforms. Yet these problems are not intractable. What is perhaps more important is that as the US managed care health system falters, it becomes incumbent upon an Australian government to preserve the features of affordable medicine.

Where the USTR has been mandated to act via petitions from industry groups, Australia can have no expectations that its role as alliance partner has any bearing on the trajectory of a dispute. As an analysis of the bilateral negotiations has revealed, the USTR has been utilised as part of the armoury of the pharmaceutical companies to protect and further their interests. Once again, for Australia, it appears that the multilateral story has been the most potent in the construction of a defence against these pressures. Australia's efforts in the 1990s in negotiating the flexibility within the system attempted to regulate the behaviour of the transnationals and preserve the unique aspects of Australian biotechnology and related health system delivery. Evidence suggests however, that the US, at the behest of the corporate world, has the clout to write the system, and its bilateral negotiations through its Free Trade Agreements have worked towards shoring up the rights of the major powers.

Chapter 5

New Depths: The *Collins* Class Submarine Project

Such was the luck of the *Collins* class submarine project that when Building K was demolished at Russell Hill, Canberra in August 2000, it was *reported* that the classified documents which surfaced unexpectedly in the deconstruction were those belonging to the submarine project.[1]

While this incident was indicative of the troubled public history of these submarines, the submarine project also provides an insight into how the Howard government's relationship with the US figured in both its international and its domestic policy. Between 1996 and 2003, the Howard government re-emphasised the relationship with one of Australia's traditional allies as the cornerstone of security policy. So significant was this orientation, that in 2003 two alliance analysts claimed that '(t)he theme of defense self-reliance has been superseded', by an emerging 'strategic interdependence' with the US.[2] On the signing of the submarine cooperation statement in 2001, then Defence Minister, Peter Reith, stated that this was 'further evidence of this Government's commitment to the historic alliance between Australia and its close ally and friend the United States.'[3] The *Collins* project was thus captured within a transition process whereby the government sought to establish greater intimacy with the US.

In the domestic arena, the Howard government also utilised an upgraded relationship with the US to assuage public concerns of uncertainty and insecurity. Through this analysis of the *Collins* project, we see the construction of a 'crisis' through the government's emphasis of flaws in the submarines. This 'crisis' would also serve a dual purpose as, through any accentuation of the project's faults, it could disparage the Labor opposition (who initially sponsored the project) and seek to arrest its increasing electoral threat. So, in spite of Navy and defence industry recognition that Australia had constructed an exceptional boat, the government publicised the faults in the boats, not only to promote US involvement in the project, but also to damage the electoral opposition. It was also clear that the government used the project to persuade the electorate that, in the end, only the Coalition was

---

1 Lincoln Wright, 'Secrets Blow About Building Site', *Canberra Times*, 23 August 2000, p. 3. N.B. I have not confirmed the veracity of this report.

2 Rod Lyon and William T. Tow, 'The Future of the Australian–US Security Relationship', *Strategic Studies Institute, US Army War College*, Carlisle, December 2003, p. 34.

3 The Hon. Peter Reith MP, Minister for Defence, 'Australia and US sign submarine cooperation statement', *Media Release*, 12 September 2001.

capable of delivering an adequate weapons and intelligence-gathering platform in the maintenance of security.

Originally, this project was imprinted with the motif of independence, both strategic and commercial, under Labor's press. As the project was born in an era of Labor government, any publication of the submarines' faults, or supposed faults, thus would imply criticism of the ALP, particularly of the Leader of the Opposition and former Defence Minister, Kim Beazley. In the year following the formal establishment of the *Collins* project, Project 1114 – New Submarines (20 February 1982) the newly elected ALP government in Australia embarked upon a review of its relationship with the United States. In September 1983, it had conducted a review of the ANZUS Treaty and in June 1984, it attempted to scrutinise more comprehensively the Joint Defence Facilities. Even though Prime Minister Hawke was a strong supporter of the alliance, the left of the Labor Party ensured that US proposals for MX missile testing in the Tasman Sea were rejected, as was support for Reagan's 'Star Wars' designs.[4] Cognisant of the directions of Nixon's 1969 Guam Doctrine that laid greater responsibilities for regional security with allies in the Pacific, the Hawke government commissioned Paul Dibb's *Review of Australia's Defence Capabilities* in 1986 and its less stridently independent White Paper, *The Defence of Australia* the following year.[5] Later manifestations of this thinking also appeared in *Australia's Regional Security*, and eventually in proposals of former Foreign Minister, Gareth Evans for the ASEAN Regional Forum.[6] Independence and self-reliance were the themes that welled from the times. Although perhaps ominously, in his critique of the later development of ensuing policies, Graeme Cheeseman warned of the possibilities of increasing logistical reliance on the US,[7] it was within the context of Australia's quest for greater self-reliance that the submarine project evolved. This chapter, then, examines the submarine project not only as it discloses Australia's initial broader attempts to balance its desire for independence with a later preternatural desire for a secure relationship with a more powerful ally, but also as it is a revelation of the interrelationship between the Howard government's domestic and international policies.

The *Collins* Project

As the concept of 'self-reliance' was one of the Labor Party's central intellectual organising themes in defence policy in the 1980s, the submarine project, as a major

4 The 'Star Wars' programme has been regarded as a precursor to the current missile defence projects.

5 Department of Defence, *Review of Australia's Defence Capabilities, Report to the Minister for Defence by Paul Dibb*, March 1986, AGPS, Canberra, and the Department of Defence, *The Defence of Australia 1987*, Australian Government Publishing Service, Canberra, 1987.

6 Department of Defence, *Australia's Regional Security*, Australian Government Publishing Service, Canberra, 1989.

7 For a critique of the success of these policies, see Graeme Cheeseman, *The Search for Self Reliance: Australian Defence Since Vietnam*, Longman Cheshire, Melbourne, 1993.

defence project, was to be a primary example of the concept in practice. Former Defence Minister, Kim Beazley, reflected that at the time three key planks were essential in realising this vision. These were: a) rigorous defence planning, b) self-reliance within the broader context of Australia's alliances and c) that self-reliance was only possible with the development of Australian defence industry capabilities.[8] In this respect, the acquisition of the submarines was a timely project. But not only was it ideally placed to enhance and expand the capabilities of the domestic defence industry, in addition to contributing to the revival of the naval shipbuilding sector, it was a 'perfect' opportunity for the ALP to embark upon a major capital works initiative. Australian industry was to be a significant beneficiary of Project SEA 1114.

Defence procurement thus displayed the independence insignia. And as the Department of Trade sponsored a trade union reconnaissance assignment to Western Europe to examine the workings of corporatist industrial relations,[9] the *Collins* project was ripe to marry both strategic and industrial independence objectives.

Defence force planning required that Australia maintain its regional military superiority whilst naval requirements specifically noted the necessity for the submarines' conflict response, surveillance, intelligence gathering and deterrence capability. As 90 per cent of Australia's trade was conducted via shipping, it would also offer an invaluable trade protection role. In particular, for Australia, these functions could be performed by submarines with relative impunity where it lacked air and sea superiority. Australia's distinctive geographic and oceanographic environment also required the submarines to function in situations of great deviation in temperature, density, salinity, humidity and climate. With strategic interests extending from the Persian Gulf to the North Pacific, and a requirement that the submarines' range extend to 9000 nautical miles, the RAN preferred large conventional submarines. In addition to the range and payload, these new boats would also need highly advanced sensors and weapons suites. The surveillance criteria required that the boat could maintain slow pace and depth in littoral and estuarine waters. The increased size of the boat would also offer better habitability conditions for crew. Given these demands it was unlikely that military off the shelf technology would be able to supply a boat and instead a new design was necessitated.

Yet this would be a daring project for Australia. The complexity of the design and construction of this boat was enormous. Certainly, it would mark an extraordinary challenge. This was particularly so as both the US and UK, even with established industries, had experienced extensive difficulties with the *Seawolf* and *Upholder* projects respectively. Combat system, noise, and welding problems besieged the former. Budget extensions, delivery delays and weapons systems inadequacies plagued the UK project. In particular, the Royal Navy had encountered substantial

8 Kim Beazley, 'The case for submarines 7 and 8', *Press Release*, Adelaide, 23 July 1996.

9 Department of Trade, 'Australia Reconstructed', *ACTU/TDC Mission to Western Europe, A Report by the Mission Members to the ACTU and the TDC*, AGPS, Canberra 1987.

problems with its combat systems programmes.[10] Specifically, for the *Collins* constructors, not only was the noise signature going to require particular attention (as it did in any submarine project) but as the performance of the sonars in tropical littoral waters was even more difficult, Australia's world class sonar industry would face significant challenges.

At the conclusion of the source selection process on 18 May 1987, Kockums/ Australian Submarine Corporation (ASC) was contracted to supply six Type 471 diesel electric submarines. Options were retained to construct two additional boats. US defence titan Rockwell International was chosen to provide the combat data system. The contract also specified that 70 per cent of the platform work and 45 per cent of the combat system were to be conducted in Australia.[11] Robert Ray, former Minister of Defence recorded that the project was to benefit Australia through:

> job creation but also through technology transfer, creation of new skills, improved quality practices and...development of modern management techniques and the introduction of new and more progressive industrial relations practices.[12]

At this time it was noteworthy that Australia's alliance partner, the US, expressed no objection to Kockums with its links to the Swedish Navy, a neutral country armed force, being selected as the platform constructor. Neither did it preclude Kockums from working with the US combat system house on the project.

What was of greater concern was the need to manage a sweeping assortment of risk factors inherent in the project. Responding to the Auditor-General's Report 1992–93, the Department of Defence (hereafter Defence) documented some of these as the innovative but untried design of both the platform and combat system, which also incorporated pioneering technology in areas such as the Integrated Ship Control Management and Monitoring System (ISCMMS) and the towed array. Complicating the design arrangements too, was that any problem inherent in the combat system would affect the broader operation of the submarines. As the *Collins* submarines intended to incorporate a completely integrated operational system, the combat system was then crucial to the overall functionality of the vessel. Without a fully operational combat system, the integrity of the other ship functions such as navigation, radar and particularly the sonar *could* be compromised. For all those involved in the project at this stage, the set components had been allocated, and the task was to make it work.

Concerns also focused on the inexperience of the new consortium and the workforce in addition to the need to manage the separate production centres together

10 Paul Dibb and Terry Roach, 'Collins: The Submarine We Had To Have', *Australian Financial Review*, 17 February 1999, p. 17.

11 Commodore Geoff Rose, 'Introduction of Underwater Platform Technology (An Australian Perspective)', *Paper for the Defence Asia Forum 1997 at the World Trade Centre*, Singapore, 16 January 1997, p. 2.

12 Robert Ray, Minister of Defence, *CPD*, *Senate Hansard*, 17 December 1992, p. 5411.

with the local industrial environment.[13] Unstated, but of significant concern, was the monopsonistic arrangement that saw the Australian government and RAN as both contractor and sole purchaser. This arrangement, coupled with the fixed price contract, complicated the project's business relations.

In 1986, the RAN discussed their requirements with their US Navy (USN) counterparts. While they viewed the project as 'challenging', the feedback on the realisation of the project was minimal. In addition, Australia's access to USN submarine platform and combat system technology was restricted through US arms export embargoes. These restrictions also applied to US exports to Australia's European suppliers.

A Genuine Shipwreck or Pathological Politicisation?

Given the technological and production demands coupled with the innovative nature of the project in Australia, there was never any doubt that this was a risky venture and that problems would invariably arise. Yet, at least from 1987 onwards, the *Collins* project managers had identified the risks associated with the project. Nevertheless, the hostile publicity surrounding the project was extraordinary. Clearly, the political contours of this project exemplify the intricacies of the government's interest in devising international strategy with a local audience in mind.

By 1999, the government had commissioned two reports into submarine capability. Yet both of these, authored by the Joint Committee of Public Accounts and Audit (JCPAA) and the Australian National Audit Office (ANAO) had mostly documented issues and solutions that were being managed by the ASC.[14] Nonetheless, the then Minister for Defence, John Moore commissioned the McIntosh-Prescott Report to review the project.[15] That many of these issues had been both well documented and addressed by Defence and the ASC, and that the new report also relied on the project office as the primary source of information on the submarines highlighted the political nature of the analysis and the politicisation of the project.

Unfortunately for those involved, one of the consequences of this continued criticism was to expend valuable resources on repetitive reporting. Moreover, some in the Australian industry claimed that this additional expenditure on US sourced material would have been much more effectively allocated for local solutions to any remaining issues. Regrettably, too, it had the effect of depleting crew and project team morale and hampering recruitment. Yet the RAN itself claims that:

---

13 'Response by Department of Defence', read by Robert Ray, *CPD, Senate Hansard*, 17 December 1992, p. 5411. See also The Commonwealth of Australia, Audit Report No. 22, 1992–93, *New Submarine Project*, AGPS, 1992.

14 The Commonwealth of Australia, Audit Report No. 34, 1997–8, *New Submarine Project*, was tabled on 25 March 1998. The Joint Committee of Public Accounts and Audit, Review of Auditor-General's Report, No. 34, 1997–8, *New Submarine Project*, was released in June 1999.

15 Malcolm McIntosh and John Prescott, 'Report to the Minister for Defence on The Collins Class Submarine and Related Matters', Commonwealth of Australia, Canberra, June 1999, p. 6.

> (t)he greatest single strength of the Navy is the calibre of its officers and sailors. Yet recruiting, training and retaining the right people will always be its greatest challenge. History shows that ships with the best sailors invariably win the battle at sea. Maritime warfare in the 21st century is no different.[16]

In a sector where submariners are difficult to recruit, it seemed difficult to reconcile John Moore's attacks on the submarines. That the submariners' and submarines' successes in international exercises were not well lauded either, and at times not even acknowledged, further exacerbated the problems. Moreover, it irrevocably skewed the public view of a remarkable project.

If the USN was interested in the *Collins* to complement their force structure, it was also evident that the US military suppliers were eager to further their claims. As eventually became evident to some, the *Collins* combat data system would need replacing. Although the ASC had advised Defence that the combat system software releases had not been delivered on schedule in 1993, both Defence and the RAN decided to persist with the supplier. Yet the proper functioning of the combat system was vital for the boat's operation as it integrated the navigational, surface system (comprising radar, ship identification and periscopes), the sonar and data processing system, electronic surveillance and the tactical data handling system (TDHS). This latter system remained crucial as it collected and processed information from the previous four systems and was ultimately responsible for target engagement. To be sure, the provision of such innovative and sophisticated technology for a boat that also deployed such complex sonar suites was an ambitious task: one that appeared much underrated by Rockwell and its associated subcontractors.[17] Moreover, their initial choice of architecture eventually precluded the installation of much more advanced technology as it became available through companies such as Thomson Marconi Sonar.[18]

Modifications wrought by those involved in the project kept the boats functioning and crews continued to be trained. Concurrently, the Maritime Systems division of DSTO had established the Combat System Research Centre in Adelaide to best manage the ongoing issues. A practicable solution to the combat system was achieved that enabled the submarines to function very effectively, if not perfectly, as the ASC, the RAN and Kockums would have wished.

Eventually, in February 2000, the Department of Defence decided to release a Request for Proposal to four combat system suppliers and ASC for a new combat system. Government approval was eventually provided and, as stated in the Defence 2000 White Paper, all submarines would be fitted with a new combat system, with work beginning in 2001 and completion planned for 2005–2006.[19]

---

16 RAN, 'Plan Blue: Australia's Navy for the 21st Century' <http://www.navy.gov.au/publications/planblue/html/planblue4.htm>. Accessed November 2004.

17 Information from interviewee.

18 Information from interviewees. Thomson Marconi Sonar was previously Thomson Sintra Pacific. In 1996 Boeing assumed control of Rockwell International's defence arm.

19 Department of Defence, 'Defence 2000: Our Future Defence Forces', Canberra, 2000, p. 90.

Subscribing to US Assistance

Nevertheless, the political discrediting of the submarines also created the space whereby the government could argue its case for the allocation of further funding and the necessity for US involvement in the project. Founded on the relationship between Vice Admiral Don Chalmers and USN, Chief of Naval Operations, Admiral Jay Johnson, Chalmers instigated the process whereby US assistance was sought. Early in 1998, Australia's then Chief of Navy and Admiral Jay Johnson convened to discuss a range of issues, the *Collins* being one. Even if the ASC and some others involved in the project were not seeking US assistance, the US Chief's response to assist the RAN was accepted. As discussed later, the *Collins* project was, after all, of interest to the US. On 10 September 2001 in the Pentagon, Vice Admiral David Shackleton and US Admiral Vern Clark signed the Statement of Principles for Submarine Cooperation. Both John Howard and US Secretary of Defence, Donald Rumsfeld, were present at the signing. Upgraded relations with the US and greater cooperation with the USN were regarded as desirable by the Coalition. Greater intimacy was integral to the government's management of foreign policy and played to its domestic audience as much as allaying any international risk.

Although the ASC and its subcontractors continued to address the problems, as a prompt and public response to the McIntosh-Prescott report in July 1999, John Moore approved additional funds of $80 million for a combined RAN/USN programme that would seek to rectify some of the operational problems. Moore would deftly address the 'crisis'. By December, with the McIntosh-Prescott Report in hand, Moore had approved $266 million for HMAS *Dechaineux* and *Sheean* to give Australia two operational submarines when the *Oberon* class, HMAS *Otama*, was retired in 2001. Approximately half of the funds were intended to incorporate new technology and the remainder to address the other performance difficulties including improvements to the sonars, TDHS, weapons control, noise signature, visual and communications technology, together with upgraded training and personnel initiatives.[20] The submarine was tested hydro-acoustically in Alaska. Propellers were sent to the US for analysis. Some of the flow noise problems were partially resolved through the addition of new fibreglass fairings fitted to the fin and other parts of the submarine. The funds also allowed for the trial of some USN submarine combat system components.[21]

US aid was also pursued by the Navy in effecting an interim solution for the Rockwell's combat system.[22] Under Project SEA 1446, the USN delivered two sets of augmentation equipment to assist with the combat system problems. Rear Admiral Peter Briggs, new Head of the Submarine Capability Team (formed as result of recommendations of the McIntosh-Prescott Report) conceded however, that this

20 John Moore, Minister for Defence, *Media Release*, 'Submarine Upgrade Proceeds', MIN 357/99, 9 December 1999.

21 John Moore, Minister for Defence, *Media Statement*, 'Reform of Defence Acquisition', 1 July 1999, MIN 188/99.

22 McIntosh and Prescott reported that the combat system was inadequate and now obsolete, with a consequence that the sonars were only about 25 per cent effective. Thomson Marconi Sonar, producers of the sonars claimed that when the combat system was fully operational then the sonars would also perform as intended.

was only an interim solution based on 'flawed foundations'.[23] Flawed foundations proved a correct analysis as the system, based upon the USN's capabilities with nuclear submarines, generated too much heat for the conventional submarines. Eventually this system would need to be replaced. And although HMAS *Dechaineux* and HMAS *Sheean* were thus 'fast tracked' with the new federated system which sought to achieve a minimal level of operational capability by the end of 2000, the combat system augmentation was still not optimal. Peter Briggs, nevertheless, paid tribute to the US Navy for their complete support in assisting Australia's ability to have two minimally operational submarines at a time when the last of the *Oberons* were phased out.

The Sub Plot: US Strategic Stakes in the Littoral Battlespace

It should not be mistaken that the US had only assumed an interest in the *Collins* in 2000. It appears instead that the USN was vitally interested for force capability reasons in the submarine technology developed in Australia. Although most certainly it would exert a powerful presence in the selection of the new combat system and sale of the ASC, the US military had kept abreast of the *Collins* project from inception. As the USN was cognisant of the value of the conventional submarine yet unable to persuade the Administration to construct these boats in the US as it might jeopardise the nuclear industry, the next best option was to foster allied engagement in their construction and operation.[24] US Joint Chief of Staff, John Shalikashvili, who was in Australia to attend the Australia–US Ministerial talks, also attended the commissioning ceremony for HMAS *Collins* in 1996. Through the 1990s, the US military had also altered its maritime mindset from the Carrier Battle Group anti-sub warfare and anti-submarine operations focus of the Cold War to the littoral battlespace of the 21st century navy. No longer did a single defined enemy preoccupy the US military, instead operational intent was reoriented to a much less homogenous cache of littoral based enemies, those of disaffected nation-states or terrorist and criminal groups, as aided by both increasingly technologically sophisticated weaponry and an atavistic arms market.

So, by the 1990s, the USN had reoriented itself to a very different strategic view. Navy policy documents stated that:

> (t)he primary purpose of forward-deployed naval forces is to project American power from the sea to influence events ashore in the littoral regions of the world across the operational spectrum of peace, crisis and war…Our attention and efforts will continue to be focused on operating in and from the littorals…Seventy-five per cent of the Earth's population and a similar proportion of national capitals and major commercial centers lie

---

23 Richard Scott, 'Final countdown for new Collins combat system', *Jane's Defence Weekly*, vol. 34, no. 2, 12 July 2000.

24 Andrew Millar has offered this as an opinion on the US submarine industry and allied engagement. *Personal Communication*, 17 November 2003.

in the littorals. These are the places where American influence and power have the greatest impact and are needed most often.[25]

Commensurate with this, the USN had planned the construction of the smaller nuclear powered submarines designed for operations in both coastal waters and open ocean. Nevertheless, the delivery of the USS *Virginia* (still twice the size of the *Collins*) was not scheduled until 2004.

It should also be noted that the US submarine force although pre-eminent, did not keep pace with its Cold War force structure. The *Seawolf* class, the most advanced US attack submarine in 2002, was originally intended as a fleet of 29, but was reduced to three with budget constraints during the 1990s. To enhance US capability, however, America looked to its allies. Rear Admiral Al Konetzni, commander of the US submarine forces in the Pacific in 2000 explained:

(w)e are pushing forward our relationship with Australia so it's as strong as the one we have with the UK in the Atlantic...Our nuclear assets are limited, but the missions aren't. Since 1997, we have retired about half of the Navy's fast attack boats, leaving me with 26 subs for the entire Pacific...That makes it all the more important to work closely with our allies.[26]

By 2001, the US in its Quadrennial Defense Review Report stated that:

(a)nti-ship cruise missiles, advanced diesel submarines, and advanced mines could threaten the ability of US naval and amphibious forces to operate in littoral waters. *New approaches for projecting power must be developed to meet these threats.*[27]

The US too, was attracted to the rationalism of Australia's two ocean policy. In upgrading the WA naval base HMAS Stirling and relocating the submarine fleet there, the Australian government had five objectives in mind. First, Neutral Bay would not be able to accommodate the *Collins*, and any east coast location imposed additional time constraints upon the submarines' usual operational tasks. Second, it could more easily facilitate its sovereign responsibilities (and later assertiveness), with regard to the Cocos and Christmas Islands in the Indian Ocean, Heard and MacDonald Islands in the Southern Ocean and the Ashmore and Cartier Islands (south of Timor) of which it became more acutely conscious in 1999. Third, it could oversee the Indian Ocean sea lines of communications, where over fifty per cent of Australia's seaborne trade (by displacement) was carried. Fourth, the Navy had more ready access to the Northwest shelf, which harboured extensive offshore oil and

---

25 United States Navy, 'Forward...From the Sea: The Navy Operational Concept', March 1997, pp. 1–2. One of the interviewees has also observed that joint exercises such as RIMPAC have often served to remind the USN of the risks presented by conventional submarines.

26 Vago Muradian, 'Top US Admiral Lauds Quality of Australian Collins Subs', *Defense Daily International*, vol. 1, no. 30, 27 October 2000.

27 US Department of Defense, Quadrennial Defense Review Report, Washington D.C., 30 September 2001, p. 31. Italics in original. See also Clark A. Murdock, 'The Navy in an Anti-access World', in Sam J. Tangredi (ed.), *Globalization and Maritime Power*, Institute for National Security Studies, National Defense University, 2001, Chapter 25.

gas resources. Fifth, this RAN initiative was premised on both logic and economic viability. Australia's strategic interests would be best served through the relocation.[28] Although the US Navy's base in Diego Garcia established its presence in the Indian Ocean, with instability in both in South Asia and Southeast Asia in 1999, the need to fortify its presence and influence in the Indian Ocean and sea routes to South and Northeast Asia was emphasised. Shoring up its links with the Australian Navy's resources was one method of ensuring this. After 2001, more established links in the Indian Ocean provided better access to the subcontinent, West Asia and the Middle East.

Horden Wiltshire, former Commanding Officer of HMAS *Sheean*, has recorded of the *Collins* submarines that the 'media smoke screen has disguised the full potential of the platform which, in an uncertain strategic environment, remains one of the most versatile and potent in the Australian Defence Force'.[29] The US too was soon to discover just how potent. More positively for those associated with the *Collins* project, such was the much lauded but little reported, success of HMAS *Waller* at the RIMPAC 2000 naval exercises off Hawaii in May, that the US interest was heightened. Despite being restricted by some aspects of its noise performance and limitations in the combat system, *Waller*, in these structured events, pursued and 'sunk' a Los Angeles class nuclear submarine and in taking periscope photographs of the aircraft carrier, *Abraham Lincoln*, demonstrated that it could enter into torpedo range of the carrier denying detection.[30] Just why there was such a dearth of publicity surrounding *Waller's* success may indicate further the strength of the interest in securing US involvement.

Importantly here, *Waller* operated with the original combat system as modified by Australian subcontractor, SonarTech, and the original Kockums platform. It did not utilise either of the two augmentation systems proffered by the US, nor operate with any US alterations. Noteworthy too, even though the exercises were highly planned and the US group knew that *Waller* was in the designated target area, they were still unable to locate it. New Minister for Defence, Robert Hill, recorded later that the:

> Americans are finding them exceptional boats...in exercises with the Americans they astound the Americans in terms of their capability, their speed, their agility, their loitering capacity, they can do all sorts of things that the American submarines can't do as well...[31]

---

28 Sam Bateman, 'Australia's "two ocean" policy', *Business Times*, 29 July 1995, p. 4. I am also grateful to some of the interviewees for the information in this section.

29 Horden Wiltshire, 'Submarines: an Australian view', in David Wilson, *Maritime War in the 21st Century: The Medium and Small Navy Perspective*, RAN Sea Power Centre, Canberra, 2001, p. 257.

30 Robert Garran, 'A deadly exercise in stealth', *The Weekend Australian*, 23–25 December 2000, p. 1. See also No author supplied, 'RAN Collins submarines now on track', *Asia–Pacific Defence Reporter*, December/January 2001, pp. 12–13.

31 Senator the Hon Robert Hill, Minister for Defence, Interview with Matt Abraham and David Bevan, 5AN, transcript, *Media Release*, MIN 681/02, 27 November 2002, pp. 2–3.

It was increasingly evident that Australia had much more to offer the US in conventional submarine technology and operations in littoral waters than the reverse. Thus, for allied operations in the littoral and estuarine waters of South East Asia and elsewhere, it was apparent that the *Collins* class submarines were most certainly a valuable asset. After 2001, the intelligence-gathering role of the *Collins* became noteworthy in profiling terrorist activity in both the region and that of the Persian Gulf. Further, it provided special force insertion capability. With the new and increased threat levels, this particular capability made the *Collins* an even more desirable acquisition.

While it was advantageous for the US to have an ally well equipped and less likely to call upon it for assistance, there appeared to be more flesh on the bare bones of its attention and support. In July 2000, William Cohen and John Moore signed the Defence and Trade Strategic Initiatives (DTSI). This was 'a statement of principles between two allies designed to enhance defence cooperation in the Asia–Pacific and Australian access to US technology'.[32] More specifically, it included the principles for Australia's exemption from most arms export regulations. Canada and Britain remain as the only two other countries with this status. Moore mentioned that the DTSI also allowed for intimate access to US submarine technology that Australia had sought for some time from the State Department and the Pentagon. If Australia were to receive specialised assistance to improve the performance of its submarines, how then would the US benefit from the exchange? In part, the US may have expected Australia to support its proposed National Missile Defence (NMD) system. Under the umbrella statement of enhanced security cooperation in the Asia Pacific, Cohen explained that the US outlay would facilitate a more seamless and swift exchange of information and technology. When questioned later about Australia's role in NMD he added that, should the US executive wish to proceed with the NMD system, 'Australia will continue to play an important role in shared early warning'.[33] While acknowledging that the NMD was a domestic political issue in Australia, the new American Ambassador to Australia, Edward Gnehm, claimed that US domestic politics would precipitate a renewed effort to complete the NMD. He expected that Australia, as responsible ally would provide the necessary assistance to the US.[34]

Strengthening Australia's role in the provision of early warning information had become of even greater import to the US in the previous two years – and not just in relation to the possibilities inherent in the NMD. In the 1990s, many countries in the region developed or expanded their submarine fleets. In the maritime battlefield of the future, the USN perceived that possible foes may well be diesel submarines equipped with air independent propulsion (AIP), enabling prolonged periods of

32 Transcript of the Joint Press Conference with US Defence Secretary William Cohen and Defence Minister John Moore following the signing of a statement of principles between the two allies designed to enhance defence cooperation in the Asia–Pacific and Australian access to US technology, Sydney, 17 July 2000, p. 1.

33 Transcript of the Joint Press Conference with US Defence Secretary William Cohen and Defence Minister John Moore, 17 July 2000, p. 2.

34 Paul Kelly, 'New messenger, same strategic alliance', *The Australian*, 20 September 2000, p. 35.

submerged operations. With the increase in disputes over territorial claims in the South China Sea, the development of special economic zones and the advance of long range anti-ship missiles, the submarine had become a higher priority for some in the region. China was modernising its blue water navy to extend its influence not only in the South China Sea but also the Taiwan Strait and the Sea of Japan. Indeed the Chinese defence budget had increased by approximately 50 per cent in real terms in the five years since 1995.[35]

More generally, analysis of the arms acquisition enacted in the 1990s in Asia reflected a maritime dimension. And although traditional security concerns have directed much of the acquisition programmes, emergent regional security issues such as piracy, illegal immigration, incidents at sea, management of environmental pollution, transnational criminal activity, legal and illegal exploitation of aquatic food stocks and seabed resources have begun to assume a greater prominence as security concerns in Asia. Indeed, the Convention of the Law of the Sea has accelerated the formal uncertainties in relation to exclusive economic zones and continental shelf boundaries. At present there are collateral claims on the southern Kurils/Northern Territories, Tok Do/Takeshima, and Senkaku/Diaoyutai lands in addition to concomitant continental shelf disputes between China, Japan and Taiwan in the East China Sea, and Spratly and Paracel Island disputes of the South China Sea.

By 1998, Asia Pacific maritime security had become of such concern to the US that it increased its surveillance of regional navies via the Pine Gap facility. Internal US Navy documents revealed that early in the year, the 'US Naval Security Group Command (NSGC) has entered into a host nation partnership at the Joint Defense Facility, Pine Gap, Australia, that requires assignment of a cadre of Navy cryptologic officers and technicians.'[36] In establishing the NSGC, Pine Gap now hosted a group responsible to the National Security Agency in addition to the CIA, which had previously been the sole operator of Pine Gap. Furthermore, in 1999, two more radomes were erected at Pine Gap with antennas that could detect the launch of ballistic missiles.[37]

It was also in 1998, following the Sydney AUSMIN meeting, that an AUSMIN Defence Acquisitions Committee was established to coordinate Australia's increased access to US high technology. As interoperability was espoused as crucial to the success of future alliance and coalition operations, it was imperative that Australia had the technology to facilitate cooperative ventures. One area of jurisdiction and coordination for the Acquisitions Committee was that of submarine warfare.[38]

35 Defence Intelligence Organisation, 'Defence Economic Trends in Asia–Pacific 1999', Canberra, 31 July 1999, p. 5. The official defence budget for China in 1999 was RMB104.65 billion (US$ 11.2 billion in 1995 terms).

36 Letter from the Commander of the US Naval Security Group Command to the US Chief of Naval Operations, 29 January 1998, quoted in, Cameron Stewart, 'Top US spy unit sent to Pine Gap', *The Australian*, 28 January 2001, p. 1.

37 Robert Garran, 'The Dome', *The Weekend Australian*, 10–11 February 2001, pp. 17 and 20.

38 William T. Tow, 'The Future of Alliances: AUSMIN as a "Case Study"', in Des Ball (ed.), *Maintaining the Strategic Edge: The Defence of Australia in 2015*, Canberra Papers on Strategy and Defence No. 133, SDSC, RSPAS, ANU, Canberra, 1999, p. 286.

Contested Waters: The Necessity for US Assistance?

Purchase of the new combat system was a process principally conducted by the Department of Defence, with representations by other departments, including Treasury and the Office of Asset Sales (an arm of the Department of Finance). Two contenders were short-listed by the Defence Department, Raytheon and STN Atlas.

In May 2000, Raytheon had acquired Boeing's naval systems division. Raytheon had been working with Boeing to solve the *Collins* combat system problems but with the announcement that the system was to be replaced, Raytheon considered it better placed to have assumed Boeing's work on the project and established a skill base and infrastructure centre in its new operations in Sydney.[39] Raytheon's Combat Control System (CCS) Mk2, the combat system currently utilised by the USN submarine fleet, would form the basis of their tender system for the *Collins*. Proponents of this system argued that in choosing the CCS Mk2, the RAN would have access to a pre-eminent level of technology and a large parent navy. Moreover, this presented the RAN, not only with assistance in the event of difficulties, but also with the prospect of access to a defined growth path in the development of new technology. Its proponents then continued, and continue, to argue that the desirability of belonging to the networked US system was preferable to any system that operated in isolation. Advantages of joint training were also identified. Arguably, too, this system, in addition to providing command decision aid for current weapon employment, offered a growth path for *Tomahawk* cruise missile acquisition. Deflecting criticism that their combat system was an unproven derivative of a system for the larger nuclear powered boats, Raytheon made much of its combined efforts with the USN to adapt the system for the smaller crew of the *Collins*. In this, the human/machine interface had been adapted to suit the *Collins*. It was also contended that as the combat system had been subject to the US operational and technical evaluation process, it had undergone a rigorous and comprehensive testing process.[40]

While this might have been true of the system designed for the US nuclear attack submarines, it was inescapably evident that the system for the *Collins* remained untried and embraced a different philosophy. If a generic system could be used as the basis for the *Collins* system, there was still the issue of risk in its adaptation for the conventional submarines. Specifically, it appeared as though the major challenges for Raytheon would be in the interface of the new combat system with the current *Collins* technology systems, particularly the sonars. Moreover, the system needed to operate in a much smaller boat staffed by fewer sailors.

Peter Briggs, too, had observed that Australia was not the first to 'wade into this swamp'; both the Americans and the British had experimented with the creative process in combat system production. When questioned in 1999 about the feasibility

---

39 Eric Abetz, Parliamentary Secretary to the Minister for Defence, *Media Release*, 'Abetz opens Raytheon's new naval and engineering centre', Parlsec 289/00, 13 October 2000.

40 Terence Roach, former submariner and defence sector consultant, argues the case for the CCS Mk 2 in 'Opportunity knocks for the Collins class', *Asia–Pacific Defence Reporter*, October/November 2000, pp. 38–39.

of replacing the combat system Peter Briggs responded that a nuclear submarine combat system 'would probably not be the answer for us', but if the proposed architecture for the next generation US nuclear submarine was being developed as commercial technology also for use in conventional submarines then it might be considered.[41] It was expected that this would be the basis for their *Collins* proposal. However, both the British and the US eventually reverted to more reliable adaptations of off-the-shelf technology. John Moore stated that:

> (t)he combat systems of the British and American submarines went through an evolution not dissimilar to this…The difference is that they cut their losses a lot earlier than we did, abandoned that route effectively…[42]

However, McIntosh and Prescott had recommended that it was indeed time for Australia to choose a new system engaging off the shelf equipment.[43] Short-listed candidate, STN-Atlas, proposed exactly that. Developed for the conventional submarine market, the STN-Atlas ISUS-90 system was an adapted off the shelf modular combat system networked using open architecture. Ten of the world's conventional submarine fleets had successfully implemented the ISUS system; these included Germany, Italy, South Korea, Turkey, South Africa and Greece. Furthermore, ISUS-90 had also been interfaced with US, UK, German and Italian weapons. The most intimate of US allies, Israel, operated the Dolphin class submarine, as designed by HDW and utilised the ISUS 90 that controlled the deployment of the US Harpoon missile. COTS technology was also not without its detractors, however. Procurement of spare parts was sometimes problematic.

Nonetheless, in constructing the argument for the STN-Atlas ISUS-90 system, naval consultant Graeme Dunk first dispensed with the claims made for the Raytheon system. He suggested that the assertions were often made that if Australia did not purchase its hardware from US sources that it risked the withdrawal of access to US technology. For Dunk, this reeked of an uncontested fragility in Alliance relations. Instead, he perceived it more likely that:

> the US is prepared to promote its industrial and commercial activities under the guise of alliance relationships; and that the Australian submarine community sees itself as an extension of the US submarine community, and thereby uses technology access as a convenient argument.[44]

Moreover, he regarded the procurement of the Raytheon system as an orphan system operating only under the umbrella of a nuclear submarine philosophy. So, controversially, it remained that the Australian government through its purchasing

41 *Transcript of Press Conference*, Rear Admiral Peter Briggs, Head Submarine Capability Team, Russell, Canberra, 23 July 1999, p. 15.

42 John Moore, Minister for Defence, *Transcript of the press conference on the release of the McIntosh-Prescott Report*, 1 July 1999, pp. 5–6.

43 Malcolm McIntosh and John Prescott, June 1999, p. 21.

44 Graeme Dunk, 'The Collins combat system', *Asia–Pacific Defence Reporter*, December/January 2001, pp. 14–15.

agencies had secured its options for both an independent and proven, if European, operator, and its ubiquitous and powerful ally.

As regards US political support for US defence industries, Japan would recall only too well US Defense Department's pressure to acquire more US made hardware. Exemplifying this were the inter-agency discussions in 1991. After bilateral defence consultations, Yukihiko Ikeda, Defence Agency Director, was requested by US Secretary of Defense Dick Cheney to increase direct purchases of US military hardware. This followed on from a dispute regarding the Japanese plans to construct a fighter plane in the late 1980s, which was resolved by a joint venture with US companies.[45]

When questioned in an Australian Senate Hearing regarding possible US pressure on purchasing choices, Michael Roche, Under Secretary for Defence Acquisition, answered cautiously. In responding to a specific question suggesting that unless Australia bought US sourced equipment then technological assistance might not be as forthcoming in other areas, Roche stated that he sought to:

> avoid saying that there are other pressures…I am saying instead, in positive terms that there is an objective process going on here that is assessing the technology available in various countries against the need of the Collins class.[46]

However, the short listing of the *Collins* Replacement/Upgraded Combat System contenders was, nevertheless, contentious. While STN Atlas Elecktronik was regarded by the evaluation team as the prime candidate, Raytheon Systems Company was also short-listed, despite its third ranking behind Underwater Defence Systems International, led by the French, Thomson-CSF (now Thales).

So clear, however, were the government's objectives in welding together their relationship with the US that it terminated the selection processes for both the combat system and torpedo selection. In July 2001, Minister for Defence Peter Reith stated instead that the Australian and US Navies would enter 'into a Statement of Principles arrangement to achieve a shared goal of maximum cooperation and synergy on submarine matters.'[47] (This was the document referred to earlier as signed by David Shackleton and Vern Clark.) Unsurprisingly, then, a year later, the government announced its intention to purchase the $400 million Raytheon system. This would be sourced through the US Navy.[48] That it would provide access to the

---

45 Further examples of specific industry requests may be found in, Gwen Robinson, 'Pressure to buy US', *Asia–Pacific Defence Reporter*, July 1991, p. 16, and Desmond Wettern about the need for US companies to relinquish complete reliance on the Pentagon for business, in 'US defence industries seek new markets', *Asia–Pacific Defence Reporter*, July, 1991, pp. 33–34.

46 Question and answer exchange between Senator Chris Schacht and Michael Roche, *CPD, Senate Hansard*, Foreign Affairs, Defence and Trade Legislation Committee, 29 May 2000, p. 109.

47 The Hon. Peter Reith, MP, Minister for Defence, 'Submarines Combat System', *Media Release*, MIN 244/01, 9 July 2001.

48 Senator, The Hon. Robert Hill, Minister for Defence, 'Replacement combat system for the Collins Class', *Media Release*, MIN 479/02, 13 September 2002.

US real time operational network was persuasive for its proponents. Furthermore, the government would also acquire the US, Mk 48 Mod 7 ADCAP torpedoes. These would be developed through a joint US–Australia programme.

Tomahawk Missile Deployment

As an adjunct to the prospective purchase of the new combat system, it is interesting to note that the manufacturer of the new generation *Tomahawk* missile, the *Tactical Tomahawk*, for the US Navy, was Raytheon. It appeared then that Raytheon was well able to argue its primacy should Australia enter into a new phase of armament policy and arm the *Collins* with these missiles. Cruise missiles in the Asia Pacific theatre, however, was a delicate proposition. Former Foreign Minister Gareth Evans postulated in 1987 that the degree of instability created by the US deployment of *Tomahawk* cruise missiles was a moot point.[49] But Des Ball was in no doubt of the destabilisation implications of its presence.[50] Ball's contention was echoed by former head of US strategic armed forces, General Lee Butler, who realised the threat of a regional arms race should Australia purchase the *Tomahawk*.[51]

Short-Term Nationalisation and Long-Term Alliances

Another commercial issue also captured broader US interest. Concurrent with the procurement of the combat system was the sale of the ASC. As the construction phase of the submarine project drew to a close, the government grappled with the future of the ASC. A perception had existed that one of the difficulties for the management of the *Collins* project had been that the Australian government was both part producer and customer. That it was the sole purchaser further complicated the arrangements. And in a climate more inclined to rationalisation and revenue raising, the government looked to a sale of the ASC. This sale, however, could not be judged solely on commercial exigencies. Infused instead, with strategic, economic and political stresses, the government had a complex problem to resolve. A number of questions arose. How to balance Australia's quest for self sufficiency in its defence industries, maintain the high quality skills and resources acquired during the project itself, maximise its technological advantages and retain a sense of its broader insurance against more powerful foes? How could this be enacted and achieve a positive domestic political outcome ensuring that employment would be maximised

49 Senator Gareth Evans, *CPD, Senate Hansard*, 'Northwest Cape: Communications with Submarines', Question on Notice, No. 619, 18 February 1987, p. 216.

50 Cruise missile deployment, however, was but one of Ball's concerns for regional security. He regarded acquisition of new armament technologies such as the purchase of ballistic missiles and weapons of mass destruction as 'disturbing' features of regional security. See Des Ball, 'Strategic Planning for the Defence of Australia in 2015', in Desmond Ball (ed.), *Maintaining the Strategic Edge: The Defence of Australia in 2015*, Canberra Papers on Strategy and Defence No. 133, SDSC, RSPAS, ANU, Canberra, 1999, p. 8.

51 Stephen Spencer, 'US expert warns against Tomahawk purchase', *AAP Newsfeed*, 7 October 1997.

while selling the asset at a commercially acceptable price? More complex still, the alliance lurked in the waters. How this could be achieved in an environment where the government and USN sought to influence the result? It was the perennial alliance dilemma of balancing the needs of both Australia and the US. And for Australia, how it conducted its relationship with an ally of much greater strength was the enduring challenge of the asymmetry in the bilateral relationship.

The sale process was complicated further in 2000, however, when HDW, the German conventional submarine manufacturer, purchased Kockums' Pacific shares. As the world's leading supplier of non-nuclear submarines, the company was constructing submarines under contract to Turkey, Italy, and Brazil in addition to its production of the new German Type 212 submarine. HDW was also in the process of delivering the Dolphin class to Israel, the Type 209 to South Africa, Type 209 to South Korea and the Type 214 to Greece. It is believed that the new company had a multibillion dollar order book.[52]

Yet in a move that alienated HDW from the sale process, the Australian government exercised its rights to purchase all ASC shares and effectively nationalized the company. It was reported, nonetheless, that in 1999, HDW believed it had tacit approval from Moore, Finance Minister John Fahey and Industry Minister, Nick Minchin, to purchase these shares. However, six months later, Moore and John Prescott would not agree to the original conditions. Under the original Kockums shareholder agreement, which it would inherit, HDW would also inherit the right of veto on technical matters. It could thus override other shareholders. The Commonwealth, nevertheless, was unhappy about the degree of control that HDW would assume. Strangely though, the government made little attempt to negotiate any solution to this issue. Indeed Prescott's discussions, with HDW in Germany, were entirely unsuccessful. It is not entirely clear at this point, however, why Moore and Prescott did not pursue these talks to a more fruitful conclusion. What is clear, nonetheless, is that at the time, the question of US involvement in the project was running parallel to the ownership issue of the ASC.

HDW did not welcome the Australian government's move to withhold approval for the transfer of shares. But not only was HDW surprised and unhappy with the government's decision-making. Other internal players were dissatisfied with the possible outcome, including Prime Minister and Cabinet Departmental chief, Max Moore-Wilton. The decision failed to please the ASC management who believed that HDW were best and well able to ensure continuity for the Adelaide shipyard through diversion of work from their Kiel shipyards. Further to this, the Australian Industry Development Corporation (AIDC), shareholder in ASC on behalf of the government, strongly objected to the nationalisation strategy, instead favouring the sale to HDW. But the AIDC board letters to Moore, Minchin and Fahey, met with minimal response. Other ministers, however, expressed concerns that the market was disqualified from ensuring continuity of work for the Osborne shipyards by

52 No author supplied, 'German Government Spurs Defense Industry Alliances', *Defense Daily International*, vol. 1, no. 32, 10 November 2000.

Coalition government intervention.[53] Thus, the eventual sale was intended to retain Australian majority ownership but with significant US industry involvement. Put simply, the government's argument of continued access to the US, took precedence over an assurance of additional work.

John Moore (then Defence Minister) claimed at the time that it was a necessary ploy to ensure sustainable access to US submarine technology.[54] As it appeared too, the government entertained some notion that one of the US submarine constructors may engage in the eventual purchase through General Dynamics/Electric Boat Corporation or Northrop Grumman/Newport News. Yet to seasoned observers this initially was unlikely given their core business in the production of nuclear boats. However, should the US experience a renewed interest in the production of conventional submarines either for itself or export, then the ASC with its submarine technology might become an attractive purchase. Chicago One Equity Partners' attempt to acquire 75 per cent of HDW in 2002 appears not to have resulted in US control of German submarine technology. Speculation at the time suggested that US military supplier, Northrop Grumman, was the driver for this bid. If so, Northrop Grumman's initial but not sustained play for Australia's air warfare destroyers may have been connected to a renewed interest in the ASC for that reason.

The Opposition Submerged

It has been observed that one of the central problems an Australian government faces in naval shipbuilding is to find a balance 'between often irreconcilable pressures.'[55] Certainly, a tension between a desire for a more independent strategic posture and one that asserted the centrality of the US alliance has emerged from the handling of the *Collins* project. Explicit in this project have been the problems that have arisen in domestic politics as the government attempted to mediate between the production of an effective submarine platform and its desire both to exert its role in the success of the project and to affirm the US alliance. This was clearly evident two days prior to the 2001 federal election. Former Minister for Defence, Peter Reith, argued at a business lunch in Adelaide that the *Collins* were 'six reasons why Kim Beazley shouldn't be allowed in The Lodge.' Later that same day at the launch of *Rankin* he praised the ASC for 'its remarkable achievement'. The 'Rankin and her sister submarines will keep Australia at the forefront of submarine technology'.[56] The politicisation of the project was similarly evident in the continued criticism of the then Leader of the Opposition, Kim Beazley, as Reith had earlier stated that:

53 Peter La Franchi, 'Australian Government Strategy for Sub Company Rejected from Within', *Defense Daily International*, vol. 1, no. 3, 21 April 2000.

54 Patrick Walters, 'US technology is sub plot', *The Defence Review* in *The Australian*, 28 June 2000, p. 2.

55 Mark Thomson, 'Setting a Course for Naval Shipbuilding and Repair Industry', *A Presentation to the Maritime Building, Repair and Maintenance Conference*, 26–27 March 2003, p. 10. Paper accessed via the Australian Strategic Policy Institute.

56 Terry Plane, 'Reith shows two faces in one day on Collins subs – Election 2001: 2 days to go', *The Australian*, 8 November 2001, p. 3.

> (m)ost Australians will remember he is the man who is responsible for the Collins class submarines and we are still trying to fix up the problems that he created at a very significant cost to the taxpayer.[57]

Clearly, through further criticism of the *Collins* submarine project, the Coalition could target Beazley. As Beazley had enjoyed popular support for much of the pre-election period up until early September 2001, from the government perspective it was vital that he be neutralised electorally. As John Moore had effectively publicised any fault in the submarines previously, Reith could reasonably expect that discrediting Beazley through this project would be successful.[58] Thus, both John Moore and Peter Reith in their public rhetoric to rectify the 'dud subs' had acted to allay the domestic threat and sustain the Coalition's incumbency. Former ASC Managing Director, Hans J. Ohff, pointed to government intrusion in the project for this reason and cited John Moore's tenure as Defence Minister as the 'most difficult time in the life of the project.'[59]

Unfortunately, for both the submariners and ASC personnel, they needed to continually battle this manifestation of governmental risk management. RAN Rear Admiral K.J. Scarce, then Head of Maritime Systems and now Governor of South Australia, took to the papers in this skirmish and publicly defended the submarines:

> (t)oday, Australia's submarines are regarded as arguably the most capable conventional submarines in the world – in my book, it is submarine performance that is the true measure.[60]

So, when Tore Svensson of Kockums Pacific Technology wondered, '(j)ust why a submarine hailed by leading naval officers throughout the world is subject to a concerted campaign of derision at home is hard to understand',[61] there was much more than just the government's IP dispute with Kockums beneath the surface.

US Commercial Interests

Issues of US commercial interest in submarine technology aside, what complicated the government's ability to make autonomous decisions on procurement were the statements emanating from the US on the need for their involvement in the project. As ironic testimony to the eventual success of the Collins project, the US began to

---

57 The Hon. Peter Reith, MP, Minister for Defence, transcript of the doorstop interview, Melbourne, 6 October 2001, Media Release, MIN 412/01, p. 2.

58 The Hon Peter Reith, Minister for Defence, 'Kim Beazley's Record', *Media Release, MIN 410/01*, 6 Oct 2001, p. 2. The Hon Peter Reith, Minister for Defence, 'Kim Beazley – Not a Good Defence Minister', *Media Release*, MIN 425/01, 1 October 2001, p. 3.

59 Hans J. Ohff quoted in Robert Garran, 'Sub deal sinks beneath US secrecy', *The Australian*, 20 December 2001, p. 2.

60 Rear Admiral, K.J. Scarce, 'Measure the Collins-class by performance,' Letters to the Editor, *The Advertiser*, 16 July 2003, p. 18.

61 Tore Svensson, 'Ask why they are trying to sink our super subs', *The Advertiser*, 16 July 2003, p. 20.

exercise its presence in the decision-making processes for both the ownership of the ASC and the choice of combat systems and torpedoes. US naval analyst A.D. Baker referred to the 'heavy-handed pressure from the US Department of Defense in the prospective sale of the Australian Submarine Corporation at Adelaide, the selection of the new torpedoes for the Collins class, and the choice of the new command system'.[62]

In order to glue US involvement, senior officials plunged into the fray. New US Ambassador to Australia, Edward Gnehm, called on Australia to install a combat system compatible with US hardware.[63] And as the tender and sale process intensified, a high level US Defence official (on instructions from William Cohen) and four senior naval officials informed John Moore in November 2000, not only of the preferences the US held on both issues but also of the consequences for Australia if it did not bend to these desires. First, the US had expressed objections to the possible presence of European equity partners in the ASC. It foreshadowed insurmountable difficulties in technical cooperation should the Europeans become involved in the company. Safeguards were thought to be unavailable to protect US technology and intelligence utilised on the submarines, from its European competitors. Second, US Admiral 'Skip' Bowman, Director of the Naval Nuclear Propulsion Program, would not countenance non-US built torpedoes being fired at US submarines in exercises, on safety grounds. Third, the US believed the new combat system should be fully compatible with US systems in order to maximise the military partnership. Failure to acquiesce, for Australia, would preclude any strategic submarine partnership.[64]

At this point, it is worth acknowledging one dynamic and reiterating another. First, though the US defence industry was undoubtedly competitive in marketing its products in the 1980s, it had not reached the same intensity in aggressively seeking opportunities as it has done more recently. By the mid-1990s, US commercial interests were also actively supported by an Administration seeking to enhance commercial claims and to reduce its budget deficits. With the change in US Administration in 2001, trade and security became much more intimately connected. Second, whatever the US response, it was the RAN, together with the Australian government, who initially approached the USN for assistance. Former senior members of the RAN assiduously maintain that it was for the mutual benefit of both navies that assistance was solicited.[65]

Taking the lead interest in a package of combat systems, heavyweight torpedo supply and ASC sale, had been the US Navy. With industry partners Raytheon and Electric Boat, the USN sought to construct a 'co-operative development program'. And cooperative it would be. It appears that in the US, Electric Boat, manufacturer exclusively of nuclear submarines, may have needed to be persuaded by the USN to

62 A.D. Baker III, 'World Navies in Review', International Navies Focus, *US Naval Institute Proceedings*, vol. 127/3/1, Annapolis, Maryland, 2001, p. 33.

63 Roger Martin and Robert Garran, 'US early warning on defence', *The Australian*, 11 October 2000, p. 2.

64 Robert Garran, 'US threat to sink strategic alliance', *The Weekend Australian*, 23–25 December 2000, p. 1.

65 Information from interviewees.

participate in the project.[66] More broadly, associated with the reduction of funds to maintain the numbers of submarines in the US fleet has been the lack of available purse for the US Naval Sea Systems Command to complete the development of the CCS Mk 21D combat system. Similarly, these constraints also apply to the US in its production of the new ADCAP torpedo. At present, the US still needs to develop this capability for littoral operations. Australia's sweeping experience in these areas has become attractive to the US in the development of specific technological expertise (which is also precisely the kind of expertise offered by Sonartech). So, again the choice of the US torpedo would assist the US in extending its capabilities and extending its influence in the littorals.[67]

Confronted with a battle of some proportions to win the combat system contract, the US had employed a fleet of tactics. Even Malcolm McIntosh and John Prescott (as appointed by Moore) had recommended that the project, with a history already damaged by flirtations with untried technology, not be subject to any further purchasing of experimental technology. Instead, they recommended that the system of choice should utilise commercial off the shelf, proven technology. Moreover, the Defence evaluation and acquisition teams rated the Raytheon proposal as a lesser prospect. In order to counteract this, the USN and Defense Department sent high-level representatives to Australia to further their claims. The government thus was shortly confronted with performance or alliance imperatives.

The new Minister, Peter Reith, together with bureaucrats from the Department of Defence, toured the US to consider the American proposals. Although the formal recommendations were delayed, Undersecretary for Defence Acquisition, Michael Roche, the ADF's tender evaluation working group, the source selection board, and the submarine capability team preferred the STN-Atlas system. This, however, was contested by the Chief of Navy, Vice-Admiral, David Shackleton. Shackleton argued forcefully for the Raytheon system as it was necessary to enhance navy operational relations with the US. His concurrent concern was that Australia had no comparable operational alliance with either the Swedish or German Navies and that US apprehension over foreign access to US technology would compromise existing arrangements and preclude Australian purchase of future US technology. John Moore, too, regarded the technical cooperation with the US and the ownership of the ASC as issues sitting heavily on the procurement choices confronting Australia. A deferral of the combat system recommendation from the Department of Defence to the Minister, gave the Australian government, military and bureaucracy time to grapple with the exigencies of the issue and to ponder the storm warnings – and not only those of international origin.

What of the co-operative development scenario? During the course of the *Collins* project Australia had acquired much sought-after technology. Taiwan was in the market for at least six diesel attack submarines. Although it was possible that

66 Geoffrey Barker claims that in Defence industry circles, Electric Boat was thought to be under pressure to assist Australia, in 'Suboptimisation', *Australian Financial Review*, 25 July 2000, p. 42.

67 A.W. Grazebrook, 'US pressure in RAN submarine competition', *Asia-Pacific Defence Reporter*, August/September 2000, p. 38.

the ASC with US capital could construct the boats, it remained a highly dubious political enterprise for Australia. This was particularly so as the Chinese Foreign Ministry stated:

> (w)e hope, and are confident, that the Australian side will scrupulously abide by the one-China policy and by no means participate in the sale of weaponry to Taiwan in order to avoid creating serious harm for Sino-Australian relations.[68]

Despite USN opposition, it seemed that the two US nuclear submarine constructors may have been considering the contract. These were General Dynamics' Electric Boat and Northrop Grumman's Newport News. One of these tenderers had its diesel submarine technology and construction experience enriched by their partnership with the ASC – a liaison that did not escape the Chinese either.

The ASC

Alliance issues, however, were clearly not the only seas to be navigated. Employment and economic issues were also at the forefront of the ASC sale. For the government the complexity of the problem was to marry its strategic priorities (once decided) with the exigencies of a commercial sale and a satisfactory employment outcome. Yet, already in circumventing HDW's participation in the sale, strategic concerns had overridden economic interests that included maximising both employment opportunities and the prospects of a profitable sale. Marginalisation of HDW, had initially relegated economic and possibly employment concerns as secondary to the alliance relationship.

Persistently problematic has been the sale of the ASC. By January 2002, the new Defence Minister Robert Hill was continuing to explore the relationship with Electric Boat. While discussions ranged over their option of a 40 per cent share holding and a consultancy service role, the privatisation deal remained in doubt.[69] Later that year, the government stated that it sought to assign Electric Boat, manufacturer of US nuclear submarines, as a capability partner. To that end, the corporation commenced a 'scoping study of the ASC's capabilities in order to assess where it might be able to add value to the corporation.'[70] By October 2002, Electric Boat had agreed to provide specialist management and technical advice for the ongoing maintenance of the submarines at a cost of $20 million.[71] However, the corporation declined to purchase shares in the ASC. Logically for the nuclear submarine builders there were

68 Lynne O'Donnell and Sid Marris, 'Beijing warns on sub sales to Taiwan', *The Australian*, 22 April 2002, p. 7.

69 Senator, the Honourable Robert Hill, Minister for Defence, Doorstop transcript, The Jefferson Hotel, Washington, DC, 10 January 2002, Department of Defence.

70 Senator Robert Hill, Minister for Defence, and Senator, Nick Minchin, Minister for Finance and Administration, 'Australian Submarine Corporation – Engagement of capability partner for a scoping study', *Media Release*, Joint 134/02, 9 April 2002.

71 Senator Robert Hill, Minister for Defence, and Senator, Nick Minchin, Minister for Finance and Administration, 'Electric Boat Corporation signs as capability partner to Australian Submarine Corporation', *Media Release*, MIN 536/02, 3 October 2002.

few persuasive reasons to purchase the ASC shares. Technically, as capability partner, it would have access to the submarines but commercially, the sale was complicated. In 2003 the unresolved intellectual property issues with Kockums, including those of the propeller technology, were still outstanding, there was an absence of orders for new submarines and the Department of Defence took some time to settle its budget allocations for the through-life maintenance of the *Collins*. Endeavouring to focus the process in January 2004, Ministers Hill and Minchin appointed Carnegie Wylie to advise on the sale of the ASC. At this point, it was unlikely that Electric Boat was either interested or able to locate an appropriate Australian partner. Tenix, a seemingly suitable candidate, desired a controlling interest and remained in private ownership, and ADI with its French partner Thales, again raised the question of European ownership. The US had continued to remain sensitive to any prospective loss of intellectual property.

One of the features of the *Collins* project (and embedded in the original vision) had been the extraordinary opportunity it offered Australia to realise, demonstrate and reward the technological expertise and entrepreneurial elements of its educated workforce. Only occasionally in the life of a small country does it have the opportunity to pursue a project of this enormity and deliver upon its aims so well. As a multibillion dollar project, it could act uniquely in the attempt to redress some of the vulnerabilities of Australia's economic profile. Public support of the ongoing project by government and an ongoing commitment to its workforce, in both industry and navy, would thus seem not only desirable but also responsible. Yet political objectives remained paramount.

Conclusion: Increased Intimacy

A significant feature of the alliance for Australia has been the entry it has provided for the 'preferential access to US technology'. This has been of import in the development of Australia's high technology defence strategy.[72] This was maintained in the Defence 2000 policy document and is necessitated to a point by the peculiarities of Australia's demography and geographic and oceanographic environment. Would the rejection of the US combat system proposal jeopardise this? If it did, it then would indeed indicate more than the *moue* of fragility in alliance relations. The more likely result is that it may occasion a pause in submarine cooperation rather than a dramatic seizure of defence cooperation.[73] Even so, if faced with this prospect, does Australia not possess the sophisticated skills to resolve diplomatically issues of difference with the US?

Could it jeopardise Australian access to cutting-edge military technology and systems? The choice of a European submarine combat system does not exclude Australia from force planning machinery and systems, nor would allied planning interfaces be short-circuited at this level. NATO exercises are conducted utilising both European and US technology. European and US submarine technologies are utilised

72 Des Ball, 1999, pp. 14–16.

73 Worth remembering here is that the British furore over rejection of their bid for the submarine platform soon dissipated.

together elsewhere in the world.[74] Moreover, as Des Ball has argued, the RMA is not applicable to all defence contingencies and less relevant to low level situations and the 'new strategic agenda', which may well be the threat more germane to Australia.[75] What was evident here, it seems, was the government's utilisation of the US alliance not only to resolve the 'crisis' and dispense with political opponents but to further entrench Australia's strategic and cultural ties. Moreover, it remains indicative of the difficulties for the smaller power in asymmetrical bilateral relations.

It also appears that the need for greater intimacy has taken precedence over an independent conceptualisation of Australian defence strategy that has not been evident to date in the sale process for the ASC. If the *zeitgeist* of the 1980s had emboldened an independence of strategic thinking and practice, by 2000, the Coalition had reaffirmed its desire for US intimacy. This is despite the swelling evidence that Australia had achieved many of the 'national interest' objectives initially prescribed for the submarine project. As a major capital works initiative, it did provide for Australia, extensive job creation, extraordinary technological gains, and valuable new skills development. Increasingly too, it is perceived as delivering on its naval objectives, and thus revealing the significant achievements of Australian industry. While this may take some time to permeate into the public consciousness after its history of poor media coverage and political manipulation, in the RAN, the USN and the defence industry, the *Collins* is regarded as an exceptional conventional submarine, one with few rivals. And while the project did encounter significant difficulties, for a high-risk venture of this scale and complexity, it would have been naïve to anticipate otherwise. How this was managed and *resolved*, however, by all the stakeholders, was of greater importance. In part, something of what was to be gained for Australia was the problem-solving experience necessary for the manufacture and maintenance of a successful product for the RAN and for the reinvigoration of a successful Australian shipbuilding industry.

Poised at a juncture where the realisation of 'self-reliance through industrial capability', may have been before the horizon, the Howard government chose to relinquish its opportunity to do so, via the effective circumscription of the contenders in the sale process. Consequently, the pathways to a slate of options in shipbuilding and export development in Australia were also contained. Through this project, the government has chosen to pursue greater intimacy with the US and attempted to shore up relations. It has done so in the mediation of threat from above and from below, while attempting to ensure its electoral survival. Now, however, even though the *Collins* project may well be redeemed, alliance relations have become more pervasive and the strength of Australia's independent defence posture had been eroded.

---

74 Although this would not be with the same degree of intimacy as the Australian–US relationship.

75 Des Ball, 1999, pp. 15–16.

Chapter 6

Iraq: Australia–US Global Partnership?

Staying in the Willard Hotel, just a few blocks from the Pentagon, John Howard was present in Washington on 11 September 2001 when the third hijacked plane, American Airlines Flight 77, was crashed into the west wing of the Pentagon. Howard's original purpose in Washington was to galvanise presidential authority for the FTA negotiations and to deliver an address to a joint sitting of the US Congress. With the FTA negotiations temporarily sidetracked by the attacks, what was eventually delivered instead was the Coalition's promise to intensify the alliance. For Howard, it would have been impossible not to have been affected by the experience of the capitol and the US under attack. During the return flight to Australia, Howard contemplated the invocation of the ANZUS Treaty for the first time since its ratification in San Francisco in 1952. He was later to claim that the events of 11 September 2001 and the 2002 Bali bombings changed the US and Australia irreparably. More specifically, despite the tragic events, Howard adeptly used his presence in Washington to foster his relationship with the executive, intensify the strategic relationship and enhance the discussion of economic ties.[1] Further, once the motivation for the removal of weapons of mass destruction was undermined as a reason for the invasion of Iraq, Howard cited Australia's need to support the US at a time of crisis as a primary catalyst for Australia's role in the war coalition.

Clearly, alliance relations had assumed a place of preference in the government's threat mediation strategy. For both material and cultural reasons, the Howard government had chosen to prioritise the US as the centrepiece of its bilateral strategy. Its material assessment of US force capability, Australia's historical and cultural connections, and the resonance of the alliance in the electorate had been the catalysts for the government's prioritisation of the US alliance. However, its response to the terrorist attacks (where the US would be supported not just in Afghanistan and in its Global War on Terror but through the highly contentious war in Iraq) raised questions regarding the implementation of an overly ambitious threat mediation strategy for Australia and for the government. Moreover, since 11 September this approach to Australia's strategic policy, where Australia assumes a role as global ally also with vital strategic interests in the Middle East, appears as a case of strategic overstretch.

This chapter examines the dimensions of threat mediation in the response to the terrorist attacks. I consider both the international situation and the domestic concerns in the formulation of Australia's intensified alliance policy, and the deployment of

1 Donald A. DeBats, Tim McDonald and Margaret-Ann Williams, 'Mr Howard Goes to Washington: September 11, the Australian–American Relationship and Attributes of Leadership', *Australian Journal of Political Science*, volume 42, issue 2, June 2007, p. 239.

the ADF through the Iraq War and the government's decision to identify global interests in its strategic policy as consequences.

'We are all Americans'

On 12 September 2001, the Parisian newspaper *Le Monde* declared in its headline statement its solidarity for the US, the country with which France felt 'so close and to whom we owe our freedom'.[2] These words resonated throughout much of the western world and were indicative of western governments' support for the US. 'We are all Americans' emotively captured the empathy for the US. European unity was also expressed through the eighteen NATO allies' activation of the mutual defence clause in Article V of the NATO agreement. Support for the US response to remove Osama bin Laden's al-Qaeda network and the Taliban regime in Afghanistan through Operation Enduring Freedom was wide-ranging, including the international commitments for the basing of US forces, the border security of Afghanistan, the allocation of military assets and the sharing of intelligence information. This is not say, however, that all states and peoples were at one with the US. Dissent was graphically evident in some of the joyous scenes from some sections of the populations in Indonesia and the Arab world on the day of the terrorist attacks.

After Howard's return journey from Washington, he announced that as the US was subject to attack Australia would respond through the invocation of Article IV the ANZUS Treaty. The Prime Minister stated that this was to:

> underline the gravity of the situation and our steadfast commitment to work with the United States in combating international terrorism. The Australian government will be in close consultation with the United States Administration in the period ahead to consider what actions Australia might take in support of the US response to these attacks.[3]

Military consultation was close indeed as almost immediately some of Australia's Special Air Services (SAS) leadership group relocated to the US military's Central Command (CentCom) at MacDill Airforce Base in Tampa, Florida. Politically Howard did not deviate from his stated course throughout the following six years, even if in consultation with the US in its early stages of the formulation of its planning, minimal information was provided to the Australian public by the government.

Australia's initial response was to commit 1000 troops to the military action in Afghanistan, including 150 from the SAS. In addition, to the commitment of 4 FA-18A fighter planes, patrol, surveillance and refueling aircraft, three frigates to patrol the Persian Gulf and an amphibious command ship, intelligence gathering capabilities as part of the Echelon programme were oriented to the operation. Certainly, though the niche role of the SAS was significant, as was the intelligence collection, the government's backing has been politically valuable to the US particularly as

2 Jean-Marie Colombani, 'We are all Americans', *Le Monde*, 12 September 2001, p. 1.

3 John Howard, 'ANZUS Treaty: Application of ANZUS Treaty to terrorist attacks on the United States', *Media Release*, 14 September 2001, <http://www.pm.gov.au/news/media_releases/2001/media_release1241.htm>.

international support evaporated for its war in Iraq. It is this deployment in Iraq that remains as the most contentious aspect of the mediation strategy.

From Afghanistan to Iraq

From the outset, the Australian government, together with the UK, was the most ardent of the US backers. Through Howard's immediate acknowledgement in October 2001 that the response to the US attackers needed to be broad in scope, the leeway was provided for state-based retaliation against Iraq. This in part explains the minimal engagement from the government in the global debate on the issue in the ensuing period. At this time internationally the debate raged as to the most appropriate response to the attacks Dealing with the al-Qaeda network and its sponsor, the Taliban, through intervention in Afghanistan was largely acceptable and supported by many countries. However, to overthrow Saddam Hussein by an invasion of Iraq was not.

Yet, if the issue of the appropriateness of the response had already been settled for the Howard government, clearly it was not internationally, where the norms of state sovereignty and non-interference prevailed. There was no doubting Saddam Hussein's explicitly tyrannical and oppressive behaviour. But despite Saddam Hussein's horrific treatment of his own people in crushing dissent through the use of chemical weapons and in his war with neighbouring Iran, international states baulked at removing his regime as part of the War on Terror. This too, was despite his invasion of Kuwait in 1991 sparking the first Gulf War and the subsequent flaunting of UN resolutions in the attempt to assess, document and dismantle any possession of weapons of mass destruction. Moreover, Hussein's inability to comply with the weapons inspectors' demands did not resolve the case against him. Frustrating the UN teams and the international community did not, for all UN members, constitute an adequate reason for removal; and one that would violate those principles of state sovereignty. The case would need to be clearer.

Yet while the US administration moved over the following eight months to describe the nature of state-sponsored terrorism, the Australian government made only brief, if important, statements of support for the US position. Other than that, it chose to observe proceedings. Responses to Bush's State of the Union speech on 29 January 2002, where he linked Iraq, Iran and North Korea as 'an axis of evil' were muted. Through this address, Bush linked these states to international terrorism and WMD development. As such they were potentially threats to the US and its allies. Furthermore, Bush argued that they may be responsible for transferring that technology or hardware to terrorist groupings. This dramatic portrayal diluted the allied attempts to engage these states in discussions on these issues. Where the Europeans had been working with Iran; Japan, South Korea and to some extent Australia, were attempting to engage North Korea in talks on these concerns.[4]

---

4 Ron Huisken, 'The Road to War on Iraq', *Canberra Papers on Strategy and Defence*, No. 48, SDSC, ANU, 2003, p. 8.

Through this period, it appeared publicly as though the US administration was attempting to resolve the dilemmas in the nature of its response. Bush's intimation in his State of the Union address that pre-emptive defence was now part of US strategy was reinforced later in statements made in the US and internationally by both Secretary of Defense Rumsfeld and his deputy, Paul Wolfowitz.[5] Yet whatever immediate plans the US hawks had for a military assault on Hussein were temporarily dissipated by international distaste for action. Many of the Europeans especially were concerned that concerted efforts were needed to resolve the Palestinian issue. Iraq may have been in breach of its UN commitments, but it was clear that Israel had also defied numerous UN resolutions. At this stage, it was also evident that the Chinese and Russians were opposed to any escalation of the response to include Iraq. Moreover, many states felt that it was highly desirable that the Afghani offensive would need to be secured before the next phase in the military response was attempted.

However, Bush had already made it clear that state-based responses were on the cards. And the next card to be dealt after Afghanistan would be Iraq. Toward the close of 2001, Bush had argued, 'if you harbour a terrorist, you're a terrorist…If you develop weapons of mass destruction that you want to terrorise the world, you'll be held accountable.'[6] The neoconservatives in the administration were preparing for the Iraq assault even though it would take some time for the invasion to materialise.

Around this time in Australia, the government expressed its interest in curtailing potential threats, particularly those of WMD, through the use of pre-emptive action. And even though Defence Minister Robert Hill was also clear that there had been no connection established between the al-Qaeda network and Iraq, the government supported the US Administration's interest in pursuing WMD's in Iraq. Ultimately it was this latitude in allowing for the pursuit of Iraq despite the failure to connect it to the terrorist group responsible for the 11 September attacks that gave the Howard government the space to join the US in the war.

Hill's support for the US strategy of pre-emption was more formally articulated in a revision of Australia's policy when the Defence Minister spoke in favour of its use in November 2002. In suggesting that it was opportune for the international community 'to seek an agreement on the ambit right to self-defence better suited to contemporary realities' he argued for the immediate need for the government to install a policy of pre-emption in its self-defence armoury.[7] This was given impetus the following month when Howard confirmed his Defence Minister's approach. Although Howard had placed tight limits on the possibilities for the deployment of a pre-emptive approach, he nonetheless advocated its utilisation in the absence of other options. These statements created concern for some within Australia and were viewed with disquiet in a region where the growth of terrorist cells was causing

5 Philip Shishkin, 'Russia's backing of US's war on terror won't extend to Iraq', *The Wall St Journal Europe*, 2003, p. 3.

6 Matthew Engel, 'US attack opens new phase of war', *The Guardian*, 27 November 2001, p. 1.

7 Robert Hill, John Bray Memorial Oration, University of Adelaide, Adelaide, 28 November 2002.

increasing apprehension. It also added to a view easily manipulated that Australia continued to ride shotgun for the US.

Australia's Foreign Policy Challenge

During this time the Foreign Minister was able to launch the latest of the DFAT White Papers, 'Advancing the National Interest: Australia's Foreign Policy Challenge'. The launch proved a notable challenge in itself as the document had not concerned itself with these 'biggest picture' issues for Australia. These were primarily crucial issues of mediation for Australia: the test for Australia in managing its relationship with its great but wounded ally; of managing its relations with an international community deeply divided over the nature of its response to the terrorist attacks and the discordant feelings of many of the international states with US unilateralism. Even if the Iraq issue was not a subject of primary discussion for Foreign Affairs and Trade, it was clear through this period that the government was a wholesale supporter of the US position in acting pre-emptively in Iraq. By 10 August 2002, Australian Brigadier Ken Gillespie and a team of military officers were back in Tampa, Florida to prepare for a range of military contingencies to deal with Iraq.[8] However, this dedicated backing was increasingly becoming questioned not only internationally but also domestically. As a government so astute in responding to the domestic environment, it was no surprise that at this point it paused to recalibrate its public position. Once more, the UN processes were articulated as a highly desirable vehicle for responding and these needed to be tested before any near unilateral action was warranted. The difficulty of this position, however, was that while the US was also forced to proceed at least some way down this path it was not enamored with this accession to international demands. If the UN chose to remain seized in reflection on these matters, the US administration was seized with the need for action (Colin Powell's reluctance notwithstanding). Australia's pathway was thus necessarily to conflict with the great majority of the UN members.

As the leaked confidential British Downing Street memo was to confirm, the US administration continued in its endeavour to construct the case against Saddam Hussein. Director of SIS (MI6), Richard Dearlove's reflection on his recent talks in Washington to the UK Defence Secretary, Foreign Secretary, Attorney-General, Intelligence and Military Chiefs, disclosed his assessment that:

> the intelligence and facts were being fixed around the policy. The NSC (National Security Council) had no patience with the UN route, and no enthusiasm for publishing material on the Iraqi regime's record. There was little discussion in Washington of the aftermath after military action.[9]

8 Tony Wright, 'The Road to War: War in Iraq Week 2', *The Bulletin*, 8 April 2003, p. 36.

9 Matthew Rycroft, 'Iraq: Prime Minister's Meeting, 23 July', 2003, as reported by David Manning, 'The secret Downing Street memo: Secret and strictly personal – UK eyes only', *Times Online*, 1 May 2005.

Though these discussions continued to percolate away in private, the Australian public were increasingly vocal in their concerns that US restraint be encouraged, due UN process be followed and issues of regime change and reconstruction be contemplated much more deeply than they were countenanced. Always attuned to the public reaction, the Howard government became much more publicly concerned with directing the US down the UN road. Howard responded midway through 2002 by shedding its complete support for the US, at least temporarily, and advocated a return to the multilateral approach. The government stated that war should always be the 'last resort' and this would need to be evident before any Australian troop commitment was confirmed. Part of the process advocated here was to re-engage the UN weapons inspector teams. Hussein must be made accountable to the UN, and the UN needed to be more strident in its approach.

Not only had Downer argued that Australia's diplomacy at the UN had been to push for forceful UN engagement but prior to Bush's UN address on 12 September, John Howard had telephoned the President to set out Australia's interest in maintaining UN involvement in managing the Iraq threat. This interest was intensified as many states continued to be fearful of US unilateralism and its disregard for the international community. Bob Woodward has recorded the ongoing US displeasure with the moribund UN processes. He noted that in the Bush-Cheney exchanges prior to the General Assembly speech, Cheney agreed that Iraq should be the primary focus but that in the UN forum Bush should contend that 'it's not about us. It's about you (the UN). You are not important.' This echoed the sentiments expressed in the previous month where he argued with regard to Iraq that 'the risks of inaction are far greater than the risks of action' and that the weapons inspectors return to Iraq was manifest futility.[10] Although Colin Powell had believed that the US position on this was not as Cheney's international publicity 'wrote large', he was increasingly powerless to counteract the potency of the neocons within the administration. Bush then argued at the UN that the 'purposes of the US should not be doubted…All the world now faces a test and the United Nations a difficult and defining moment…Will the United Nations serve the purpose of its founding or will it be irrelevant?'[11] Nonetheless, Howard rightly supported the public courting, at least, of the UN. But the new UN approach would need to be forthright, forceful and wrapped in time constraints. It was prepared to engage multilaterally but the provisos were clear.

Following these developments, two options were approved. First, in the following month the US Congress provided authority for the administration to attack Iraq and thus for US unilateralism. Second, the UN Security Council passed Resolution 1441 unanimously on 8 November 2002, which showed the UN was attempting to provide the mechanism by which the Iraq issue could be addressed. It called for Iraqi disarmament by December 8 or Iraq would encounter 'serious consequences'. The problem was that the mechanism in its ambiguity proved faulty. Initially it was regarded as a win for both the British and for Powell who had run hard at the process. However, the US regarded 1441 as an end point of many resolutions. If compliance

---

10 Bob Woodward, *Bush at War*, Simon and Schuster, New York, 2002, p. 335.

11 George W. Bush, Address to the UN General Assembly, New York, 12 September 2002.

was not met, this constituted the final authority to act. However, others, particularly the French, considered that chief weapons inspector Hans Blix would need to report on the Iraqi WMD compliance and if inadequate then the UNSC would need to construct a separate authorisation for war. Only the UNSC could rule on this.

Yet, as Ron Huisken observed, the challenge for those on the UNSC opposed to US unilateralism on Iraq was to use the Security Council to achieve an effective but peaceful solution without antagonising the US. Management of this required adroit diplomacy from the international group.[12] Although 1441 had temporarily placated both groups involved, at some point it would be tested. This occurred when Blix delivered his reports on Iraqi compliance. Whereas while he found that Iraq had not complied completely, neither was it clear to the inspectors that WMD stocks and delivery mechanisms were in Hussein's possession. He recorded instead that the United Nations Monitoring and Verification Commission (UNMOVIC) had an increasing ability to discover the answers. The answers, however, were too far away.

Australia, the US and the UK rested their public case on their belief that Saddam Hussein was in possession of large stocks of chemical and biological weapons. That he had used them previously added weight to their argument. Added to this was speculation that Iraq possessed mobile weapons laboratories, thus making detection more difficult. Now they were concerned that he was in possession of launchers and warheads that extended the threat beyond its internal application. This was made more perilous by a claim that Hussein had connections with al-Qaeda with the implication that these WMD could be passed on to the terrorist network. All three governments attempted to inflate the threat by affirming the story that Iraq had attempted to acquire uranium oxide through a source in Niger.[13] Powell, however, failed to include the story in his UN address. But more importantly, Powell had failed to convince the UNSC both of the exact WMD threat posed and of the need to act immediately. The satellite imagery and intercepted phone conversation evidence presented did, however, bolster support in US domestic constituencies for the oncoming war.[14]

At this point, the US proceeded ceremonially with the UN process but forcefully in the military build up in the Gulf. Bush had seemingly acquiesced in the UNSC process but only until it was apparent, by 10 March, that both the French and the Russians would exercise their veto to dismiss it. Any UN approval and hence majority international support, for any invasion in Iraq was lost.

Bush, Blair, Spanish Prime Minister Aznar, but not Howard, met in the Azores on 16 March for the final stages of the war planning. This meagre coalition acknowledged

12 Ron Huisken, 'The Road to War on Iraq', *Canberra Papers on Strategy and Defence*, No. 48, SDSC, ANU, 2003, p. 18.

13 George W. Bush, President delivers State of the Union, The US Capitol, The White House, Washington D.C., 28 January 2003, <http://www.whitehouse.gov/news/releases/2003/01/20030128-19.html>, John Howard, Ministerial Statement: Iraq, *House of Representatives Hansard*, 4 February 2003, p. 10645, and British Joint Intelligence Committee, 'Iraq's Weapons of Mass Destruction: The Assessment of the British Government', 24 September 2002, <http://www.number-10.gov.uk/output/page271.asp>.

14 Bob Woodward, *Bush at War*, Simon and Schuster, New York, p. 355.

the failure of the UN process and agreed to proceed alone. The following day Bush restated Iraq's weapons threat and its terrorist connections. Bush then declared his 48 hour ultimatum for Hussein and his two sons to remove themselves from Iraq. On 19 March 2003 the Coalition of the willing forces officially entered Iraq.

Australia's instant intimate involvement in a Global War on Terror occurred with the deaths of 88 Australians in Bali on 12 October 2002. The tragedy, the deaths of over 200 people and the wounding of many more, wrought at the hands of terrorist cells operating through Southeast Asia, served to solidify the government's resolve for action. Moreover, the bombings gave the government the opportunity to connect Australia's response to that of the US. Howard argued that:

> (w)e now understand, after the events in Bali and those of 11 September 2001, that we are living in a world where unexpected and devastating terrorist attacks on free and open societies can occur in ways that we never before imagined possible.[15]

Consequently, the government was interested in intelligence and security cooperation in the region with the US in much more hardnosed and immediate ways. Further, it was able to justify to a domestic audience an uncompromising response to terrorist activity as it interconnected with US global military strategy. Australia's intimate experience with this terrorist tragedy also had the immediate effect of uniting many behind the government and galvanising support for its wide-ranging strategy to confront the terrorist threat.

Australia's involvement in the prospective war in Iraq remained contentious however. If many wanted the government to act upon the terrorist threat there was still difficulty in translating this into a justification to attack Hussein. Yet four months after the Bali bombings, on 23 January 2003, the Australian government deployed the HMAS *Kanimbla* and additional forces to the Gulf. On the basis that if war transpired, the Australian forces would need time to acclimatise to the region. Robert Hill also maintained that the deployment of forces would provide effective pressure on Hussein to comply with the UN resolutions.[16] However, it was increasingly difficult to escape the inevitability of the invasion. By this time Australia's military command team, previously stationed in Tampa, had relocated to Qatar with its US CentCom counterparts. A spring offensive was desirable to the US for climatic reasons but also to ensure the allied support (including those in the Middle East such as Jordan) did not decay. Arguably too, it would also reduce the risk to the world economies.[17]

Just prior to the commencement of the war Howard connected the Bali bombings to the Iraq campaign. He stated:

15 John Howard, Ministerial Statement: Iraq, *House of Representatives Hansard*, 4 February 2003, p. 10645.

16 Robert Hill, Transcript of doorstop interview with Senator Robert Hill, Commonwealth Parliamentary Offices, Adelaide, 22 January 2003.

17 Christopher Meyer, interviewed for 'Blair's War', Frontline, *PBS*, 18 March 2003.

> (w)e lost 88 Australians in Bali because of the willful act of international terrorism, and we all had to grapple with that…I will…be asking the Australian people to bear those circumstances in mind if we become involved in military conflict in Iraq.[18]

Furthermore, he hastened to add that the Iraq war would 'make it less likely that a terrorist attack will be carried out against Australia'.[19] However, Australian Federal Police Commissioner, Mick Keelty, before being reined in by the government, was clear that Australia's participation in the war in Iraq had made Australia a bigger target. This was given impetus by confirmation that Australia's intelligence services had advised the government that the Iraq campaign would increase the jihadist terrorist threat and serve to increase recruitment to terrorist cells both in Australia's region and globally.[20]

On 19 March SAS forces including those of the ADF acted to shut down forces in southern and western Iraq. They secured the oilfields located in these areas and importantly negated Iraqi capability in attacking Israel, Jordan and Saudi Arabia. This was vital in containing any possible escalation of the war into a wider Middle East catastrophe. Shock and awe proceeded in the US Operation Iraqi Freedom. The US had sent approximately 125,000 troops to the region, with the UK deploying a force of around 26,000. Australia's Operation Falconer, part of the coalition force in the Gulf, consisted of about 2,000 ADF personnel. Included in the deployed forces were around 500 of the Special Forces Task Group, Australia's contribution consisted of naval, army and air force personnel with 14 F/A-18 aircraft, Hercules transport planes, Orion patrol aircraft, Chinook helicopters, navy frigates and transport ships. The force also included navy personnel stationed in the Gulf as part of the Multinational Interception Force which had been deployed to enforce UN sanctions against Iraq; this was additional to a range of specialist teams.

Post War?

Twenty-one days later the US claimed military victory. On 17 April 2003, Robert Hill announced the scaling back of military forces in the Middle East. Although WMD had not been located, the government celebrated that Australia had contributed to the liberation of the Iraqi people from a tyrannical dictator. Indeed the rationalisation of involvement in the war was now recalibrated to acknowledge the human rights gains and the birth of a new democracy in the Middle East. Troops were to begin returning home the following month. Howard immediately ruled out the use of the ADF in reconstruction, despite US requests. However, Robert Hill later left open

18 Philip Hudson and Caroline Overington, 'Howard links Iraq war to Bali', *The Age* 10 March 2003, p. 1.

19 John Howard, *Transcript of the Prime Minister, the Hon John Howard MP, Address to the Nation*, 20 March 2003.

20 Tom Allard, 'PM was told war would spur terrorism', *Sydney Morning Herald*, 23 August 2004, p. 1.

the opportunity for small-scale involvement in response to US expectations.[21] US pressure was maintained on the allies to remain in Iraq to assist with the reconstruction process. General Richard Meyers, Chairman of the Joint Chiefs of Staff publicly voiced the request with: '(w)e don't think it ought to be a US job alone and so we would appreciate any help that the Australian government felt they were prepared to give.'[22] Moreover, it was clear that as an occupying force and transitional authority Australia had some responsibilities to assist with the welfare of the Iraqi reconstruction. After repeated pressure from the US and also the UK, Howard agreed to retain some forces to assist in advisory capacities in the reconstruction effort.[23] Over the next two years, this amounted to around 880 personnel. However, as the effort to win the peace did not eventuate with anywhere near the same efficiency, Australia remained under continued pressure to recommit forces. This materialised in February 2005 with Australia's redeployment of 450 troops serving to protect a Japanese engineering team in Al Muthanna province in Southern Iraq as their 1,350 Dutch protectors returned home. By mid-2005, 1,370 ADF personnel formed part of Operation Catalyst in Iraq, with annual cost estimates at around $402.5 million. Australia remained under persistent pressure from both the US and the British to recommit troops. Though Howard had astutely limited the troop deployment in Iraq by mid-2007, 1575 ADF personnel were deployed in Iraq and a further 970 in Afghanistan.

As of August 2007, approximate estimates of civilian deaths in Iraq numbered 70,000. Coalition of the willing troops killed numbered around 3,954; of these 3,659 were US troops. Australia had suffered two casualties. An Iraqi government had been installed in the National Assembly with some view to power sharing. But the road to post war reconstruction remained bloody and problematic. Despite the troop 'surge', central Baghdad was far from secure. Ambushes were commonplace. Public beheadings provided grisly testament to the opposition's power to terrorise. Equally distressing over the longer term was the local people's inability to reconstruct a durable normal life. Demonstrative of the disturbance to the patterns of a basic existence extended to the deterioration of the medical system where doctors increasingly were choosing to leave Iraq because of their inability to practice safely.

The deaths of Sergio Vieira de Mello, highly respected Special Representative in Iraq of the UN Secretary General, and twenty-one of his officers in the suicide bombing on 19 August 2003 against the UN offices in Baghdad struck the UN hard. It was the worst attack on the UN itself in its 58 year history. Certainly, the UN only had a tenuous presence in Iraq after the divisive split on the 1441 resolution, but it had nevertheless, reentered the fray. This attack effectively reduced its capacity to commit further people and resources to an invasion that many of its members had refused to support.

---

21 Peter Hartcher and Geoffrey Barker, 'Tension builds over postwar role', *The Weekend Australian Financial Review*, 5–6 April 2003.

22 Peter Hartcher, 'US calls on Australia to play peacekeeping role', *The Weekend Australian Financial Review*, 5–6 April 2003.

23 Reuters, 'US wants Australian peacekeepers in Iraq – reports', *The New York Times*, 30 April 2003.

The London bombing in July 2005, Bush, Blair and Howard's prominent featuring as foremost enemies of the jihadist groups on global websites, and the intelligence agencies' statements of the inevitability of further terrorist strikes on the coalition's domestic populations, were reminders of the extended nature of the battlespace. Spain's removal of its forces from Iraq after the Madrid bombings were a reminder of how effective attacks on democracies can be in effecting a retreat in military policy. Many of the terrorists appeared to originate in countries where US troops were stationed. Removal of the US military presence principally in countries in the Middle East remained a principal goal of al-Qaeda, thus overriding the religious or values-based argument as the central and sole source of conflict.

Exacerbating the military and political campaign for the coalition forces was the deterioration of the situation in Afghanistan by mid-2005. Elected leader Hamid Karzai had been unable to establish effective or complete control in a country that had for years resisted all foreign intervention. Security outside Kabul was tenuous with narcotics dollars sustaining some of this resistance. Parliamentary elections scheduled for 18 September were challenged by rejuvenated Taliban forces that had inflicted further casualties on both civilians and US troops since the early part of 2005. Afghan Foreign Minister, Abdullah Abdullah called for the return of Australian Special Forces and engineers to assist in the retrieval and stabilization of the situation. As Australian forces were not operating at the same tempo that they had been in 2004, with the winding back of operations in both East Timor and the Solomon Islands, the government announced the deployment of 150 personnel in a Special Forces Task Group. Further options for a provincial reconstruction team were to be prepared and submitted to the government by the ADF.[24] That Australian forces were returning to Afghanistan in some ways further echoed Powell and Franks' assessment that in the end, militarily, there was no substitute for troops on the ground. Even if the initial aerial strikes in Afghanistan had proved remarkably successful, combat troops were irreplaceable.

Local Fallout

As much as Howard continued to drive the Australian agenda in the response to the terrorist attacks, the Labor Party continued to be sidelined. Initially, with Kim Beazley as leader and an ardent supporter of the US alliance, it was difficult to see how any Beazley Labor government would not have supported the role in Afghanistan. The Iraq War was much more difficult for Labor. By the time these events unfolded Simon Crean headed up the Party. Crean's subsequent demands that the government explain its arguments for supporting any prospective US invasion of Iraq met with a dramatic response from the Foreign Minister that probably surprised even his colleagues. Downer's implication that Crean was guilty of appeasing Hussein escalated the debate within Australia. However, soon after the Iraqis threatened to withdraw commercial contracts to Australia. Suddenly 500,000 tonnes of Australia's

24 Robert Hill, Minister for Defence, 'Special Forces to Deploy to Afghanistan', *Media Release*, 113/2005, 13 July 2005.

wheat trade to Iraq was jeopardised. It was only after intense negotiations between the two countries that the wheat trade deals were reconfirmed.

Crean's support of the ADF in their personal involvement demonstrated that Australian politicians had learnt something from the tragedies of the Vietnam veterans' experiences. Though Crean was unable to back the unilateral deployment of the ADF without UN sponsorship, he nonetheless offered his support for the ADF and their families. At the departure of the Australian troops for the Persian Gulf, he endeavoured to discriminate between the two positions.[25] It was not an easy distinction to convey, however, and his position was not without its critics at a sensitive time when the *Kanimbula* was departing for the Middle East and Australia was embarking upon war. However, Crean's position was one that was vindicated by the events that transpired in Iraq.

As Labor's leadership jam intensified, new leader and maverick politician, Mark Latham, melodramatically enlivened the alliance environment. His announcement in 2004 that if elected he would remove all Australian personnel from Iraq by Christmas caught even senior Labor members by surprise. Contrary to then shadow foreign minister Kevin Rudd's message that Australia needed to fulfill its transitional authority responsibilities, Latham claimed a festive season exit strategy for Australians in Iraq. Predictably, this drew a dramatic response from the government, particularly as it intersected with their alliance policy. Latham, however, only widened the political target with a lurid and personal assault on the US President and his perception of Howard as completely subservient. By claiming that Bush was the worst ever US President, he instantly drew the US into the grist of local politics. US ambassador Tom Schieffer responded by asserting his preference to work only with the Howard government while Richard Armitage, author of 'our relationship has never been stronger or closer',[26] weighed in with a verbal mugging of Latham. Consequently, Latham was forced to revive the fortunes of leadership rival, Kim Beazley, by reinstating him as shadow defence minister. Beazley, always regarded as a security conservative and well liked in Washington, was needed to reconstitute the ALP's affinity with the US. For the Labor Party, however, Latham's dramatic attacks had circumscribed the space in which it could reasonably and effectively criticize either the government's policy in Iraq or US unilateralist strategy.

The government's threat management strategy, however, was suffering under the weight of the Iraq deployment. An Australian association with unilateralist US foreign policy was of increasing concern to the Australian public. Public opinion on the broader issues involving the US was mottled. Even though the government had garnered electoral ballast for its perceived authority on broad security policy in an uncertain threat environment, the deterioration in post-war Iraq continued to erode its buoyancy. As the Lowy Institute's findings later revealed, the public held more sophisticated views than might at first touch be anticipated. While those 1000 people surveyed remained explicit supporters of Australia's US alliance, they

25 Simon Crean, *Transcript of speech at the farewell ceremony for HMAS Kanimbula*, 23 January 2003.

26 Richard Armitage, 'Deputy Secretary of State Armitage delivers remarks at the Asia Society Forum', *FDCH*, Sydney, 13 August 2003.

were much more concerned with the current US foreign policy and practice. Ivan Cook for Lowy disclosed that when asked about potential threats from the outside 57 per cent of respondents were worried about US foreign policies. This concern rated more highly than illegal immigration, China's rising power, world population growth and local failing states. Intriguingly, it rated on a par with concerns over Islamic fundamentalism. Moreover, 68 per cent felt that the government took 'too much notice' of the US. Juxtaposed against this was the view of 72 per cent of those surveyed that the US alliance is either 'fairly' or 'very' important. Moreover, 68 per cent felt that the government took 'too much notice' of the US.[27] A reasonable deduction here might be that these Australians, who generally approve of Australia's US alliance, expect Australia's support of the current US global strategy to be more selective. This analysis was reflected in Lowy's 2007 survey where Australians felt positively toward Americans, but not toward George W. Bush and his policies.[28] Credibility for this reasoning was also seemingly evident in the design of the Coalition's 2004 electoral campaign when any publicity of Australia's involvement in the Iraq War was minimalised. That Labor made little of it revealed just how effectively the Coalition was able to manipulate the connection between the alliance generally and support for the current US policy. Concurrently, it was also evident just how damaging Latham's tactless approach had been electorally for Labor.

The Defence Ring Cycle

Accordingly, a debate then opened as to the appropriateness of Australia's long held defence strategy. For some time the concentric circles stratagem prevailed in ADF structuring and procurement decision making. Prioritisation was given to securing Australia's shores, then extending this to the immediate region. Defence of the sea-air gap to the north of Australia was paramount as threats to Australia would emanate 'either from or through' the archipelago to the north. However, Robert Hill soon conveyed the view that the 'rings around Australia' security strategy was up for review, arguing that '(i)t probably never made sense to conceptualise our security as a series of concentric circles around our coastline, but it certainly does not do so now.'[29] The new approach was likely to include a renewed interest in reorienting ADF capabilities to more distant offshore operations. Obviously, Hill was not trawling for a strategy that would trash the immediate defence of Australia. Instead, he argued that:

> we wouldn't junk that because that is the ultimate threat, but what I'm saying – although it's the ultimate threat, it's less likely than more likely. We now have the highest level

27 Ivan Cook, 'Australians Speak 2005: Public Opinion and Foreign Policy', *Lowy Institute for International Policy*, Sydney, 2005, pp. 13–14.

28 Alan Gyngell, 'Australia and the World: Public Opinion and Foreign Policy', *Lowy Institute for International Policy*, Sydney, August 2007.

29 Robert Hill, 'Beyond the White Paper: Strategic Directions for Defence', *Address to Defence and Strategic Studies Course*, Australian Defence College, Canberra, 18 June 2002.

> of tempo since the Second World War but they are all outside the concentric circles or certainly the inner circle.[30]

Certainly, the nature of threat for Australia had altered to include a much more significant rise in the terrorist or asymmetric threat and Australian policy makers needed to rethink how to deal with this threat. Hill's revised strategy would thus mean much more highly mobile forces and greater interoperability with allies. In the patois of ADF language it implied ADF restructuring to enable a greater focus on 'manoeuvre warfare'.[31] If this meant addressing some of the shortfalls in ADF ability to conduct operations such as those in environments such as East Timor then this would be an appropriate policy. If, as the *Defence Update* of 2005 suggested, it meant a restructuring to address jointly some of the asymmetrical threats emanating from terrorist cells in the region then it was an apposite change. Instead, it marked the beginnings of a policy role that included ongoing global operations for Australia. By the time the *Defence Update 2007* was crafted, the government's ambitions had inflated to suggest that Australia's vital strategic interests included the Middle East. It presumed too that Australia, as partner to the US now in both the Asia Pacific and the Middle East regions, had the resources and global influence to conduct such a wide-ranging policy. If the government continued to construct policy around global US military strategy, demanding interoperability with the US, then it would need an ADF equipped to do so.[32] Australia's mediation strategy in defence now incorporated a global reorientation that would demand a significant outlay of resources and a belief, albeit misplaced, that it commanded power in the global environment.[33]

No Better Friend

Part of the threat mediation strategy for the government was to ensure the prominence of the US for both domestic and international audiences. 'America has no better friend anywhere in the world than Australia', remarked John Howard to a joint sitting of the US Congress in June 2002.[34] Howard had understood implicitly that the US had changed as a result of the 11 September assaults. In fact, Howard later argued that as regards Australia's motivation for participation in the Iraq War:

30 Robert Hill, interviewed on *Lateline, ABC Television*, 11 July 2002.

31 Paul Monk, 'Defence: the Seamless Challenge', Austhink, <http://www.austhink.org/monk/seamless.htm>. Accessed 12 July 2005.

32 Hugh White, 'Old, New or Both? Australia's Security Agendas at the Start of a New Century', in Derek McDougall and Peter Shearman (eds), *Australian Security after 9/11*, Ashgate, Aldershot, 2006, pp. 13–28.

33 Andrew O'Neil, 'Ambitious strategic policy misfires', *The Advertiser*, 10 July 2007, p. 20.

34 John Howard, *Transcript of the Prime Minister, The Hon John Howard MP address to the Joint Meeting of the US Congress*, Washington D.C., 12 June 2002.

> (o)ur alliance with the United States is unapologetically a factor in the decision that we have taken. The crucial, long term value of the United States alliance should always be a factor in any national security decision taken by Australia.[35]

If the justification for the war gravitated from WMD eradication to regime change and liberation of the Iraqi people, the constant in the communiqués was that due homage to the US alliance was vital. Foreign Minister Downer's own take on it was that failure to support the US at this time could seriously splinter a relationship that was crucial to Australia's security, especially in a fragile region. Any failure by Australia to back the US would have been viewed very seriously with the consequential result of the alliance being weakened 'very substantially'.[36] Moreover, the government argued that support for the US was critical if Australia were to maintain a position of influence on US policy. Recall that the government had claimed that it had endeavoured to persuade the US to seek UN approval for its Iraq operations.

In this respect, the government's interpretation of alliance relations to some extent mirrored those of Tony Blair. While Blair's agenda was to restore peace more generally in the Middle East with a concurrent implicit interest in finding resolutions to the previously intractable Israeli-Palestinian crisis, Blair also advocated support of the US on the issue of democratic values as it stood near friendless in the international community. He argued that meant 'that when America is fighting for those values, then, however tough, we fight with her – no grandstanding, no offering implausible and impractical advice from the touchline'.[37] Part of this argument was that the US as the world's superpower needed to be supported. However, though the argument over the exercise of influence on US policy was much more credible from Britain as a UNSC member and nuclear weapons state than from the south west Pacific, both governments felt the uncertainty and inadequacy of their strategic position. Both leaders could smartly recall the US role in their country's survival of World War Two. Their relative interests may not have been entirely synonymous with the US, however, their overarching principle here remained that the strategic relationship was more valuable than one military campaign. Whether this one operation was right or wrong was superseded by the perceived prospect of longer-term benefits.[38]

Existing here were two concepts worthy of discussion as they are intended by products of the government's mediation strategy: reciprocity and influence. The notion of reciprocity was inherent in the motivations for both governments. But this would always be a gamble on future security dynamics. Reliant on a dice that would roll a US prepared to entangle itself in distant conflicts, a scenario that matched national interests and an administration prepared to argue the domestic costs, the Howard and Blair governments could only hope for compatibility at any future time and place.

---

35 John Howard, *Transcript of the Prime Minister, The Hon John Howard MP, Address to the House of Representatives*, Parliament House Canberra, 18 March 2003.

36 Tom Allard, 'Going to war secured US alliance, says Downer', *Sydney Morning Herald*, 3 March 2004, p. 7.

37 Glenn Frankel, 'From memos, insights into ally's doubts on Iraq War: Blair's advisers foresaw variety of risks, problems', *Washington Post Foreign Service*, 28 June 2005, A01.

38 As argued by Michael Clarke in Glenn Frankel, 28 June 2005, A01.

What of influence? That the neoconservatives in the US administration were prepared to invade Iraq despite profound reservations within the State Department was demonstrative of the difficulty in diverting US powerbrokers. Even if it could be argued that Blair achieved a stay of execution in temporarily orienting the US to the UN, it is difficult to see how either the UK or Australia dramatically altered the course of US action. Reinforcing the US determination to enact the unilateralist exercise of power was Donald Rumsfeld's statement that 'the mission determines the coalition and the coalition must not be permitted to determine the mission'.[39] Here the possibility of allied influence is negated. Also, however, the longer-term coalitions are deemed dynamic entities, thus underlining ambiguity of the relationship.

'Guns *and* Wheat?'[40]

One of the government's intentions with its threat mediation strategy was to improve Australia's security and prosperity. Preservation of alliance relations was one government concern in its deployment to Iraq. Preservation of its $1billion wheat trade was another. The complicating factor in this deliberate mediation approach was that the US was its strategic friend and ally but in the wheat trade in Iraq, it was the competitor. The peak US wheat body, US Wheat Associates, had coveted the lucrative Iraqi trade for some time. However, not only was the US an unattractive strategic supplier for Iraq, Australia, through its wheat exports to Iraq since 1948, had oriented the Iraqi preference for its hard, dry wheat variety. By 2003, AWB Ltd, Australia's monopoly wheat exporter had also oriented Saddam Hussein's regime to its exports because of its willingness to agree to Iraq's sanction-busting kickback scheme where Canada had not. As AWB accepted Iraq's inland transportation fees as high as $45–$56 per metric ton, which it paid to Alia transportation, a Jordanian based trucking company, Saddam Hussein's regime effectively sidelined the UN's Oil-for-Food programme. Eventually in 2005, Paul Volker's Independent Inquiry into the United Nations Oil-for-Food Programme (IIC-OFFP) recorded that AWB's kickbacks provided $290 million to Iraq and constituted 14 per cent of the illegal funds. AWB was the chief perpetrator of global companies providing illicit funds to Saddam Hussein.[41] Consequently, Australia's wheat trade exports to Iraq were reviewed.

Until 2005, and despite warnings including those from a DFAT officer in New York, the government vigorously defended the Australian exports and the AWB as its agent. Australian concerns regarding the loss of the trade to the US were heightened at the onset of the war as the US prepared to offer up to 600,000 tonnes of wheat as aid. Industry regarded this proposal as a precursor to the re-entry of the US suppliers into the market. Yet as the war began in 2003 Downer had told the AWB that his 'primary concern' was that the US would 'conclude that (Australia's) sacrifices on the battlefield

39 Donald Rumsfeld, 'US Secretary of Defense holds media availability', transcript, *Federal Document Clearing House*, 23 September 2001.

40 Paul Kelly's term 'Guns and Wheat', *The Australian*, 15 April 2006.

41 Independent Inquiry Committee into the UN's Oil-For-Food Programme (IIC-OFFP), 'Manipulation of the Oil-For-Food Programme by the Iraqi regime', *United Nations*, 27 October 2005.

entitled its farmers to the Iraqi wheat market'.[42] Perhaps the US, increasingly isolated internationally over its preemptive actions in Iraq, was persuaded by Downer's concerns. The only senior non-US administrator initially appointed in the reconstruction phase was former AWB CEO, Trevor Flugge, to head up the Ministry of Agriculture. Further, when Australian Ambassador Michael Thawley persuaded the US Congress (temporarily at least) not to pursue Australia's transactions in the maintenance of its market share, it appeared as if Australia's alliance strategy had commercial effect. As with the steel tariff exclusions it appeared as if Australia's material contribution to the war produced commercial spin-offs. Like that study though, it may also be the case that commercial concerns were also very much a part of the bargain. An argument made elsewhere suggests that the retention of the Australian wheat marketing monopoly may have been part of a broader trade off in the AUSFTA agricultural negotiations where a much lower bargain for Australian producers was accepted.[43]

Conclusion: Threat Mediation Overplayed

Domestic spin-offs had been one of the results of the threat mediation strategy for the government. But, by talking up the alliance, expectations are eventually raised. This has both strategic and domestic consequences. Though the government had achieved some greater access to defence technology and heightened intelligence sharing, there existed domestic repercussions for its policies. First, the government's assiduous rhetorical support for the US following the 2001 terrorist attacks meant that eventually the smaller ally had limited the options under which it could manoeuvre. If the government managed deployment astutely in the first instance, it was ultimately less able to retreat when requests for specific military assistance were made in the sustained Long War. Eventually, this persistent requirement for Australian deployments in Iraq and Afghanistan forced Australian defence policy writers to entrench an unsustainable global role for Australia in subsequent Defence Updates. Second, the flawed US strategy of invasion of Iraq with its inability to reconstruct Iraq, the escalating list of casualties, the rebalancing of power in the Middle East to Iran, the attendant Abu Ghraib and Guantanamo debacles, undermine US credibility and legitimacy both internationally and locally. This disquiet, taken together with the ongoing demands on the Australian Defence Force, is reflected in the Lowy Institute's poll indicating concerns with US foreign policy. What they also suggest is the increasing inappropriateness of the Australian deployment in Iraq as a threat mediation strategy. Such was the nature of the government's ambitious twin policy approach of guns and wheat too, that the government ignored suggestions that the AWB was violating the OFFP sanctions without thought to the implications in Iraq. Ironically as well, Australian farmers have lost much of their wheat export trade to Iraq to US farmers. Ultimately, these strategic and domestic consequences of the deployment to Iraq reveal how the government overplayed its threat mediation hand.

---

42 Caroline Overington, 'Mr Not Responsible', *The Australian*, 7 May 2007, p. 7.

43 Richard Leaver, 'The New Trade Agenda' in Carl Ungerer, *Australian Foreign Policy in an Age of Terror*, UNSW Press, Kensington, NSW, 2007.

Chapter 7

Steel Blues

Alliance relations were becoming more pervasive in 2001: but just how persuasive would soon be tested in the next trade dispute. If the US was a central component of the Howard government's management of risk in foreign policy then it was necessary to display cause for its choice. Reciprocity was required for mediation to be effective domestically. US imposition of safeguard measures for its steel industry in 2002 provided an opportunity to analyse how the Coalition's threat mediation could operate with a change of Administration in the US, with a refocus on the interlinking of trade and security issues, and importantly with its direct linking to US commercial interests. In this way, the government's bargaining would move beyond the culturally enclosed approach deployed in its previous disputes. As the steel tariff dispute speaks of the primacy of US domestic politics in the bilateral relationship, an explanation of the relevant US domestic politics is significant in determining how much leeway any Australian government might have in implementing its brand of threat mediation in foreign policy.

Australian Steel Blues

So pressing were the domestic political pressures for the new Republican President, George W. Bush, that in March 2002 tariffs ranging between 8 and 30 per cent were introduced on a container of steel imports. These safeguard measures remained in place for 21 months before their Presidential revocation in December 2003. While the Howard government intuitively surmised that the Republican President's free trade credentials read more emphatically than those of his opponent's prior to the Presidential elections in 2000, in this steel dispute, the demands of the specific US internal political context overrode the immediate free trade bent. Though the Administration may have had in mind a longer term need to construct support for Trade Promotion Authority, its immediate concern was to respond to the crisis in traditional steelmaking communities.

With a sweep of congressional elections scheduled for later in 2002, the Republicans were concerned to consolidate their electoral position by granting short-term assistance to steel communities in key states. Moreover, with a balance of trade crisis in the US of over US$437 billion, together with the intensity of the nationalism promoted post-11 September 2001, the US administration exhibited no patience for further consensual negotiations in addressing the overcapacity of global steel production. Yet Australia's Howard government was dismayed that their long-time ally should implement tariffs that would detrimentally affect the Australian steel industry. The Australian steel industry had made efforts to respond to the imperatives of global demand and had rationalised extensively over the previous two decades. The initial US tariff decision reflected US insouciance toward any cultural claims of friendship made by allies where this intersected with US domestic demands. However, the Howard government, together with BHP (BHP Billiton after 2001), successfully lobbied the US to waive the majority of tariff applications to Australian exports. To manufacture any result in the eventual tariff negotiations Australia needed to understand both the difficulties of structural readjustment within the US and how Australia's commercial relationship with US steel manufacturers could be crucial in staving off further plant closures. This would be particularly so in BHP's relationship with some West Coast manufacturers. Politically, it was essential that the government could demonstrate some US responsiveness to Australia's enlistment in the US military reaction to the terrorist attacks. For the government, it was vital domestically that the US be seen to reciprocate Australia's elevation of the bilateral relationship. Thus, this dispute is worthy of consideration, given the interplay of a raft of domestic and external issues integral to the bilateral relationship at a time when Australia supported the US in its 'war against terror'.

US and the Global Steel Trade Since 1960

To comprehend fully the imposition of the 2002 tariffs it is necessary to understand historical forces at work. At the intersection of the historical use of protectionist practices aimed at both assisting the processes of industrialisation and maintaining employment and an increasingly interdependent world economy, stand the convulsions surrounding the tariffs imposed by the Bush Administration on steel imports. Liberalising forces inherent in the Uruguay Round of world trade talks continued to impel participants to restructure, yet easing the national dilemmas of structural adjustment has been problematic for most governments. While the production of steel has been one of the crucial components at the base of industrial and military development in the US for a significant part of the twentieth century, technological change has been a partner to the decrease in demand. In the period between 1989 and 1999, world GDP grew around 30 per cent, yet because of the substitution of lighter materials for steel, production in 1999, of 788 million metric tons, mirrored the 786 million metric tons produced in 1989.[1] Even despite this attempt to reflect decreased demand, persistent global overcapacity, and market subsidies still plagued the industry. As traditional producers downsized, the late industrialising countries have increased productivity. As a consequence, real steel prices over the past thirty years have cycled downward.

Protection of the steel industry in the US has long been a political issue, both domestically and internationally. Responding to narrow sectional interests, the US chose protection, thereby enforcing little industry consolidation. Rejecting a radical

1 International Iron and Steel Institute, 'World Steel production, 1950 to 2000', 18 June 2001, <http://www.worldsteel.org/trends_indicators/figures_1.html>. Accessed April 2002.

approach to address longer-term competitiveness, the US government supported the status quo in the industry, as is evident in a snapshot of US steel protection history.[2]

In protest against the subsidisation of European steel production in 1968, US steel companies initiated a set of countervailing duty suits. As a result, the US government responded by implementing a series of Voluntary Restraint Agreements (VRAs) that forced countries exporting to the US to limit their exports to the US market. In that era of managed trade, trans-Pacific tensions also intensified. Tokyo reluctantly agreed to restrain its exports. Although these arrangements became redundant with the recovery of steel prices in 1974, by the conclusion of the 1970s US protection against both Japanese and European imports reappeared in the form of the Trigger Price Mechanism (TPM). Here, steel imports were subject to a system of minimum prices and anti-dumping investigations. However, the TPM was ultimately regarded as ineffective in the provision of sufficient protection and the VRAs were reinstated against a range of countries, including Australia.[3]

During this time, participants at the Tokyo Round of Multilateral Trade Negotiations (1974–1979) also embarked upon discussions to formalise a new Antidumping Code as US anti-dumping laws allowed for greater success on the part of domestic plaintiffs.[4] Revision of these laws also facilitated the opportunity for private citizens to file suits. Not only did these laws facilitate a massive increase in the number of complaints filed within the US, but soon 50 other countries had also written or rewritten dumping laws. In the hothouse environment of the 1990s, where dumping complaints had risen by 50 per cent, US steel itself became a frequent target of these laws. Nonetheless, Daniel Ikenson from the Cato Institute has estimated that steel manufacturers in the US accounted for 75 per cent of all anti-dumping suits filed with the Department of Commerce.[5] It is also worth noting that these anti-dumping suits have included Canada and Mexico, US NAFTA partners.[6] Relevant here too, was that during the period of restrictive import controls, principally between 1972 and 1981, wages in the US industry increased 179 per cent despite a decline in productivity.[7] These higher wages were later to become a crucial dynamic in the negotiations of health and pension benefits (legacy benefits) in the 1990s onwards.

---

2 Ann Capling and Brian Galligan, 'The Steel Industry', in *Beyond the Protective State: The Political Economy of Australia's Manufacturing Industry Policy*, Cambridge University Press, Cambridge, 1992, pp. 170–71.

3 See 'Steel Arrangements with the USA', News Release by the Acting Minister for Trade (Senator Walsh) on 29 December 1984, published in Richard H. Snape, Lisa Gropp and Tas Luttrell, *Australian Trade Policy 1965–1997: A Documentary History*, Allen and Unwin with the assistance of DFAT, St Leonards, 1998, pp. 495–96.

4 Gary Clyde Hufbauer and Ben Goodrich, 'Steel: Big Problems, Better Solutions', International Economics Policy Briefs, *Institute for International Economics*, No. 01-9, July 2001, p. 1.

5 Daniel Ikenson, in J.P. Cassidy, 'Bush steel tariff move impacts 'Rust Belt' voters', *The Hill*, 6 March 2002, p. 4.

6 David Phelps, American Institute for International Steel, at the *Cato Institute Policy Forum*, 'What's Wrong with the Steel Industry Again?', 20 February 2001, pp. 3–4.

7 William H. Barringer and Kenneth J. Pierce, 'Paying the Price for Big Steel', *American Institute for International Steel*, Washington, 2000, p. 36.

Existing problems with global overcapacity were exacerbated in the 1980s by the reduction in demand resulting from the global recession in 1981–82 and increased production of high quality but low cost steel from new exporters, Brazil, Korea, Taiwan, and traditional exporter, Japan.[8] Continued friction between the US and Japan was fuelled by US analyses that manufacturing in Japan was operated by cartels coordinating production and engineering high domestic prices to sustain cheap export product.

Fin de Siècle Steel Problems

By the 1990s, overcapacity in the steel trade remained unresolved. The Ukraine and India also emerged as substantial exporters with massive potential and assisted by government encouragement. An estimated 25 per cent of the global steel industry in the 1990s was government-owned and insulated in varying degrees to market pressures. As a strategic industry, not only did the steel trade offer employment and arguably foster national security, it also generated hard currency.[9] Mainland China too, fostered the development of its steel industry as part of its modernisation programme. Despite being beleaguered by poor product in the 1990s, Chinese manufacturers endeavoured to improve the quality of finished product and in the process rapidly increased their export volumes. Eventually, their domestic demand for steel eased global pressures. But arguably too, Russia's emergence as a major steel exporter was the most significant factor in the 1998 steel crisis. As a legacy of the old command economy, Russian manufacturers produced more than demand decreed and, at times, at prices unrelated to the cost of production.

In response, not only did the US invoke further anti-dumping and countervailing duties, but also sponsored attempts to find multilateral solutions. Nonetheless, US imports of steel increased substantially in 1997–98 as the Asian financial crisis hit and, as Brazil and Russia were also confronted with economic slowdowns, steel was diverted to the US from other markets.[10] Steel imports rose dramatically in 1998, recording an increase of 33 per cent from 1997, itself a record year for US steel importation. Import penetration by 1998 was only marginally less at an increase of 30 per cent.[11] Compounding the increases in volumes was the decline in prices, as aided by the decline in value of foreign currencies. Export revenue, denominated in US dollars, became vital for many countries affected by the financial crisis.

The Multilateral Steel Agreement discussions, which aimed to terminate the subsidisation of global steel production, also floundered in 1997, leading to renewed domestic pressure on the US administration to act unilaterally.[12] However, as part of

8 Ann Capling and Brian Galligan, 1992, p. 170.

9 Tim Treadgold, 'US Tariffs A Kiss of Death For BHP Steel', *Business Review Weekly (Australia)*, 14 March 2002, p. 14.

10 Janet Plume, 'Decision time on steel; Restrictions on imports would have spillover effects on carriers and ports', *Journal of Commerce*, 7 January 2002, p. 32.

11 USTR, 'General Steel Policy', 1999 Annual Report, Section III, p. 164, <http://www.ustr.gov/sectors/industry//steel.shtml>. Accessed April 2002.

12 Gary Clyde Hufbauer and Ben Goodrich, 2001, p. 2.

the renewed multilateral negotiations sponsored by the OECD in 2001, to address the glut in global steel production, 39 countries agreed to cut 97.5 million tons per year. However, this marked a reduction of only about one third of the 250 million ton excess. Furthermore, this process would take a number of years to reduce capacity.

While world steel production decreased in 2001 by an estimated three per cent, it was reflective of the decline in industrial production in OECD countries of just over two per cent. Industrial output in Japan contracted by approximately seven per cent and correspondingly steel production fell in response to weakened domestic demand.[13] Production in the US was also affected by a contraction of industrial production of over three per cent and the continued strength of imports buoyed by the strong greenback.[14] Though traditional steel producers had made some attempts to scale back production, it was offset to some degree as new producers and late industrialisers increased theirs.

Steel manufacturing in the US in 2002 was a US$50 billion industry, directly employing 154,000 workers, with steel mills in most states of the US. For those directly or indirectly employed in the steel industry in the US, with the apocalypse of crisis upon them, global steel reductions by 2010 were a distant and dismal horizon. Lethal dynamics of the high dollar, increased imports, domestic recession, high wages, low prices and the liability of health insurance and pensions for workers and retirees was decimating the industry and with it the steel communities. These exacerbated the structural inefficiencies of the old mill manufacturers. In some instances historical, structural location problems that arose from the sourcing of raw materials created dramatic inefficiencies for manufacturers. The growth of competitive mini-mills also increased the profitability pressures on the traditional integrated producers. These mills, which produced steel from scrap metal, generally employed non-union labour and required less worker hours in the production processes. In 1991, the mini-mills manufactured 21 per cent of crude steel in the US. In 2001, this had increased to 46 per cent. This was likely to increase to 51.6 per cent in 2002.[15]

US domestic steel prices in the last quarter of 2001 were at their lowest for twenty years. In the three years from 1998–2001, companies responsible for 30 per cent of steel-making capacity had filed for bankruptcy. Perceptions were rife that because of the closure of Asian markets post-1997 financial crisis, steel producing countries not only in Asia but also from elsewhere, including the Commonwealth of Independent States, had increasingly sought to exploit the US market and thus threaten the US steel cities.

13 ABARE, 'Minerals and Energy', *Australian Commodities*, vol. 8, no. 4, December quarter 2001, pp. 602–03.

14 ABARE, 2001, p. 603.

15 Gary Hufbauer and Ben Goodrich, 'Steel Policy: The Good, the Bad, and the Ugly', International Economics Policy Briefs, *Institute for International Economics*, January 2003, no. PB03-1, p. 5.

US Domestic Politics

Complicating the Administration's decision-making on steel protection was its entanglement with the Trade Promotion Authority Bill (TPA). In December 2001, the TPA passed the House of Representatives with a majority of one. Reputedly, the promise of protection for the steel industry assisted in securing the legislation's passage.[16] With the result in the Senate also closely contested, and the possibility of a second vote required in the House after Senate amendments to the President's negotiating power contained within TPA, support from those elected in steel-producing states and those who favoured protection of US manufacturing more generally, was vital. In recalling Democrat Senator Max Baucus' opening of the Senate Finance Committee meeting in 2002, it was clear that TPA and steel protection were explicitly connected:

> I want to tell the administration in the strongest possible terms that the support of Congress and the apparent successes of last year could both melt away very quickly if issues like those phasing the lumber and steel industries are mishandled. Enforcement of trade laws and handling of secretarial disputes is the real asset test that Congress applies to an administration trade policy.[17]

In seeking to address the steel crisis, prior to the tariffs, Bush had announced three directives on 5 June 2001. First, USTR Zoellick, Secretary of Commerce, Donald Evans and the Secretary of Treasury, Paul O'Neill, would endeavour to negotiate reductions in global steel excess with US trading partners. Second, this group was also to attempt negotiations to determine rules to govern the future trade in steel. Third, USTR Zoellick was to initiate a Section 201 investigation under the 1974 Trade Act. Each of these was claimed to be WTO consistent.[18]

In this instance, Section 201 was used to identify whether foreign steel imports were a catalyst for serious injury or could pose a threat. As was evident in the lamb dispute, imports can be fairly traded but still be seen to cause injury and thus subject to 201 trade remedies. In contrast to anti-dumping laws, Section 201 allows for the trade remedies to be imposed on individual exporters not directly responsible for the injury. In their findings the US International Trade Commission (ITC) commissioners determined that in 16 of 33 steel product categories, injury was evident and those manufactures were eligible for trade restraints. However, in making their recommendations to Bush, the commissioners had failed to agree on a common strategy to restrain imports. Commissioner Okun recommended quotas; three commissioners recommended 20 per cent tariffs, while commissioners Devaney and Bragg considered high tariffs appropriate on specific items.[19] Spared

---

16 Gary Hufbauer and Ben Goodrich, 2003, p. 3.

17 Max Baucus, testimony in the 'Hearing on Lumber and Steel trade Disputes', *Senate Finance Committee, FDCH Political Transcripts*, Washington D.C. 13 February 2002, p. 4.

18 The White House, 'Statement by the President Regarding a Multilateral Initiative on Steel', *Office of the Press Secretary*, 5 June 2001, p. 2.

19 US International Trade Commission, 'ITC Details Determinations Concerning Impact of Imports of Steel on US Industry', 11 December 2001, <http://www.usitc.gov/er/nl2001/

definitive consistent advice, Bush was thus provided with the space, both legally and politically, in which to act.[20]

Moreover, Zoellick attempted to defend the ongoing use of Section 201 investigations as they created the latitude not only in which specific industries could restructure, but also in which broader US goals of trade liberalisation could be enacted. Zoellick argued that 201 was necessary to construct the consensus for ongoing reductions in tariffs. In effect, 201 safeguards helped 'persuade US industry to accept significant cuts in US tariffs and other market opening measures'.[21]

It is also worth considering the impact that the terrorist attacks had on the US psyche and decision-making. Prior to the attacks, in August 2001 (after the 201 launch), Bush was explaining to Pittsburgh steel workers that steel was already a national security issue. Moreover, he expressed concern that the military might be 'over-reliant' upon foreign steel.[22] After 11 September, these considerations gained momentum. In the national psyche, security, unity, and patriotism were salient motivators in the post September 11 environment.

With the pressing issues of worker and industry security, the immediate Congressional and longer-term Presidential elections, the trading surrounding TPA, a restrictive steel Bill within the Congressional process and a climate of acute US nationalism following the terrorist attacks in the previous year, Bush chose to impose a system of tariffs and tariff rate quotas. In doing so, he claimed that this action was taken,

> to give our steel industry an opportunity to adjust to surges in foreign imports, recognising the harm from 50 years of foreign government intervention in the global steel market, which has resulted in bankruptcies, serious dislocation, and job loss. We also must continue to urge our trading partners to eliminate global inefficient excess capacity and market-distorting practices, such as subsidies.[23]

ER1023Y1.PDF>. Accessed 6 April 2007. US International Trade Commission, 'Summary of Commission Remedy Recommendations', 11 December 2001, <http://www.usitc.gov/er/nl2001/er1207y1c1.pdf>. Accessed 6 April 2007. See also US International Trade Commission, 'Certain Steel Products Trade Data', 11 December 2001, http://dataweb.usitc.gov/scripts/steel.asp>. Accessed 6 April 2007.

20 Gary Hufbauer and Ben Goodrich, 'Time for a Grand Bargain in Steel?', International Economics Policy Briefs, *Institute for International Economics*, Washington D.C., January 2002, p. 5.

21 US Department of State, Office of the United States Trade Representative, 'USTR Robert Zoellick defends Bush Action on Steel Imports', p. 2.

22 President George Bush, transcript of remarks by the President to Steelworkers Picnic at Mon Valley Works, US Steel Group, Pittsburgh, Pennsylvania, Office of the Press Secretary, 26 August 2001, p. 2.

23 President George W. Bush, 'President Announces Temporary Safeguards for Steel Industry', *Statement by the President, The White House, Office of the Press Secretary*, 5 March 2002.

Notably, the statement was framed within the Administration's rhetoric that free trade was the 'cornerstone of the economic agenda'.[24] However, that the legacy costs issue was still outstanding ensured that the disquiet was not fully quenched. US Steel Corp plans to buy Bethlehem and National Steel was arguably dependent on this issue being resolved.

More severe than the international trade commissioners advised, the tariff system implemented ranged from 8–30 per cent, mostly at the upper end but dependent on the specific steel product. These 'safeguard measures' were to remain in place for three years. It appeared that those countries excluded from the trade remedies were the US' FTA partners and also WTO developing countries that exported small shipments to the US. However, the US retained the discretion to review the exclusion provisions. Importantly for Australia, the decision also allowed for product exclusion requests to be considered within 120 days. This was aimed at ensuring access for US consumers for particular products.[25]

Zoellick reiterated that the decision needed to be taken in context of ensuring support for the free trade agenda. He claimed that the Administration needed to address the 'fear' and 'anxiety' accompanying the change that had been attributed to the forces of globalisation. In promoting free trade thus, 'the United States ha(d) to manage the homefront and the international front.'[26] For Zoellick it was vital to create coalitions.

Clearly the Bush Administration's ability to deliver any tariff exclusions to Australia was based not just on its policies to assist those people affected by plant closures but also by its perceptions of how this would affect its chances of re-election. Australia's Howard government was thus dependent upon the exigencies of US domestic politics in achieving any waivers for Australia and a construction of the argument for a synchronisation of interests.

Immediate International Reactions

One of the difficulties with the Howard government's practice of prioritising the US relationship has been that the Bush Administration had exhibited decidedly unilateral preferences. This, however, has not appeared to unduly concern the Coalition, nor to arrest its taste for alliance affairs. The Europeans, however, readily contested US unilateralism.

The Europeans sought to test the US actions against WTO rules. Moreover, compensation for losses in EU exports would be pursued through the WTO process. In separate actions, Japan, Korea, China, Switzerland, Brazil, New Zealand and

24 President George W. Bush, 'President Announces Temporary Safeguards for Steel Industry', *Statement by the President, The White House, Office of the Press Secretary*, 5 March 2002.

25 President George W. Bush, The White House, 'Fact Sheet: Regarding the Presidential Action on Steel', *Office of the Press Secretary*, 5 March 2002.

26 *Press Briefing by US Trade Representative Robert Zoellick*, The James S. Brady Briefing Room, 5 March 2002, pp. 2 and 8.

Australia, had initiated WTO consultations with the US. In testing the prospects for a joint action, the EU held talks with these countries, and with Norway and India.[27]

That US unilateralism was a constant source of angst in the international trade system is well documented. However, Zoellick's trade diplomacy in Doha in November 2001, had done much to assist in the establishment of a renewed agenda for trade talks. This, nonetheless, was not enough, as Zoellick's free trade posture soon was swamped by the electoral interests of the Administration sensitive to a broader resistance for liberalisation. So, too, was any goodwill emanating from Doha as the US and EU returned to their more familiar roles of pugilists. Poor diplomacy had soured the opportunity for further global trade liberalisation, it was clearly poor diplomacy. More broadly, the unilateralism of ballistic missile, global warming, biodiversity, and international criminal justice decisions were compounding the perceptions that the US was solely a self-interested global participant.

For all the rhetoric of claim and counter claim in this altercation, the WTO offered a procedure for dispute settlement. Yet, as the US was well aware, the establishment of the panels, the submission of the reports, the decision-making process and the review of appeals, if necessary, were time consuming. Finally, prior to the final WTO decision, President Bush terminated the measures. Accompanying the announcement were Robert Zoellick's comments on the success of the safeguards in assisting the domestic industry to respond to the barrage of imported steel.[28]

Steeling for Change: The Australian Steel Industry Restructures

The Australians, particularly as assisted by BHP Billiton, had lobbied the Administration and had addressed the ITC Commissioners in seeking exclusions for Australian steel exports. Australian Ambassador to the US, Michael Thawley, argued to the ITC that Australia had already completed the process of restructuring that was now necessitated in the US. In doing so, he briefly described the structural adjustments made by the Australian steel industry in the latter half of the 1990s. Twenty thousand jobs had been shed in gutting the industry, with the closure of the Newcastle mill reducing Australia's production by 20 per cent. In 2001, Australia did not subsidise its steel industry.[29] Once the ITC had made its recommendation to the President, both the Australian government and BHP Billiton raised the intensity of their lobbying, attempting to limit any prospective impact on BHP Billiton's $450 million exports to the US. DFAT indicated that it had argued two details to the US administration. First, as the US was concerned with global overcapacity and subsidised production, DFAT contested that the Australian steel industry had

---

27 European Commission, 'The European Commission's strategy to respond to the US decision to impose protectionist duties on steel imports', DN: MEMO/02/59, Brussels, 18 March 2002, p. 3.

28 Remarks by Robert B. Zoellick, United States Trade Representative on the decision by the President to terminate steel safeguards, 4 December 2003.

29 Embassy of Australia, *Office of Public Affairs, Testimony by the Australian Ambassador to the USA, Michael Thawley, Before the International Trade Commission*, 6 November 2001, Washington, D.C., pp. 1–2.

endured a process of 'significant rationalisation'. Moreover, it cited BHP Billiton as the third most competitive producer of slab steel in the global trade. Second, in general, Australian produced slab steel and feedstock was mostly utilised by West Coast mills.[30] As Thawley had argued to the ITC, the US mills had long-term arrangements to import the products as they were unavailable in the US.[31] In aiming for greater efficiencies and thus in the purchase of a future, the West Coast mills played a crucial role for the Australians by testifying to the necessity of the imported Australian feedstock.[32]

Bureaucrats in the Australian Embassy in Washington had worked assiduously with BHP Billiton to argue the Australian case and revoke the tariffs. Given the extent of structural adjustment in this sector undertaken in Australia, it was even more pressing that the Coalition demonstrate that its foreign policy choice of upgraded alliance relations was effective.

Concessions for The Big Australian

This dispute is indicative of the observation that bargaining between non-state actors is just as crucial in understanding relations in the international arena.[33] Both state and non-state actors were affected by the tariffs and both acted to alleviate the situation. Given that Prime Minister Howard, Trade Minister Mark Vaile and the Australian steel industry had 'lobbied hard to persuade the Bush Administration that Australian exports were part of the solution to helping the US steel industry'[34] (via their supply shipments), the government's disappointment at the tariff decision was palpable.

BHP Billiton too was frustrated by the decision, especially as its projections for steel exports to the US in 2001–02 were approximately 700,000 tonnes, less than the 800,000 tonnes in 2000–01. Mindful that it was intending to publicly list BHP Steel Limited in July 2002, Kirby Adams, President and CEO of BHP Steel, was careful to cite the positives.[35] He noted that tariffs had not been imposed on slab products, which comprised 40 per cent of exports to the US in 2002. By imposing a quota system, Bush had allowed for US mills to process slabs to retain cheaper imports. Further, both Adams and BHP Billiton CEO, Paul Anderson, claimed that the tariff decision had already been anticipated and thus had been incorporated in their strategic plan. Astutely, BHP Billiton had also invested in a 50 per cent interest in North Star BHP Steel, based in Delta, Ohio. As a low-cost mini mill operator,

---

30 DFAT, 'Background briefing by DFAT Officials on Trade Minister's forthcoming visit to US', 22 January 2002, pp. 1–2.

31 Embassy of Australia, 2001, p. 2.

32 Embassy of Australia, 2001, p. 2.

33 Susan Strange, '*Cave! Hic Dragones*: a critique of regime analysis', in Stephen D. Krasner (ed.), *International Regimes,* Cornell University Press, Ithaca, 1983, pp. 353–54.

34 The Hon. Mark Vaile, Minister for Trade, 'US Get(s) Precious Over Steel', *Media Release*, 6 March 2002.

35 BHP Steel produces flat products, while OneSteel Ltd, as producer of long products, was spun off BHP Billiton in October 2000. The same was also to occur for BHP Steel as it was eventually separately listed from BHP Billiton.

producing 1.5 million tonnes per annum, it would be a beneficiary of the higher prices for steel in the US market.[36]

At this juncture, the government worked assiduously to demonstrate the value of its alliance priority and effect results. Vaile, together with the Minister for Industry, Tourism and Resources, Ian Macfarlane and the Minister for Justice and Customs, Senator Chris Ellison, coordinated a summit of steel industry stakeholders to discuss the tariffs and the appropriate responses. Not only were participants, both capital and labour, concerned by the immediate effects of the tariffs on exports, but also by the prospects of trade diversion and the impact on upstream product exports. Consequently, along with a range of secondary proposals, the government initiated consultations with the US as a precursor to WTO action, and the participants agreed to the monitoring of both trade diversion trends and threatened dumping on the Australian market.[37]

Left with the product exclusion clause in the 201 decision as its only opportunity window for immediate action, both the government and BHP Billiton attempted to restate their objections to the tariffs. BHP Billiton had conducted a sophisticated campaign and coordinated the lobbying. The company had worked hard to educate Congressional members from the US west coast of the crucial nature of the Australian imports to the sustainability of west coast mills and hence steel communities. It was cheaper, too, to import the materials from Port Kembla than from some US midwest producers. In particular, BHP Billiton, the government and DFAT, argued that Steelscape a former BHP Billiton US subsidiary located in Kalama in Washington State was designed purposely to process their Australian hot rolled coil. As this feedstock was constructed to exact specifications, it was vital for the mill's continued function. Exemptions thus were sought to preserve the 250,000 tonnes of coil exported from Port Kembla.[38]

Despite being one of 1,200 firms seeking exclusion from the tariffs and opposition from a number of congressional representatives in steel states, the Administration granted Australia an exemption for hot rolled coil products. The USTR was authorised to consider the possibility of exclusions under Section 203 on the basis that the request did not contravene the safeguard measures objectives. Each case was assessed individually, with approval dependent on the necessity of a particular product for the US market and the attendant inability of the US to supply it.[39] It

36 Kirby Adams and Paul Anderson, quoted in BHP Billiton, 'BHP Steel Vows to Meet Challenge of US S.201 Impact', *News Release*, Melbourne, 6 March 2002.

37 The Minister for Trade, Mark Vaile, the Minister for Industry, Tourism and Resources, Ian Macfarlane, and the Minister for Justice and Customs, Senator Chris Ellison, 'Steel Industry Meeting – Communique', *Joint Media Release*, Canberra, 19 March 2002.

38 BHP Steel, 'BHP Steel Secures Tariff Exemption for Exports to Key US Customer', *News Item*, Melbourne, 11 March 2002. Grupo IMSA of Mexico bought Steelscape from BHP in 2000, however, BHP continued as feedstock supplier.

39 US Department of Commerce: ITA, 'Product Exclusion Requests Under Section 203', 4 June 2002, <http://ia.ita.doc.gov/steel/exclusion/>. Accessed 10 April 2007.

is also worth noting that the intensity of the political pressure in the US for the safeguard measures related to the import of flat-rolled products.[40]

Vaile had contacted US Commerce Secretary Evans to persuade him of Australia's case and eventually it was Evans who spoke to Mark Vaile on 10 March to convey the decision. In keeping with the US claims that the tariffs were WTO consistent, the explanation of the decision needed to adhere to WTO guidelines that the exclusion was made on the basis of a technicality and not acknowledge preferential treatment for specific countries.[41] Thus, the ITA lists of exclusions record only company and product details, not countries. This result ensured that approximately 80 per cent of BHP Billiton's exports to the US would remain outside the new tariff barriers. Hot rolled coil, which would be re-rolled by Steelscape, would be exempt from the US trade remedy. Eventually, over 85 per cent of Australian steel exports (over $400 million) were excluded from the tariffs.[42] However, the $100 million in a range of high-value cold rolled steel, plate, tin plate and other steel products exports remained subject to tariffs.[43] Kirby Adams immediately thanked Howard and Vaile as well as the Australian Embassy in Washington for their personal commitment to the process.[44] Vaile responded:

> (t)he Government was very pleased that the US Administration listened to our concerns and responded in a way that reflected both the depth of the bilateral relationship and our mutual commercial interests in this sector.[45]

The government at last was able to demonstrate some benefits of its alliance policy, even if commercial arrangements were at the heart of its success.

Tariff and Product Exclusions: Commercial and Political Patterns

After the storm of the tariff decision subsided, it became possible to discern patterns of exemptions. Commercial decisions were crucial, but it could easily be construed that Bush and Zoellick were also attempting to use the tariffs for broader purposes. Seemingly, the tariffs and their exemptions would be utilised to pursue both domestic

---

40 Gary Clyde Hufbauer and Ben Goodrich, 'Next Move in Steel: Revocation or Retaliation?', International Economics Policy Briefs, *Institute of International Economics*, Washington D.C., no. PB03-10, October 2003, p. 5.

41 Sid Marris, 'PM's 'win' leaves BHP in the queue', *The Australian*, 12 March 2002, p. 1.

42 DFAT, 'Trade 2003: A statement of outcomes and objectives by Mark Vaile, Minister for Trade', Canberra, 2003, p. 35.

43 See Department of Industry, Tourism and Resources, 'Steel International Context', accessed 12 June 2002, via <http://www.industry.gov.au/> for the specific restrictions on all Australian steel products to the US over the three year period. Also Tim Colebatch, 'BHP Gains Relief From Steel Tariff', *The Age*, 12 March 2002, p. 3.

44 Kirby Adams quoted in BHP Billiton, 'BHP Steel Secures Tariff Exemptions for Exports to Key US Customer', *News Item*, Melbourne, 11 March 2002.

45 The Hon. Mark Vaile, MP, Minister for Trade, Australia, 'US Gazettes Australian Exclusion from Steel Import Restrictions', *Media releases*, 6 April 2002, MVT023/2002.

and international aims. Internationally, both trade and security goals could be served by astute decision-making with trade policy tools. Friends were to be rewarded and enemies left unassisted. If Bush needed to construct internal political capital through the imposition of tariffs, it appeared that Zoellick was offered an olive branch, at least to maintain the pretext of his free trade credentials and was given some limited scope to pursue his broader aims of negotiating free trade agreements. Just how convincing others regarded the exclusions remained open to discussion, however. In Brasilia, in March 2002, to discuss the proposals for the Free Trade Area of the Americas (FTAA), Zoellick reminded his audience that the US had 'created' exemptions for 90 per cent of Brazil's steel exports to the US.[46] Brazil as a co-chair of the FTAA in the talks scheduled to begin in October 2002, was crucial to the success of the talks. Moreover, in exempting those countries with established free trade agreements with the US (eg. Canada, Mexico, Jordan, and Israel) others, including Australia, would be induced to see the merits of exclusive trade agreements with the US.

Constructions of trade coalitions, however, were not the only gambit in the play. Broader US security concerns seemed to be relevant too. Despite Russian complaints, the US argued that its safeguards allowed 'generous' quotas for Russian steel.[47] In its new security agenda, Russia would be vital to assist the US in its 'war on terror'. Turkey too, was exempt. Not only was Turkey persuaded to assume the leadership of the peacekeeping force in Kabul in mid-2002 (at least in name) Turkey, despite its reservations, was also regarded by the US as a likely platform for any possible continuation of the war against Iraq.

Throughout 2001, the Australian Prime Minister had assiduously promoted the intimacy between Australia and the US. Eager to dispel the memories of his previous visit to Washington in the throes of another trade dispute, and the shortest of shrifts in his meeting with Clinton, Howard's meeting with Bush on September 10, reputedly was extensive in conversing on shared interests. As noted, Howard was keen to utilise foreign policy to create domestic outcomes in his government's threat mediation strategy. Thus it was important to maximise opportunities that played well in the local environment. Revelations of close relations with the US President were thought to enhance this. Bush and Howard's joint statement, musing that 'they greatly enjoyed their discussions, which were characterised by unusual warmth and candour', was utilised in this respect.[48]

Four very different days later, Australia invoked the ANZUS Treaty as a response to the terrorist attacks in New York and Washington D.C. Cabinet agreed that Article IV of the Treaty was relevant to terrorist assaults. The decision acknowledged both the gravity of the attacks on the US and was a sign 'to demonstrate our steadfast

46 Robert B. Zoellick, 'USTR Zoellick in Brazil Defends Steel Tariffs Decision', Speech transcript at the Brazilian Ministry of Finance, Brasilia, Brazil, 11 March 2002, p. 2.

47 Robert Zoellick, 'Zoellick Defends Bush Steel Tariffs decision in Financial Times', op-ed article in the *Financial Times*, 12 March 2002, issued by the United States Embassy in Tokyo.

48 Prime Minister of Australia, John Howard, 'Joint statement between the United States of America and Australia', *Media release*, 10 September 2001, p. 3.

commitment to work with the United States in combating international terrorism'.[49] Subsequent to that, Australian SAS troops were assigned to join their US counterparts in action in Afghanistan. For the government, if trade and security were intertwined then it might now be possible to achieve greater traction in negotiations.

Resistance then to Australian pleas for exemptions from the tariffs, after considerable lobbying, would seriously undermine the Howard gloss and the Australian commitment to the coalition against terror, even if one of the cardinal rules of American relations with Australia had been that trade and security should never mix. Within Australia, such was the promotion of the alliance to a domestic audience, either unaware of – or actively opposed to – the distinction between trade and security, that some form of reciprocity became apparent in the public consciousness. New South Wales Treasurer, Michael Egan, publicly connected the tariffs with Australia's support of the US war on terror. In commenting on the tariffs and his expectation that the US had ignored Australia's involvement in the war coalition, he observed that 'Australia has stood shoulder to shoulder with America in the war on terrorism and in every major conflict of the last hundred years'.[50] Indeed, *The Australian* newspaper in its editorial believed Mark Vaile, 'hinted that Australia might win special relief because of its unflinching support for the war on terror.'[51]

Having made much of the new bonds between Australia and the US, Howard was indeed tangibly relieved that the US had demonstrated their commitment to Australia. As he recalled, this was 'the first time, in my memory, that we've had a special deal from the United States exempting us from a trade barrier.'[52] Howard's *éclat* was such that on 14 April 2002, he was inclined to celebrate:

> it can fairly be said that the alliance between Australia and the United States, so vital to the defence of Australia in the 1940s, in World War II, of continuing fundamental relevance to our security and our defence, that alliance had never been stronger and has never been closer.[53]

In this weather, Australia decided against the pursuit of a WTO challenge against its friend.

US analyst Gary Hufbauer confirmed the importance of alliance relations in determining product exclusions for Australia. He regarded the alliance partnership as 'enormously helpful' in assisting the process but Hufbauer also considered that

---

49 Prime Minister of Australia, John Howard, 'ANZUS Treaty: Application of ANZUS Treaty to terrorist attacks on the United States', *Media release*, 14 September 2001.

50 Michael Egan, quoted in AAP Newsfeed, 'NSW: US steel tariffs will hurt local industry – Carr', 6 March 2002. Michael Baume, 'Steel Battle Requires an Iron Will', *Australian Financial Review*, 4 February 2001, p. 55.

51 *The Australian*, editorial, 7 March 2002.

52 John Howard, transcript of interview by Barrie Cassidy, 'PM to push free trade agenda in US', *Insiders*, ABC Television, 2 June 2002, p. 3.

53 John Howard, *Transcript of the Prime Minister The Hon John Howard MP Prime Minister's Closing Address Liberal Party 49th Federal Council*, Hyatt Hotel, Canberra, 14 April 2002, p. 2.

the business orientation was 'equally important'.[54] A material opportunity to foster closer links with the US had been presented and realised. So, while the concessions may have reflected the lobbying done to persuade the Bush Administration of the necessity to ensure Australian market supply to west coast steel manufacturers, it was implied that the San Francisco system of US Pacific alliances involved bonds more extensive than those of security.

This, however, compounded institutional and academic concerns with Australia's uncritical acceptance of the broader US *modus operandi*. Pascal Lamy, in Australia in July 2002, claimed that Australia, in not joining other countries in lodging a WTO complaint against the tariffs, had placed its bilateral relationship with the US ahead of principles in the international trading system. If the system was to work, then he argued that countries needed to maintain the principles of its operation.[55]

Conclusion: Commercial and Political Symmetry

As this dispute unfolded, it exposed the structural complexities of Australia's situation in the trading environment of the early 2000s. It revealed the increasing complexities of global trade and how Australia's bilateral relationship with the US is interconnected with systemic issues. In part, the dispute concerned the political willingness of a new Administration to deal with the latent effects of increased exports in 1998 and from Asian countries and Russia during the financial crises of 1997–98. As importer of last resort, the US actions served to reduce the immediate effects of the crises. It has served, then, a vital function in maintaining the global financial system, with Australia a beneficiary of this role.

However, the consequences have been manifested in the inability of the domestic steel manufacturers within the US to absorb the effects of increased imports. Already vulnerable, this left them more susceptible to the dramatic increases in the export capability of late modernising states in the global system as aided by a strong US dollar. Restructuring to adapt to these new conditions would be passed on, however, to others in the international system. In the bilateral economic relationship the argument that the asymmetry of the relationship determines that the smaller country must accept the pain of adjustment, remained relevant.[56] Australia's small size precludes it from exercising any of the leverage attained from economies of scale. Size also has necessitated the ongoing reform of its manufacturing industries for it to compete in the global trading system. Australia's steel industry has grappled with restructuring over the past two decades as a result.

By choosing to protect its industry, the US shifted the demands of change offshore. $70–100 million of Australia's steel exports to the US were subject to tariffs for 21 months. Although concessions were granted, opportunities for growth have been

---

54 Gary Hufbauer, personal communication, 4 October 2003.

55 Mark Davis, 'EU attacks Australia on steel stance', *Australian Financial Review*, 17 July 2002, p. 1.

56 Richard Higgott, 'The Ascendancy of the Economic Dimension in Australian – American Relations', in John Ravenhill (ed.), *No Longer an American Lake: Alliance Problems in the South Pacific*, Berkeley, Institute of International Studies, 1989, pp. 132–63.

constrained too, as half of the $750 million export trade has been limited to 2001 levels. Moreover, this was in a broader context where Australia's trading deficit with the US stood at $13 billion. This is not to say, however, that the US ultimately can avoid structural change in the steel industry either. As the US Administration was aware, in both industrial and political aspects of this crisis, it was using time to assuage the pain of domestic adjustment and to maximise its domestic electoral advantage in doing so. As Australian governments have discovered, significant political difficulties arise from the inflation of the US relationship. In particular, this concerns the creation of false public expectations that the partnership will deliver benefits to Australia at the expense of domestic US producers.

Timed as it was in the aftermath of the terrorist crisis for the US, the 2002 steel dispute has inevitably attracted some discussion of the interrelationship between trade and security. That Bush should talk of the maintenance of a domestic steel industry as a national security issue was designed to resonate in a country where protection and nationalism was the new political currency. As Hufbauer had observed, alliance relations were of some significance in the determination of exclusions. In Australia, where the twain of trade and security had rarely met, subtle connections were intimated. Though the tariff concessions may have been formulated to protect the steel industries within the US, and granted to a slab of countries which applied on those grounds, that the Australian government was willing to flaunt its ally status and threat mediation strategies, indicates a willingness to ferment the trade – security connections in the public arena. Although many Australian governments had discovered in the past that it was a hazardous practice to imply reciprocity across trade and security, there seemed symmetry in the interests of the Bush Administration and Howard government to foster more ubiquitous links between the ANZUS allies.

Chapter 8

Linkage Politics: The AUSFTA

According to both major political parties in Australia, prior to 2001, trade and security did not mix. According to former US Secretary of State, George Schultz, clearly they did not. When both Michael Duffy (Special Minister for Trade Negotiations in 1987) and Mark Vaile, newly appointed Trade Minister in 1999, made suggestions that the Australia–US Joint Defence Facilities might be used as bargaining chips in the agricultural disputes of the times,[1] they were hastily reminded by their Federal colleagues that in Australian foreign policy the Joint Facilities were off limits. Trade and defence policies with the US were to be conducted as discrete enterprises. George Schultz abruptly circumvented any discussion that the continued deployment of the US Export Enhancement Program (EEP) might result in Australia's cancellation of Australia–US defence talks.[2] Confirming the public distinction, Prime Minister John Howard argued in 2005 that 'both sides of politics strongly rejected the suggestion that we should use trade as a lever in our strategic alliance with the United States.'[3] But what of the reverse?

With the election of George W. Bush in 2000 and the appointment of his Administration, it seemed that Australia's security involvement in Afghanistan and Iraq might assist in its endeavours to promote trade ties. But conversely, according to new USTR, Robert Zoellick, greater trade intimacy would 'strengthen the ties of our security alliance'.[4] After 11th September 2001, the Bush Administration was acutely conscious that trade policy could be a potent tool in securing allies in its response to terrorist assaults and threatening regimes. And whereas the original San Francisco system of security alliances was designed to counter Chinese and Soviet influence in Asia after 1945, in this new global overlap of trade and security policy, the US was attempting to construct an even more potent and extensive antidote to less transparent assailants. Accompanying Zoellick to the White House were officials whose Cold War experience lent itself to the integrated use of trade and foreign policy. Vice

---

1 The US objected to the chemical content of Australia's beef exports to the US in the late 1980s and thus imposed restrictions, while in July 1999 the US had implemented a tariff-rate quota on imports of Australian lamb.

2 Gary Brown, 'Breaking the American Alliance: An Independent National Security Policy for Australia', Canberra Papers on Strategy and Defence No. 54, SDSC, RSPaS, ANU, 1989.

3 John Howard, *Transcript of the Prime Minister the Hon John Howard MP, Joint Press Conference with the Premier of NSW, the Hon Bob Carr MP*, Phillip Street, Sydney, 9 June 2005.

4 Robert B. Zoellick, 'A Pacific Partnership: Australia and America in a Globalizing World', *Remarks to the Australian American Leadership Dialogue*, Washington D.C., 10 July 2002.

President Dick Cheney, Defense Secretary, Donald Rumsfeld, and Deputy Secretary of Defense, Paul Wolfowitz were advocates of alliance structures to support US foreign and military aims. And in framing a response to the terrorist attacks, George Bush continued to reiterate the 'rewards for friends and the punishments for enemies' theme.

So, during its second term in office, the Howard government intensified its threat mediation strategy and attempted to bargain bilaterally in a much more comprehensive fashion: namely through an AUSFTA and the overlay of security and trade. However, hitches in Australia's ability to complete trade agreements with Asia were a precursor to Australia's pursuit of a deal with the US. Aside from possible financial benefits arising from a deal, ensuing difficulties in realising closer economic relations in East Asia, and Australia's perennial apprehension with isolation in patterns of global trade and a commensurate understanding of the domestic electoral appeal of a fortification of relations with the US were motivations for the government's pursuit of a formal trade agreement with the US. If its opportunity for regional trade deals in Asia was problematic, it was drawn to the US by a new Administration that actively sought 'competitive liberalisation'. Consequently, regional and bilateral trade deals with select countries were canvassed in this process.

Concurrent with the security interplay, upon the announcement of the increases in US steel tariffs, some Australian proponents of an FTA with the US observed that those countries with free trade agreements with the US were exempt from the tariffs. A certain logic then presented itself that an FTA would constitute the best means to improve Australia's global economic position, especially when the multilateral trade institutions wavered. It could be used to shore up Australia's economic vulnerability internationally and simultaneously quell political and economic demands from below. Greater integration with the US, as principal strategic ally and cultural ally, suited the government's interests, even though it could be argued persuasively that it was not the ideal bilateral trade partner.

In Chapter Two, I demonstrated how the government's initial attempts at culturally bound bargaining with the US through the leather and lamb disputes were ineffective. In Chapter Three, through the East Timor crisis, I considered the need for Australian and US interests to coincide if the Howard government was to achieve its desired outcomes. Chapter Four reiterated the importance of the US for Australia in the biotechnology sector, yet cautioned on the need to mediate that power in securing Australia's interests. Through Chapter Five I disclosed how the government had achieved greater intimacy in defence procurement and in Chapter Six, Australia's commitment to the US state based response to the terrorist attacks through its military deployments revealed an ambitious threat mediation strategy. Chapter Seven demonstrates how the government had endeavoured to leverage upon both its commitment to US security aims in addition to arguing its claims through its commercial connections.

I continue with this theme in this chapter, examining how Australia's interest in the interplay between trade and security coincided with the US Administration's interest in economic statecraft. Renewed alignment of US trade and security strategy also provided an opportunity for the Australian government to attempt to increase its bargaining leverage. Australia's support for the US 'war on terror' and its military intervention in Afghanistan and Iraq enhanced its capacity to foster a trade deal. But what might be the implications of a mix of trade and security policies, especially as Australia's wheat trade to Iraq could inevitably be a casualty of the war? As the situation in Iraq deteriorated after the initial military strike and the Australian government remained circumspect on further deployments to Iraq, Australia's leverage to conclude any deal was lessened. For the Australia–US trade agreement to be completed, there needed to be a more persuasive and material coalition of interests in the US, especially to counteract the intransigence of the US agricultural lobby. These forces appeared as both the pharmaceutical and manufacturing industries in addition to those of the Administration who saw the benefits and modeling effects of an AUSFTA extending beyond border tariffs.

An Inclusive AUSFTA Framework?

In June 2002, at the Senate Foreign Affairs, Defence and Trade Legislation Committee's Consideration of Budget Estimates, DFAT officials were quizzed about the proposals and progress of the Free Trade Agreement. Prior to the US announcement of Trade Promotion Authority (TPA) approval, vital for any US free trade deal's success, Australia and the US had completed initial discussions on the shape of the agreement. In these preliminary discussions, DFAT officials explained that Australia had always approached the WTO definition of an FTA as 'comprehensive', with all major sectors, including agriculture, on the table. It was later confirmed by DFAT that, in initial discussions with the US, the prospective FTA negotiations were intended to be comprehensive, with nothing excluded. Thus, Australia and the US would be 'looking at' chapters in an agreement on general trade, agriculture, tariffs, goods, rules of origin, trade remedies, safeguards, services, investment and e-commerce. As Australia was a signatory to the Australia–New Zealand Closer Economic Relations Trade Agreement (ANZCERTA) and the US to NAFTA, it was suggested that these agreements, together with the Canada – Chile agreement, would flag a starting point for discussions.[5]

Without doubt optimism is always the starting point for negotiations such as these. However, both Howard's and Vaile's public commentary that agricultural liberalisation was a primary focus heightened the stakes for a result.

The Australia–Asia Too Hard Basket?

It was evident that it was not just voluntarist decision-making that was propelling Australia into Zoellick's competitive liberalisation strategy. Regional disorder was complicating Australia's trade options in the late 1990s. Countries within East Asia too had established a series of proposals to establish free trade agreements, some with deliberate intent to exclude Australia. Accordingly, the Howard government,

---

5 Bruce Gosper and Steve Deady, Senate Foreign Affairs, Defence and Trade Legislation Committee, 'Consideration of Budget Estimates', *Proof Committee Hansard, Commonwealth of Australia*, Canberra, 5 June 2002, pp. 324, 357 and 360.

weary with the effort needed to formalise free trade arrangements within Asia, and unable to or uninterested in assisting APEC to foster further liberalisation, sought an 'easier' and 'more comfortable' option.[6]

Clearly, where there is sufficient motivation on both sides, be it economic or strategic, East Asian countries will continue to foster links with Australia. Amongst recent business activity, China's spectacular resource deals with Australia evidence this. While overestimating Asian sensibilities has sometimes played to Australia's disadvantage, as those with experience working in Asia sometimes describe,[7] it is evident that these deals met with China's self interest.

Yet John Fuhrman, adviser to the former Trade Minister, Tim Fischer, has written that the Howard government had been 'disappointed' by regional criticism. Australia had been a major contributor to Asian Financial Crisis packages and had worked effectively to reduce stringent IMF reform measures for Indonesia. Although Fuhrman personally remained sceptical of the benefits flowing from an Australia–US Free Trade Agreement (AUSFTA), in 2001 he observed that:

> there is a sense the easier option is the extended hand offered by the new Administration to resuscitate the US alliance and engage the US in the region…The notion of an FTA provides an opportunity to do both, and is more attractive than trying to deal with the moveable feast of Asian criticism.[8]

Some of this criticism stemmed from Australian support of US maintenance of the IMF's centrality in the financial crisis, Australia's vocal touting of its own economic successes post crisis, Downer's interpretation of Australia's practical regionalism in Beijing, as well as the near-disintegration of relations with Indonesia during the East Timor crisis. Ultimately, it contributed to the initial political opposition within ASEAN to the ASEAN–ANCERTA FTA (AFTA–CER), which was initially suggested by the ASEAN Trade Ministers themselves. Over the course of these events, significant opposition to Australia's integration with AFTA and/or ASEAN+3 (ASEAN plus China, Japan, South Korea) was generated within Indonesia, Malaysia and The Philippines.

That this occurred at a time when East Asian elites saw a need to project their own interests in global affairs compounded the regional ramifications. Not only was APEC exposed as incapable of producing a satisfactory political or financial response to the crisis, together with Washington's disposition, both of disinterest and of a competitive triumphalism, this ensured that the region would seek arrangements that provided for their control.[9] It is a measure of the lessening economic import

6 John Fuhrman, 'Political tie not worth more regional flak', *Australian Financial Review*, 6 February 2001, p. 43.

7 See for example, Michael Byrnes, *The Asia Game*, Allen and Unwin, St. Leonards, 1994.

8 John Fuhrman, 2001, p. 43.

9 Peter Drysdale, 'The Impact of the Japanese Economy on Asia and the Pacific: Does Asia Need Regional Trade Arrangements?', *Presentation to IMF–World Bank Conference on Economic Interdependence: Shaping Asia–Pacific in the 21st Century*, Tokyo, 22–23 March 2001, pp. 4–5.

of APEC that while in the past any speculation upon free trade agreements was contemplated with the APEC framework and liberalisation plans in mind, the new proposals ignored the principles of open regionalism. Japan, long a proponent of multilateral negotiations, relinquished its loyalty as it recognised opportunities for domestic structural reform and accelerated reform through FTAs. It also saw how Japanese companies were disadvantaged by preferential agreements already struck by its trading partners.[10] That many of these trade and investment proposals did little to resemble true non-discriminatory free trade agreements did not suggest this was anything to substitute for continued multilateral enterprise. Instead, policy makers were driven by a fear of isolation.

So, while the ASEAN–CER agreement may have embodied prospects for greater economic return, it appeared as if the Howard government had exacerbated the apparent regional disorder. Further, it appeared as though it may have circumscribed any options it may have had for realising gains to be wrought through an AFTA until at least Mahathir retired, Susilo Bambang Yudhoyono was installed and the necessity arose for ASEAN to create ballast in its dealings with China.

These new policy preferences also stemmed from the increasing uncertainty surrounding relations with China as a potential economic and military powerhouse. Correspondingly, it has also been assisted by the US determination to pursue bilateral trade arrangements across the Pacific. Complicating this, however, was a regional aversion to US unilateralism in trade relations. As many of the US allies in East Asia are principal sources of the US trade deficit, they have been subject to varying trade remedies to restrict their exports to the US. Yet US markets were persuasive and it had maintained its markets for imports throughout the financial crisis, despite wavering in its application to address the problem through other means. Aware of the possibilities, Washington was capitalising on its timely opportunities in the region. Zoellick's strategy in creating a climate of competition for engagement with the US, was proving effective, nonetheless, in directing foreign trade activity toward the US before Japan could resolve its internal economic problems and prior to China's maturity as a global economic centre. Moreover, these arrangements, fortifying the centrality of the US, overlapped with its hubs and spokes system of security alliances. As such they marked a comprehensive strategy against the emerging power of China.

Desperately Seeking Uncle Sam

Ann Kent observed that the Coalition's interest in revitalising the relationship with the US in 1996 was given impetus by China's threats to Taiwan during its presidential campaign in the same year. China's provocative behaviour, together with the exposed inadequacy of any regional security forum to respond, created terrain on which the Coalition could structure a return to its traditional accent on the

10 Noboru Hatakeyama, 'Japan's New Regional Trade Policy – Which country comes next after Singapore?', Second Annual Whitman International Lecture, *Institute for International Economics*, Washington, DC, 13 March 2002, p. 5.

US alliance.[11] Traditional alliance relations with the US were becoming increasingly attractive as regional trade options for Australia were circumscribed.

Through the 1990s, the US had tested Australia's seas with offers of a free trade agreement. George H. Bush, floated the idea in 1992, and the Clinton Administration again expressed an interest in pursuing the concept in May 1997. Both offers were rejected. Zoellick claimed that early in the 1990s, both political and bureaucratic leaders in Australia preferred to connect Australia to Japan, on the premise that it was the future of the world economy. In doing so, they spurned the first Bush Administration's offer which argued that Australia would be best served through an FTA with the US: an FTA which would 'strengthen its ability to compete globally and with its Asian partners'.[12] By the late 1990s, however, with Japan's future in this role eroded, and fears that Australia may be left isolated, the US overtures began to look more attractive to the Coalition.

In 2000, the Howard government then set out to initiate these proposals. It surmised that an FTA marked an opportunity to execute its bilateral approach to trade diplomacy.[13] Clearly this would distinguish the government's approach from that of its Labor predecessors. Anxious for a variation of the theme, it would denote also the 'renewed' emphasis it had placed on traditional relationships. Deftly responsive also to the traditional strains of the need for assured security in the electorate, the government seized the opportunity to further entrench its relations with the US.

For the Coalition, the prospective benefits of an AUSFTA focused not just on the possibilities of economic gains accruing in all sectors, (with growth in manufactures and services). Instead, attention was devoted to the potential for expanded investment, technology and business practice transfers. Presentation in these cultural terms was necessitated precisely because even with all sectors included in the financial modelling, massive gains were not apparent. Although a number of modeling studies were conducted on the possible gains and losses of any agreement, informed commentators including Andrew Stoler and Ann Capling declined to take much stock from their results.[14] Perhaps the most interesting of the modeling results was to show that any gains from an AFTA–CER far outweighed possible gains from an AUSFTA. Apart from this it probably will not be for some time that the financial benefits or costs of the deal become apparent.

After the FTA proposal gained the Presidential imprimatur, Australia's responsiveness to US military activity in Afghanistan and Iraq hastened the process.

---

11 Ann Kent, 'Australia and China, 1991–95: Asymmetry and Congruence in the Post-Cold War Era', in James Cotton and John Ravenhill (eds), *Seeking Asian Engagement: Australia in World Affairs 1991–95*, Oxford University Press in Association with The Australian Institute for International Affairs, Melbourne, p. 171.

12 Robert B. Zoellick, 'A Pacific Partnership: Australia and America In a Globalizing World', *Remarks to the Australian American Leadership Dialogue*, Washington, DC, 10 July 2002, p. 7.

13 Department of Foreign Affairs and Trade, 'In the National Interest', Foreign and Trade Policy White Paper, *Commonwealth of Australia*, Canberra, 1997.

14 Ann Capling and Andrew Stoler, lectures given on the AUSFTA, Flinders University, South Australia, April–May 2004, author's notes.

Richard Fisher, former Clinton deputy USTR, commented on the pace of the negotiations:

> Contrast the treatment of Australia with the treatment of Chile, where we already have an agreement that has been negotiated, but where nothing is happening. The President, rightly in my view, will reward friends first.[15]

Public hopes were also raised as to the outcome for Australia. In concluding President Bush's meeting with Australian Prime Minister Howard at the Crawford ranch in Texas, in 2003, Bush enunciated his desire to see negotiations completed by the end of 2003, ready for the Congressional approval process in the first part of 2004.

American Remix: Trade and Security

Any opportunity for Australian foreign policy management through the upgrade of US relations has been dependent on US policy activity and its preparedness for reciprocity. Australia's approach on the FTA now appeared timely as it intersected with the pattern of US enthusiasm for trade agreements globally. Though the US mix of intended free trade agreements may replicate the San Francisco system of security alliances in the Western Pacific, it was not confined to the region. As such the US was also constructing a palisade against its economic competitor in the EU. The US strategy was extending vigorously and broadly across the globe with trade deals bracing security alliances in Asia, the Middle East, Europe and the Americas.

Early in 2001, Robert Zoellick articulated his strategy of competitive free trade whereby the Administration was:

> advancing trade liberalization and America's interests – globally, regionally, and bilaterally…(further)…we should emphasize not just the economic benefits of trade, but also explain how trade is intertwined with security, political cooperation, and the spread of individual liberty and democratic values.[16]

Exponents of the Washington consensus in the Americas were earmarked for 'reward' where 'good performers will get special treatment'. The aim of this tactic was to spur others into negotiations with the US. This would apply to those performers in both the security and trade realms.

More broadly, it has been possible to identify more extensive links between US trade and security activity. After 11 September 2001, the US foreign policy focus shifted from country and regional preoccupations to more consuming and broader global concerns. Proposed plans for 'competitive liberalisation' were intimately intertwined with security objectives. In framing a response to the terrorist attacks, George W. Bush continued to reiterate ideas of dividends for allies and penalties

15 Peter Hartcher, 'What Australia won from the war', *Australian Financial Review*, 10–11 May 2003, p. 25.

16 Robert B. Zoellick, 'A Time to Choose: Trade and the American Nation', US Trade Representative, *Speech to the Heritage Foundation*, Washington D.C., 29 June 2001, pp. 7 and 10.

for antagonists. Moreover, in this Manichean world, the desire to confront the 'axis of evil' would place some limits on the new Administration's immediate desire to rectify its trade deficits with allies. Overall a pattern emerged that evidenced a synchronisation of trade and defence policy, not just in the Pacific but globally. This pattern was pervaded with Cold War overtones.

Where the Clinton Administration's record on trade arrangements was ambitious in its attempts to open markets, it felt less compelled to pursue foreign policy objectives. The Uruguay Round was finalised, NAFTA completed, the FTAA launched and the US–Vietnam bilateral trade agreement signed. Clinton's USTR, Charlene Barshefsky, vigorously hunted down market opening objectives. Once trade promotion authority was confirmed Zoellick was no less ambitious, but more acutely aware of the strategic benefits to be garnered. Searching too, for alternatives to combat the trade deficit with Asia, Washington was conscious of the opportunities that the FTAA might offer in reducing imports from the Western Pacific. In negotiating to expand its import options through the Americas, it was hoisting the ensign of competition across the Pacific.[17]

More explicit trade and security deals were also part of the strategy. The 1985 US–Israel Free Trade Area Agreement and associated agreements probably marked the high watermark in US past efforts to link the two. Between 1983 and 1988, the US converted military loans to Israel to grants, awarded considerable military contracts through the Strategic Defense Initiative and joint US–Israeli missile development programmes and formalised bilateral relations in economic, defence and research areas.[18] Strengthening ties in the Middle East continued to occupy the US. Legislation for the US–Jordan FTA was signed on 28 September 2001, at a time of ever increasing difficulty for the US to design and implement a successful Middle East strategy. Once the US was confronted by the terrorist threat, the Bush Administration was prepared to utilise trade instruments overtly in bolstering its allies. As testimony to this, consider for example how the exclusions to the steel tariffs were allocated not just as a response to specific business requirements but designed with strategic objectives in mind.[19] By mid-2002, the USTR was discussing the prospects of a FTA with Egypt with commercial objectives but also as part of the strategy to reward friends for their help in the response to the terrorist attacks, and a recognition of the vulnerability of Egypt as a partner in any Western alliance in the Middle East.

---

17 Peter Field, Australia's former chief negotiator for the Uruguay Round, suggests that the pursuit of an FTAA raises a conglomerate of competitive agricultural issues, for example the effect on Australia of increased South American exports of beef, sugar, and oranges into the US, Chilean/Argentine wine exports, and post Castro Cuban sugar exports to the US? Author discussion with Peter Field, 11 October 2002.

18 Howard F. Rosen, 'The US–Israel Free Trade Area Agreement: How Well Is It Working and What Have We Learned?', in Jeffrey J. Schott (ed.), *Free Trade Areas and US Trade Policy, Institute for International Economics*, Washington, D.C., 1989, p. 104.

19 See, US Ambassador, Tom Schieffer, quoted in Tim Colebatch, 'BHP Gains Relief From Steel Tariff', *The Age*, 12 March 2002, p. 3. Also, John Howard, transcript of interview by Barrie Cassidy, 'PM to push free trade agenda in US', *Insiders*, ABC Television, 2 June 2002, p. 3.

Immediately after 11 September 2001, the US implemented its economic strategy to assist in its response. Economic sanctions against Pakistan were lifted, debt relief was entertained. Debt forgiveness was also important for the Jordanian relationship. China and Taiwan's planned entry to the WTO were assisted and Russian WTO aspirations were reviewed. New trading preferences for Indonesian exports to the US were allocated and the US planned to offer the advantages of the technology sector agreement struck with Singapore to Indonesia. Further afield, the US and Poland completed two agreements to extend economic and military ties. A multi-dimensional response that incorporated medium and long-term constructive measures and the rebuilding of relationships with the Arab and Islamic worlds was clearly called for. The use of American soft power would be integral in this. Thus, Morocco was designated as the second Arab Muslim country to engage in free trade arrangements, with an FTA signed in 2004. More broadly, in addressing the development agenda, Washington proposed a liaison with the South African Customs Union. This incorporated South Africa, Botswana, Namibia, Lesotho and Swaziland.

Australia and Linkage Politics

Consonant with the 'benefits for allies and less for others' mantra, if an FTA was to be negotiated with Australia, its CER partner New Zealand was to be isolated. New Zealand's continued denial of US ships' entry to its harbours and failure to support the US in Iraq constituted decidedly unfriendly behaviour and as a consequence Wellington was frozen out of prospective trade deals. By contrast, Australia's negotiations were hastened by its endorsement and involvement in US military operations. So, while the first Howard governments (1996–99) had recouped little in their efforts to utilise the special and traditional relationship with the US on trade matters in the Howe and lamb disputes, it was hoping for much more in its deployment of the security card enterprise. Now US economic statecraft found a ready partner. Foreign Minister Downer stated that:

> an FTA would help engender a broader appreciation – in both countries – of the bilateral security alliance and the manner in which ANZUS, together with the web of US alliances in the region, helps to underpin the stability and prosperity of East Asia and the Pacific.[20]

Across the Pacific, the USTR also reflected that deepening the trade relationship would affirm the security alliance. Connecting with Downer's comments on the role of ANZUS he also observed that: 'Australia, the world's 14th largest economy, also

---

20 The Hon. Alexander Downer, Minister for Foreign Affairs, 'The Strategic Importance of a Free Trade Agreement to Australia–United States Relations', *Speech at the Australian APEC Studies Centre conference on 'The Impact of an Australian–United States Free Trade Agreement: Foreign Policy Challenges and Economic Opportunities' transcript*, Canberra, 29 August 2002, p. 3.

is eager to strike a free trade agreement with the United States, and not just for economic reasons.'[21]

Linkage politics, however, present some concerns for Australia. First, as the logic of bilateralism suggests, the US can exercise greater power on those issues with which it is most concerned. If '(t)he United States' bilateral alliances provide the framework for Washington to project its power and influence in a systematic and predictable fashion at critical intervals'[22] they provided a framework to secure its own interests. Focussing both security and trade interests through this channel enhances the power of the US. A further entrenchment of economic and political ties may further erode the government's ability to question its ally on security issues and call into question its own decision-making, particularly in the deployment of the ADF. Australia's unexamined support of US led military action in Iraq demonstrated this unquestioning role. Australia's acceptance of US and British policy that failed to report on either the dismantling or relocation of WMD in Iraq, detracted from the quality of decision-making processes of the Coalition government. More access but less influence would be a less than desirable feature of a future relationship.[23] Chris Reus-Smit has elaborated on this point. He has argued that current US grand strategy with its threat to international rules and frameworks, together with its recent role in 'escalating global tensions' demands a more critical assessment from Australia. The Howard government needs to reconsider how this strategy fits with Australia's necessity for the proper functioning of multilateral institutions.[24] Ironically too, an uncritical ally is ultimately of less value to the alliance, and less able to add value in the provision of regional expertise. As Keohane and Nye have noted too (and as explained in Chapter One) Australia has historically subjugated other agendas to the security alliance. When trade is tied to security, trade outcomes in parallel economies are likely to be of lesser consequence. It would hardly be surprising, that if Australia acted to further entrench relations without question, the set would be tuned for a replay of that perennial motif in Australia–US relations: 'a promise to the smaller partner but with first return to the senior partner'.[25]

---

21 Robert B Zoellick, 'Globalization, Trade and Economic Security', *Remarks at the National Press Club*, 1 October 2002, pp. 4–5.

22 William Tow and Russell Trood, 'Conclusion', in William Tow, Russell Trood & Toshiya Hoshino (eds), *Bilateralism in a Multilateral Era: The Future of the San Francisco Alliance System in the Asia–Pacific*, Japan Institute of International Affairs, Tokyo, and the Centre for the Study of Australia–Asia Relations, Griffith University, Queensland, 1997, p. 171.

23 Michael Cox has argued that whilst the US needed allies in its war on terror, the question remains as to its interest in genuine consultation with these parties. See Michael Cox, 'US Grand Strategy: Implications for Alliance Partners', *Centre for Defence and Strategic Studies, Australian Defence College Conference on United States Grand Strategy: Implications for Alliance Partners*, Canberra, 1 August 2003, p. 6.

24 Chris Reus-Smit, 'US Grand Strategy and Australia', *Centre for Defence and Strategic Studies, Australian Defence College Conference on 'United States Grand Strategy: Implications for Alliance Partners*, Canberra, 1 August 2003, pp. 3–5.

25 G.Turner, 'Looking to America: the Crocodile Dundee factor', in G. Turner, *Making it National: Nationalism and Australian Popular Culture*, Allen and Unwin, Sydney, p. 98.

Second, the interconnection of trade and security relations with the US presages greater influence for Congress. As the 1990s trade disputes revealed, trade policy in the US turns on US domestic constituencies, US trade law and Congressional representation. In these disputes the government overestimated the power of the US executive to deliver on alliance considerations. US economic statecraft is beholden to Congressional forces.

Third, it is also worth asking if economic ties are increased whether this will create pressure on sourcing of defence acquisitions and ultimately defence spending? Notable amongst the members of the American Australian Free Trade Agreement Coalition (AAFTAC) were three US military manufacturers. These were: Raytheon, Lockheed Martin, Rockwell Collins, as well as the Aerospace Industries Association. Through the latter part of Australia's *Collins* class submarine project, the Coalition's choice to enhance defence ties with the US placed constraints on the development of naval shipbuilding in Australia. Its alienation of German shipbuilder, HDW, in the tender process for the Australian Submarine Corporation (ASC), (even though it was part owner of ASC through its inheritance of Kockums' shares and replete with backorders to construct new diesel-electric submarines) was a direct response to both Coalition desires to upgrade US relations and to US pressure itself. Once the potential of the submarines was realised by the US, not only did it object to European equity partners in the project, it demanded US compatible systems. US Ambassador to Australia in 2000, Edward Gnehm, called for the installation of a US combat system.[26] Failure to comply would threaten the strategic submarine partnership.[27] This is despite NATO partners' employment of non-US software and munitions. Could Australia eventually provide weapons and military equipment or technology for US allies that it is unable to produce itself? Possible provision of non-nuclear submarines or the associated technology for Taiwan remains one controversial example of this. And even though I have argued elsewhere that the submarine project may not have been explicitly involved in the AUSFTA discussions,[28] it is conceivable that in the future, defence contracts (including those related to the submarines) may become connected to ongoing AUSFTA pressure.

Australian defence purchasing between 2001 and 2006 reveals a propensity for acquiring US materiel. The purchase of the aging Seasprite helicopters was compounded by expert strategists' skepticism of the massive outlay in expenditure to join the experimental US F-35 joint strike fighter project. Doubts were cast on the return for Australia's $16 billion investment, with questions raised on both the appropriateness and efficacy for Australia. Leigh Purnell, executive director of the Australian Industry Group Defence Council, was also wary of 'replication of existing

26 Roger Martin and Robert Garran, 'US early warning on defence', *The Australian*, 11 October 2000, p. 2.

27 Robert Garran, 'US threat to sink strategic alliance', *The Weekend Australian*, 23–25 December 2000, p. 1.

28 Maryanne Kelton, 'Sub plots: A Collins-class offset?', *Policy, Organisation and Society*, Special Edition, 'An American–Australian Free Trade Treaty?', vol. 20, no. 1, 2001, pp. 131–140.

capability or capacity in Australian industry'.[29] The decision to invest in this project immediately removed any question that European manufacturers would sell combat aircraft to Australia. Again, the Europeans were distanced from Australian defence purchasing. This move further contributed to the appearance of reluctance on the part of Australian policy makers toward the Europeans. Arguably too, Australia had ignored the role the EU could serve as a counterweight against US economic and military power.

By the summer of 2003, the Australian government had decided to purchase new tanks. This was despite the procurement of tanks not being identified in the 2000 Review which aimed at determining capability priorities for the next ten years. In 2003, the Army had operated approximately 100 German-built Leopard Tanks. Its choices for the replacement were whittled down to three, either: the Leopard 2, the Challenger 2 (UK) or the US Abrams. The consensus appeared to be that for the Australian regional environment the Leopard tanks were the most appropriate. Not only were they lighter and, as Australia could purchase more because of their lesser expense, this would allow both for greater flexibility and ease of deployment. Aldo Borgu has also questioned why the tanks became a priority for the armed forces. He argued that even for the US military, funds spent on the upgrade of SAS forces would be preferable to new tanks.[30] It would be an unusual choice then, if Australia should decide to purchase the US tanks on the basis of interoperability with US forces in activities outside the region.[31]

Moreover, while much is made of Australian access to US high technology equipment and source codes there remain many crucial questions regarding the quality and appropriateness of the acquisitions and technology transfers. Is Australia always the recipient of the best US military equipment? If not, why not? How effectively has the government driven this bargaining? That I have argued earlier that the government's culturally bound bargaining in its trade disputes with the US has proved flawed, gives rise to serious questions as to the nature of its bargaining in the more secret and expensive area of defence acquisitions.

Fourth, Australia's support for US global military operations in Afghanistan and more particularly Iraq, consumed its strategic focus and attention on the proliferation of WMD. This was to the detriment of its ability to monitor the deteriorating situation on the Korean peninsula and the evolution of North Korea's WMD programme.[32] Australia's preoccupation with US global interests impacted on its ability to assess and act upon strategic and economic concerns within its own region. One of the consequences of conflict on the Korean Peninsula would necessarily be the severe disruption of trade with North Asia.

---

29 Geoffrey Barker '$12 billion to buy experimental war plane', *Australian Financial Review*, 28 June 2002, pp. 1 and 18.

30 Aldo Borgu, 'The Defence Capability Review 2003: A Modest and Incomplete Review', Australian Strategic Policy Institute, 2003, pp. 4–6. Hugh White, 'Why fewer and bigger is bad for defence', *The Age*, 24 November 2003.

31 Paul Dibb and Richard Brabin-Smith, 'Cinderella's reality check', *Australian Financial Review*, 24 February 2004, p. 62.

32 Andrew O'Neil, 'Issues in Australian Foreign Policy: January to June 2003', *Australian Journal of Politics and History*, vol. 49, no. 4, December 2003, pp. 17–22.

Fifth, Australia's former chief trade negotiator for the Uruguay Round, Peter Field argued that while in the past Australia had been well regarded as a genuine third party in any agricultural negotiations, an AUSFTA with the US would immediately sap Australia's integrity in further negotiations. Potentially, it may be perceived as the 'cat's paw' in future negotiations.[33] Moreover, how would this play out in longer term economic and strategic relations with China and indeed, tripartite relations between the US, China and Australia? So, while there was an intersection of strategies propelling the agreement forward many questions remained.

Sixth, is this overlap between the two policy areas of trade and defence, a smart move in alliance relations? Russell Solomon, in his study of Australia–US trade policy-making through the 1980s, observed that Australia's frustration with US protection remained separated from the defence relationship. Here he argued that '(t)his has revealed an acknowledgment by Australian policy-makers of the overall weakness in Australia's bargaining power in relation to the US.' Furthermore, he claimed that not only did Australian policy-makers consider that any linkage would demonstrate that Australia has a greater necessity for the alliance, but that it may disrupt a sound political relationship and create electoral discontent.[34] This appears as a recurrent theme in the assessments of many of Australia's alliance analysts. William Tow has warned of the dangers of the inter-relationship between commercial and strategic issues in alliance relations, particularly as the commercial disputes can detrimentally affect the bigger picture.[35] Des Ball, too, has argued against it. Similarly, he has warned that 'the attempt to do too much' with the alliance may run counter to the overall relationship.[36] Inescapable, then, is the irony that in over intensifying relations with the US, the Howard government may counterproductively detract from the potency of its threat management practice in both the international and domestic spaces.

To be sure, this discussion is not necessarily about US imposition of its desires upon Australia; instead, it is concerned with the degree to which Australia creates an environment in which it can adeptly manage its opportunities and accept that the US interests are not always identical with its own. It is concerned with how Australia arranges the room in which it can manoeuvre.

Commercial Appeal

As the discussion above suggests, alliance ties alone are insufficient determinants for Australian trade outcomes. The FTA required commercial incentive. Mid-way through 2003 it seemed that Australia had secured a more significant profile in

33 Peter Field, *personal communication*, 11 October 2002.

34 Russell Solomon, 'Political Economy of Australia's Trade Policy – Making Towards the United States', *unpublished Ph.D thesis, University of Sydney*, Sydney, 1993, p. 248.

35 William T. Tow, 'Australia and the United States', in James Cotton and John Ravenhill, *The National Interest in a Global Era, Australia in World Affairs 1996–2000*, Oxford University Press, South Melbourne, 2001, p. 172.

36 Des Ball 'The US–Australian Alliance: History and Prospects', *SDSC Working Paper no. 330*, ANU, Canberra, January 1999.

Washington than it did prior to the military conflict in Afghanistan and the War in Iraq. This support was aided by Michael Thawley's assiduous work in cultivating relationships in Washington and the fine work of Congressional liaison officers based in the embassy. Further, Howard's friendship with Bush had secured greater Australian access to decision-makers in the US. At the Bush–Howard meeting in Crawford, Texas, Bush affirmed his relationship with Howard and confirmed that the FTA talks be completed by the year end. Haste, however, was of necessity. Given the political complications of completing a trade deal in a US election year, the sooner a deal could be struck and signed, the better. The better too for the Howard government: with the deterioration of the situation in Iraq in the latter half of 2003 and Australia's refusal to commit more combat troops at that time, the Coalition's cachet in the US was waning. Despite the presence of some 800–900 Australians in Iraq, some on civil and educative assignments, the US was increasingly frustrated with the Howard government. Australia's political and military support for the US had assisted in the motivations for negotiating the FTA deal, but with that power's dissipation other forces were needed to conclude it. Certainly, the deal would suit USTR Zoellick's competitive liberalisation strategy and provide a model for others, particularly in IP. It would also denote the centrality of the US in a new phase of global trade bargaining. Yet for Congress to be persuaded, commercial appeal was vital.

With particular groups within the US agricultural lobby, some, in electorally decisive states opposed to providing concessions to Australia as competitor, it was crucial that the US Administration construct countervailing coalitions. Relaxed screening processes in foreign investment and reorientation of manufacturing supplies to the US were certainly attractive to US commercial interests. Defence industries were not much discussed but continued to exert a powerful presence in the relationship. Both lead negotiators, Steve Deady and Ralph Ives, for Australia and the US respectively, had also stated that intellectual property concerns constituted critical interests to the US.[37]

Although Ralph Ives pointed specifically to US interest in digital technology, US pharmaceutical companies would be particularly concerned to ensure that Australia did not alter its patent rules on generic drugs for export. If alterations to some current patents were allowed in Australia this could enable Australian generic drug manufacturers to compete in the 'first to market' race in third countries. With the rise in middle class in Asia, capturing regional markets in pharmaceuticals such as basic antibiotics could be a multibillion dollar windfall. Commercially this constituted a highly persuasive motivation for the FTA to include intellectual property provisions to limit Australian generic drug manufacturers' capacity for early export. This would also indicate that similar provisions exist in the US–Singapore FTA only as a model for others. Confirmation of the interest in pharmaceuticals may be found in the

37 Steve Deady, Speech at International Business Week, sponsored by the Adelaide Office of DFAT, Stamford Plaza, Adelaide, 27 August 2003, and Ralph Ives, 'Competitive Liberalisation – The Australia–USA Free Trade Agreement', International Visitor Lecture, Institute for International Business, Economics and Law, at Flinders University, 21 October 2003. Author's notes on both occasions.

comments made by the US Industry Functional Advisory Committee on Intellectual Property Rights for Trade Policy Matters in February 2003. Their report also denoted that the committee includes representatives from PhRMA, Pfizer, Merck and Co., and Eli Lilly & Co.[38] This, of itself, could be persuasive enough to seal the deal. And yet not only has there been little public debate over the issue of intellectual property, particularly in pharmaceuticals, the Department of Industry has removed some of those papers from its website that had pointed to the need for alterations to the rules applicable to generic manufacturers. Bhagwati and Panagariya have also claimed that for Mexico the NAFTA price was 'acceptance of intellectual property provisions'. They also suggest that more broadly these agreements were models for further trade liberalisation.[39]

A further issue of concern to US pharmaceutical companies was the re-export of pharmaceuticals into the US at cheaper prices. Currently this is an issue across the Canada–US border. Not only is it of interest to US producers to curb this activity but also to prevent it being replicated by other countries. US pharmaceutical giants were also dissatisfied with the profits they were able to extract from the Australian market because of the limitations imposed by the Pharmaceutical Benefits Scheme (PBS). The USTR cited the lack of transparency in this process and the lack of an appeals process as 'problematic'.[40] As discussed in the biotechnology and pharmaceutical chapter, the US corporations believe they receive returns that are insufficient to compensate for the research and development costs inherent in the production of pharmaceuticals. Recovering these costs, would add to the profits from an assured entry into Asian markets. Ultimately then, PhRMA, as an extraordinarily potent and effective lobbyist in the US, was unusually concerned to seal the FTA deal. Politically in the US, it could also be used effectively to counteract agricultural opposition.

The Inevitable and the Ongoing

On 8 February 2004, Mark Vaile and Robert Zoellick signed the FTA with its acceptance by Congress later in the year. This signalled the completion of the Howard government's three year campaign. The security overlay, in addition to Zoellick's liberalisation agenda, had been successful in providing the momentum for progressing the deal. What necessitated an agreement of some form was the political capital devoted to the agreement by the Howard government. That it has been signed, however, does not signal its success. Nor does it yet flag a winning trade management venture by the Howard government.

38 USTR, 'The US–Singapore Free Trade Agreement (FTA): The Intellectual Property Provisions: The Report of the Industry Functional Advisory Committee on Intellectual Property Rights for Trade Policy Matters (IFAC-3)', Washington D.C., 28 February 2003, p. 13.

39 Jagdish Bhagwati and Arvind Panagariya, 'Bilateral trade treaties are a sham', *Financial Times*, 14 July 2003, p. 17.

40 See the section on pharmaceuticals in the USTR National Trade Estimates, Foreign Trade Barriers: Australia, 2003, p. 12.

It is important here that the first point of assessment should be the government's own rationale for entering into negotiations with the US – that it would deliver significant benefits to Australian agricultural producers. At once, because of the deal's failure on inclusivity, particularly on agriculture, the prospective financial benefits as publicised by the government will not be realised. To be sure, the rise in the Australian dollar vis-à-vis the greenback had already negated many of the early gains. How assertively Australian companies seek out opportunities will also be a determinant of the agreement's success.

US touting of the gains for its manufacturers too, would suggest that any efforts to ameliorate Australia's trade deficit with the US remain problematic. How the changes to US foreign investment in Australia may affect the economy probably will not be known for some time but this sector may proffer possibilities for the most significant economic benefit. Nonetheless, a trade agreement was not necessary to relinquish sovereignty constraints on foreign capital and any yielding on these issues always requires qualification. On the important issue of intellectual property and services, it would seem that there is still something to be negotiated, and much to be revealed. And even if the PBS pricing remains intact the costs of the scheme itself may escalate and the selection of pharmaceuticals may be subject to further pressure from the US drug companies. This was a point that Ambassador Thawley acknowledged upon his retirement when he noted that this signing of the deal was just the beginning and that the US would continue 'to push hard on a whole range of things'.[41] Some of the upside of this, however, was revealed in mid-2005 with the new E3 visa arrangements allowing an extra 10,000 Australians to work in the US.

It will be interesting to see too how Robert Zoellick's comments in Washington at the conclusion of the talks are realised in the future as he observed that:

> one of the major US knowledge based industries is research-based pharmaceuticals, and we had to work this issue very carefully given the importance and sensitivities of the PBS –the Pharmaceutical Benefits Scheme –in Australia. We are pleased that we were able to agree on some core principles, some processes, and ongoing efforts that reflect our mutual commitment to the value of innovation, the importance of research and development, and the therapeutic benefit of innovation.[42]

Agreement of standstill arrangements in some IP sectors, such as production of generic pharmaceuticals as explained previously, but also in the media sector and digital technology, can also preclude dramatic opportunities for growth of local companies.

Despite the speculation, it is largely impossible to know at this juncture what benefits and costs the FTA will deliver. Certainly, since NAFTA, Canadian–US trade has escalated dramatically. Yet at this point it remains difficult to assess the claims, often contradictory, that both governments have made for the agreement. That the

---

41 Michael Thawley interviewed by Leigh Sales, 'Trade important to US – Australia ties', *AM, ABC transcript*, 5 May 2005.

42 Robert Zoellick and Mark Vaile, 'Transcript of press conference with US Trade Representative, Ambassador Bob Zoellick, and Australian Minister for Trade, Mark Vaile, on conclusion of FTA negotiations in Washington, D.C.', 8 February 2004.

agreement is not inclusive, however, does flag the surrender of important broader political objectives – namely Australia's legitimacy in negotiating comprehensive trade agreements with others, either multilaterally or regionally. How can any future agreement with Japan, for example, ensure that agriculture is included? More specifically, Australia now agreed to some specific price mechanisms in this deal that have been previously denied to Japan. Some of the precedents that have been set here may create longer-term difficulties for any Australian government to manage.

Ironically too, as has been argued elsewhere, the consequences of the competitive liberalisation strategy as played out in this deal may have the reverse effect for Australia. Zoellick's intention was to raise the bar of liberalisation when other diplomatic tracks had been ineffective. Yet, through Howard's acceptance of the minimal liberalisation of agriculture in the AUSFTA, the Australian rail has been lowered for other deals. For Australia, this will be particularly applicable in prospective FTA negotiations in Asia.[43] No doubt regional partners will be interested in being offered the same agricultural platter of carve outs as the US menu. If so, the argument resonating loudly suggests that orthodox Australian trade policy with its assiduous agricultural focus has been forsaken by this agreement.

Also of concern are the related reports that some in the Australian trade negotiating team were decidedly discontent with the failure of the US to respond to Australian requests in the final phase of the talks. Despite the rejection of Howard's personal pleas that were unable to elicit a better deal for Australia, Vaile did not walk away as promised. Far from being unusual in the stable of Australia–US trade disputes, once again this marked the inability of the special relationship to deliver on material issues. This appears to be a recurring pattern throughout the Howard incumbency.

Indeed, there were increasing concerns that the *association* with the US has once again appeared as the priority in the final phase of the negotiations over and above the quality of the deal itself.[44] And any savvy US negotiator would have intimately understood the Australian domestic politics inherent in the deal. So, as it eventuated, for the government this was not the deal anticipated, and for the public, not the deal promised. If the government used the alliance to address issues of its own electoral survival, then it should come as no surprise that Howard was willing to sign on to a deal that was less than satisfactory. That ALP leader Mark Latham had expressed criticism of the US alliance, and was thus perceived to be vulnerable to political attack on this front also underscored the necessity of ensuring that the Coalition could demonstrate the strength of its ties with the US.[45] But ultimately and ironically in failing to secure a deal that reflected its initial intentions, even with Prime Ministerial intervention and supposed military leverage, what the final

43 Richard Leaver, 'The Australia–United States Free Trade Agreement: The Boomerang of Competitive Liberalisation?' *Paper presented at the Conference on Evolving Dynamics of Australia–East Asia Relations in the 21st Century*, College of International Affairs, National Chengchi University, 3 June 2005.

44 Christine Wallace, 'Lobbyists, negotiators stunned by Bush rebuff', *The Australian*, 25 February 2004, p. 2.

45 Kim Richard Nossal, 'Upper Hand Down Under: American Politics and the Australia–US Free Trade Agreement', *Paper prepared for the annual meeting of the Australian and New Zealand Studies Association of North America*, Toronto, 20–21 February 2004, p. 9.

agreement reveals is not the strength of Howard's alliance relations and its approach to managing foreign policy – but its frailty.

Of itself, this discussion underscores the difficulties in the government's choice of economic management with its concurrent interest in culturally enclosed bargaining. Though the security leverage achieved through the support of US military quests may have assisted in prompting the negotiations, this was inadequate too in delivering more substantive benefits for Australia. The instant brouhaha, as was predictable in any negotiation with the US with its consequent 'winners' and 'losers', highlights the inherent risks of arbitrating in foreign policy where the outcomes are material not cultural. If to date, the government has been successful electorally with its enthused intimacy with the US, the current national reflective assessment of the benefits and bankruptcies, in addition to the broader political consequences, may make electoral success harder to sustain.

Conclusion: The Trouble with Bonding

Of concern then, was the Howard government's desire to associate itself to a US trade policy that was coupled with a markedly assertive security posture. Even now, the government has yet to adequately explain Australia's continuing support for US defence policy. Instead, Australia, with its inherent structural constraints and finite space in which to manoeuvre policy, seems determined to limit its options and enhance US power.

Recall Michael Thawley's words that this agreement was just the starting point. Given the difficulties in negotiating this agreement, the future seems just as problematic as US trade policy looks set to be besieged by some potent pressures. In the medium term there appear to be looming contradictions for US policy that will affect the US capacity to deliver on any trade deals. At some point, pressure for the US to resolve its budget and current account deficits will intersect with its current predisposition to offer trade incentives for its allies in the war on terror. If so, it cannot be long before compliant allies are forced to accept the economic burden of the response to the terrorist attacks. Current USTR, Susan Schwab, will likely need to pursue the same specific market-opening initiatives that former USTR Barshefsky zealously employed to reduce the deficit during the Clinton presidency. These pursuits will further complicate trade relations between Australia, China and the US, much as was done in the 1980s. In 2002, although the trade deficit was greater than those of earlier years, there was not the same perception in Congress that other countries are usurping US pre-eminence. Thus, there was not the same degree of 'white heat' in recent trade politics as there was in the peaks of the two previous decades. And so, there was less pressure to implement Section 301 (of US Trade Law) market-opening measures.[46] This may not remain as the disposition, however, especially as there is both increasing antagonism in the international system and more particularly as the US finds the space to refocus on the emergence of China. Already US pressure on China spotlights a revaluing of the yuan and a reduction in

46 I.M. Destler, *personal communication*, 1 November 2002.

China's exports into the US. For some time Australia has felt the need to carefully manage its position in relation to both these powers. The pressure to do this well will only increase as questions arise over US economic ability to sustain its aggressive intervention and reconstruction posture.

No doubt US producer interests too, will influence the progress of ongoing phase-ins, the use of safeguards and future-related negotiations. Although agricultural trade barriers in the US will eventually need redressing, this was a difficult time frame for Zoellick to enact change. As much as the USTR was interested in reform, domestic political pressures obstructed the negotiations, even despite the support for his campaign for trade to enhance security objectives. In short, it was inopportune to deal effectively with Australia in this sector. As many knew, the bigger picture on agricultural issues was always etched on the multilateral canvass. But through this deal Australia may even have sacrificed its legitimacy in this arena. Nonetheless, that Chile could have negotiated much better agricultural outcomes in its bilateral FTA dealings with the US flags the inadequacy of the Australian approach. And that in the longer term Mexico also discovered that sugar producers in the US were able to claw back some of the concessions cited in the NAFTA agreement raises some concerns for the phase-in gains in this sector more generally. For Zoellick's own interest in real trade reform in the US, particularly in agriculture, it might have been 'the right war but the wrong time.'[47]

There was also the impetus for Zoellick's competitive liberalisation and a manifestation of his truism that '(i)n trade as in politics, one can't beat something with nothing' in multilateral trade strategy.[48] But in sum, this was inadequate to override the political capital that was needed to elicit Congressional support for the agricultural liberalisation in an election year. It was impotent in swaying the sugar and dairy producers in the US, in Florida, the state that delivered the Bush incumbencies. Across the Pacific through the AUSFTA negotiation process itself, Australia also had little to offer in tariff or quota concessions. Yet it was politically necessary for the Howard government to sign off on a deal with its alliance partner. So the offerings in the negotiations lay in the WTO plus arrangements. Certainly there were gains to be had for the US in investment and specific sectors such as quarantine relaxation, media rights, government procurement, intellectual property and pharmaceutical control. And even though the explicit linking of security and trade in US Congressional minds was persuasive in initiating the discussions, it was this, the material commercial interests, that convinced the US to seal the deal.

---

47 I.M. Destler, *personal communication*, 1 November 2002.

48 Robert Zoellick, 'Zoellick says US trade strategy advocates openness', *Wall St. Journal*, 10 July 2003.

Conclusion

'More than an Ally'?

Former US Deputy Secretary of State, Richard Armitage, as he often enjoyed doing on his regular visits to Australia, upped the ante in the descriptions of the Australia–US relationship. He thought of Australia as much more than an ally.[1] Over more than a decade in office, the Howard government had done much to intensify Australia's relationship with the United States. It did so as it endeavoured to deliver strategic and economic outcomes for Australia but also to enhance its own domestic standing. In this process the government's intentions have been primarily founded on material perceptions of threat, yet also influenced by Australia's historical and cultural orientation.

Problematic however, was the inherent uncertainty in the delivery of outcomes for the smaller power in asymmetrical bargaining. Undoubtedly, on set issues there are a plethora of factors that can shrink the relational power factor. Obviously, where the importance of the issue was lesser for the greater power, gains could be made in the bargaining process. The contextual environment could also be persuasive in determining the outcomes. Nonetheless, power politics remained as the overarching determinant of results. If the issue was of significance to the greater power then the resources and leverage it could bring to bear on the outcome was decisive. However, even if the Howard government's threat perception was materially premised, its trade bargaining initially was culturally bound. What it also created was an air of expectation and reciprocity. The government, then, needed to demonstrate publicly how the relationship was of benefit. Hence, there existed a perceived need to legalise trade arrangements and attempt to employ the use of material factors to enhance leverage in this bargaining process.

The government's natural desire to retain incumbency and its consequent attention to managing domestic politics was also crucial to its decision-making. Bipartisanship has been a feature of past Australian governments' commitment to the US alliance, and the recent Labor governments were no different in their assiduous affirmation of the relationship. Regional relations of the mid-1990s and static global trade relations of the late 1990s assisted in creating the aura of bilateral attractiveness. Fashioning an environment where the crisis dynamic of strategic and economic uncertainty was linked enabled the government to intensify these relations with some vigour. Playing to the security 'crises' of Timor, Terror and Tampa, effectively created the breach whereby the government could justify its policy of greater intimacy with the US. This

---

1 Kim Beazley's assessment of Richard Armitage's speech to the Asia Society Forum in 'Self-Reliance Before Dependency', *Australian Financial Review*, 14 August 2003, p. 63. Richard Armitage, 'Deputy Secretary of State Armitage delivers remarks at the Asia Society Forum', Sydney, *FDCH*, 13 August 2003.

was coupled with the sense that the Hawke and Keating governments had moved too quickly in reshaping Australia. Intuitively then, the Howard government acted to remove the tension from the security/identity nexus. Thus, the Coalition's choice of bilateralism with the US, despite the logic and recent trade diplomatic practice of multilateralism as the most appropriate choice for Australia, became explicable, if not entirely defensible. It also became electorally successful.

Bilateralism as a Strategy

Initially, the Howard government's endeavours in this culturally bound bargaining process were tested in the lamb tariff and Howe leather disputes. Trading on a culturally informed relationship in both instances proved inadequate to resolve the disputes along the lines that the government would have wished. It expected that the US would acquiesce in its solutions for resolution. In the Howe dispute it had hoped that the US government would allow Australia to continue to support its car leather manufacturer financially to improve its export performance into the US market. Yet this would be at the expense of local US manufacturers in Michigan and Pennsylvania. Reversing the roles, where the US sought to assist its lamb producers through imposition of tariffs, the Howard government rallied to remove them. Howard's meeting with Clinton in Washington yielded nothing. US intransigence remained consistent with its behaviour in many trade disputes with Australia in previous years. The flaw in both instances was that Australia expected that the US Administration would overrule its domestic constituencies, in these cases both represented by vocal lobby groups and legal advocates, in addition to the processes of US trade law, in favour of their small ally in the Southwest Pacific. Australia's test of the effectiveness of US trade law to protect their constituencies received a resounding response in the demonstration that the US would act to ensure its commitment to its citizens. Australian cultural bargaining was circumscribed by its failure to acknowledge the material nationalism inherent in US policy implementation.

Failure to resolve these disputes through any personal or government-to-government discussions resulted in recourse to the multilateral dispute settlement mechanism of the WTO. Ignoring Australian assumptions, the US contested Australian government assistance to Howe. Furthermore, if Australia did not act to remove all assistance to Howe, then the US, through the WTO, would consider cross-sectoral retaliation. Wine makers in Australia were mortified at the prospect. Abolition of lamb tariffs, similarly, was not achieved through bilateral intergovernmental channels. Australia, as a small power, eventually recognised the impotence of its position and retreated to the leverage of the multilateral international rules-based system. So, although the government had opened with a policy of unencumbered bilateralism, it soon discovered that its understanding of its relationship with the US was inadequate. To alter the dynamics it would also need to deploy material factors.

Events in East Timor in 1999 confirmed the importance of the US relationship for Australia. US structural power in the international system enabled Australia to intervene in the crisis. Despite the Clinton Administration's initial reluctance to supply troops, the US decision to exercise diplomatic and economic leverage over

Indonesia to facilitate the entry of the UN force led by Australia into East Timor proved invaluable. Indonesia's initial intransigence to any multilateral action created a dangerous scenario for the Australian government – to enter Timor (Indonesian sovereign territory) without consent would have been an act of war. US intervention overcame the impasse for Australia. The US too, in the protection of its own interests, needed to maintain stability in the archipelago. Although the US did not deploy the 31st Marine Expeditionary Unit from the USS *Belleau Wood*, their presence constituted a deterrent to those forces in East Timor contemplating the perpetuation of further destruction. The provision of US intelligence and crucial logistical support did much to assist the smooth operation of the military campaign. It is clear that for Australia, especially when its own resources are inadequate, the friendship of a powerful ally with a *convergent* interest is invaluable.

US attractions for Australia are many and diverse. Knowledge-based and high-tech sectors constructed on Australia's educated workforce can strengthen Australia's international economic position. US venture capital and markets are vital in this process. Concurrently, however, there exists a need for the government to mediate between these requirements and those relating to the provision of adequate and affordable health care in Australia. Pressure from the US pharmaceutical lobby group, PhRMA, aims to influence the Australian government's maintenance of particular provisions in intellectual property that enable Australians to have access to affordable medicines and preserve a viable pharmaceutical industry. Through the FTA, it has acquiesced on the issue of intellectual property protection for its generic manufacturers.

Threat mediation in this sector reveals the competing interests and choices that the government must manage. Across specific governmental negotiations, Australia acted within multilateral organisations to resist the pressure of major global powers to write the IP rules to suit their interests. Bilateralism, however, is often a US preference. Ideally suited to its great power status, the US has much to gain in bilateral negotiations.[2] In its efforts to maintain control over the processes in this sector, it has elected to avoid APEC in favour of individual negotiations with member states. On trade-related intellectual property negotiations conducted at a multilateral level, Australia has continued in its endeavours to arbitrate between the interests of the major players and developing countries in order to provide better global outcomes.

Provision of national security in all its forms – basic needs, strategic, economic – is the responsibility of all governments. In each of the sectors reviewed, in the examination of its delivery, it is clear that internal and external risks must be managed. Where the government becomes pre-occupied with its own survival, however, this becomes a much politicised process. This was no more evident than in the case of the *Collins* class submarine project. In this venture, the government's own aims conspicuously assumed primacy over the realisation of an independent shipbuilding project in Australia. The government's political status took precedence over a recognition that Australia had delivered on an outstanding high-tech project.

---

2 Coral Bell, 'The Future of American Policy in the Pacific', in Gary Klintworth (ed.), *Asia–Pacific Security: Less Uncertainty, New Opportunities?*, Addison Wesley Longman, Melbourne, 1996, p. 31.

While the US contributed to the performance of the submarines, it is debatable whether the US, with no expertise in conventional submarine construction, could be touted as the saviour of the project. Interoperability with the US is unquestionably an asset for Australia, as is the access to appropriate high technology equipment, but it cannot exist at the expense of capability. To assume that ongoing access to high technology would have been jeopardised had Australia not sought US involvement in this project overdraws the long bow. Undoubtedly, as the *Collins* project emanated from Beazley's vision (and as responsive to the RAN's requirements), the government could benefit politically from any setbacks in the project. John Moore and Peter Reith relentlessly criticised the project to disparage the then popular leader of the Opposition and created the public space for US assistance. Consequently, the government netted simultaneous political gain and more intimate bilateral ties with the US. In the wake of this study, however, were an independent multi-billion dollar naval shipbuilding industry and a major component of Australia's strategic self-reliance.

Parallel Engagement

Parallel security developments have also influenced outcomes. After the dismal trade disputes in the early years of the Howard government, if the government were to pursue bilateralism then it would need to continue to deploy material components. After the terrorist attacks on New York and Washington on 11 September 2001, Howard signaled his intent to support the US in a sustained fashion, and invoked the ANZUS Treaty. Speaking at the National Press Club not long afterwards, Howard also connected the security issues to Australia's border protection.[3] The linking of the sovereign border issue also reverberated with domestic politics. That he was present in Washington at the time of the attacks no doubt contributed to the depth of his personal response. Moreover, a change in actors in the Administration from Clinton to Bush enabled Howard to strike a much greater degree of personal affinity with a US President.

Australian SAS troops, military and medical personnel were dispatched to Afghanistan to counter Taliban and al-Qaeda networks. Here they formed part of a coalition of countries supporting the US in its response to the assaults. Empathy for the US post 11 September was abundant as many countries had also lost their citizens in the attacks. Yet that much larger coalition of countries involved in Afghanistan was whittled down significantly in the pre-emptive action against Iraq. Explaining why the government was enlisting in the war in Iraq, Howard provided two reasons. Initially he claimed to assist in the removal of Iraq's weapons of mass destruction. Second, the deployment was an affirmation of Australia's security alliance with the United States and its 'crucial' importance to Australia's regional security interests.[4]

---

3 *Transcript of the Prime Minister, The Hon John Howard MP, National Press Club Address, Canberra,* 8 November 2001, p. 2.

4 John Howard, *Transcript of the Prime Minister, The Hon John Howard MP, Address to the Nation,* 20 March 2003, p. 2 and John Howard, *Transcript of the Prime Minister, The Hon John Howard MP, Prime Ministerial Statement to Parliament on Iraq,* 4 February 2003, pp. 11–12.

Once Bush declared the conclusion of the strikes, Howard had deftly removed the majority of Australian troops from Iraq. Yet, given the enormity of the security and reconstruction task, ADF personnel still remained present in Iraq and Afghanistan in 2007. Plaudits were, of course, won from the US for this military and political support. After the contribution in Afghanistan, George W. Bush described Howard as 'a close personal friend' and one who 'sees the threats that the free world faces as we go into the 21st century'.[5] These connections deepened Australia's decision to provide material support to the US in its pre-emptive action in Iraq. By 2007 too, they had skewed Australian defence policy to a global orientation, despite its limitations of resources and influence.

Could backing for US military action realise some material responsiveness in the trade relationship and exact greater leverage in trade outcomes? Unusual in Australia's 'new' relationship with the US was the fresh attempt to publicly integrate trade and security policy. The US imposed tariff restrictions on a range of imported steel products for domestic reasons. Not only was it acting to protect an ailing steel industry and construct electoral capital in steel city communities, it was also attempting to generate the political capital to win approval for Trade Promotion Authority. Spawning the political resources for electoral success in the steel states and garnering enough Congressional votes for TPA may have been achievable, yet its ability to stave off further traditional steel producer bankruptcies was limited.

The US implementation of steel tariffs and Australia's eventual receipt of select exemptions disclose how the Bush Administration had attempted to both reward its coalition friends and coerce others to extend strategic support. The pattern of exclusions revealed international political intent. US allies, including Australia, were given reprieves in the severity and extent of tariff application. Implied in the motivations for this leniency was the nature of Australia's close support of the US. Howard's claim that Australia and the US had never been closer gave impetus to this. Nonetheless, commercial arrangements were crucial to the allocation of exemptions. That BHP Billiton exported products vital to mills in the US, and thus US domestic commerce and employment, was imperative in gaining tariff exclusions for Australia. The primacy of US domestic interests coincided here with Australia's requests. Revealed in the pattern of exclusions was a synchronisation of both US and Australian economic and military interests. Though the exclusions delivered a welcome reprieve for Australia in the immediate term, the whole affair confirmed a global perception of US unilateralism and clouded the climate for multilateral negotiations.

Some synchronicity of political purpose was also evident initially in the talks surrounding the AUSFTA. USTR Zoellick realised an opportunity to further his strategy of trade liberalisation through its union with broader US Administration security objectives. This strategy also enshrined the centrality of the US in any liberalising process. Once again, the Howard government's aims had intersected temporarily with those of the US Administration (if not Congress). For Howard, the pursuit of a trade agreement with the US was logical given the explanation of

5 'Remarks by the President and Prime Minister Howard of Australia in Photo Opportunity', *News Release, Office of the Press Secretary*, The Oval Office, 10 February 2003, p. 1.

his motivations in upgrading the relationship. Mediating threats for the Howard government had centralised the place of the US in Australia's foreign relationships. However, as these choices in mediation involved a process of culturally bound bargaining with military and industrial backing, there were obviously risks attached. Both personal and political costs were incurred by Australia's continued military commitment to the US. Even though the Howard government could cite its loyal support for US military activity as a means to sway US decision-making, it was unable to exact sufficient leverage in producing the type of deal it touted initially as the US implicitly understood the weaknesses in Australia's bargaining position. That the US has substantial deficits with which to deal but at the same time acknowledges that economic success sustains its military status,[6] will always ensure that trade gains, even for allies, are not easily bought.

There is no doubt, nevertheless, that there will be specific gains for traders. US capital and markets remain crucial for Australia's continued economic development. Yet, a longer-term analysis is necessary to document just how successful the AUSFTA will be. In the short term, however, it is possible to raise four concerns. First, the less-than-inclusive agreement detracts from Australia's ability to represent its broader interests in multilateral negotiations and commensurately sacrifices any remaining authority of the Cairns Group. It is worthwhile remembering that it is only in this multilateral arena where there is any possibility of systematically reducing the massive subsidies paid to US producers and those of EU and Japanese interests. More specifically, the proposed agreement detracts from Australia's ability to negotiate comprehensive agreements within the region. It would appear that in its mediation priorities, the Howard government was prepared to surrender this agricultural leadership.[7] Second, while opportunities for increased investment are likely, the longer-term demands that may result from specific negotiations, particularly Australia's ability to utilise new technologies and in the future realisation of intellectual property, may detract from the quality of the Agreement. Third, overall, trade is most likely to increase but it is unlikely that the trade deficit with the US will be reduced. Fourth, to date the government has signed a number of trade agreements but so far has yet to demonstrate that this outlay of political and bureaucratic capital has produced the outcomes it has desired.

Access. And Influence?

Clearly, the change in US Administration in 2000 was advantageous to the Coalition and to Howard personally. Where the Clinton Administration had been largely unresponsive to specific Howard government requests through the two initial trade disputes, and in the East Timor crisis acted in its own interests to ensure stability in Southeast Asia, the Bush Administration appeared more receptive to Howard. Open displays of friendship between the two leaders, in set pieces such as the Shanghai

6 Michael Lind, *The American Way of Strategy*, Oxford University Press, Oxford, 2006, p. 225.

7 Mark Beeson, 'Australia's Relationship with the United States: The Case for Greater Independence', *Australian Journal of Political Science*, vol. 38, no. 3, November 2003, p. 391.

APEC meetings, were often politically profitable. However, to return to the perennial question in Australia–US relations: could this translate into genuine influence when Australian interests diverged from those of the US? Problematic here for Australia was the nature of US power. Although Howard may have done much to centralise foreign policy-making in Australia, Bush, who gained office in controversial circumstances, remained beholden to many actors. Congress and domestic lobby groups, including those not always sympathetic to Australian concerns, needed to be feted by the Administration: a point that seemed less understood by the Australian government in its implementation of bilateralism with the US. Political coalitions necessary for the retention of power in the US, and to manufacture a range of US foreign policy objectives, needed to be constructed. Australian preferences were hardly a priority, and, in some circumstances directly antithetical to the interests of a number of potent US stakeholders. Particularly antagonistic were specific agricultural and IP lobby groups. Congressional legislation, such as that restricting the international trade in arms, provided further limitations on US assistance. Therefore, even if the Administration felt inclined to negotiate favourably with Australia, its ability to do so was constrained by the legitimacy of its power[8] and the Administration's need to mediate threat in the US.[9]

If it is argued that Australia's cultural interests were similar to those of the US, can it also be said that its security and commercial interests always were similar? The alliance enhances prospects for Australian influence in a region where its relative clout will decline as other states' population and economic status increases. Good management of the alliance, therefore, is crucial to Australia's long-term interests. However, serious matters circle the current bilateral policy approach. The failure to deliver the stated trade outcomes and the grave outcomes of pre-emptive action in Iraq expose a defective approach.[10] Yet contextually there is more to consider. Although US unilateralism has existed in conjunction with its multilateral policy partner throughout the twentieth century, the unilateralism of the Bush Administration was distinctive. Despite the flaws inherent in the Kyoto Protocol and the International Criminal Court, they represented the best consensual multilateral effort. The Bush Administration's retreat from each highlighted the US belief in an 'exceptionalism' that eschewed leadership. Its abrogation of the ABM Treaty reinforced this point. The US desired allied cooperation but largely determined the terms and conditions.[11] US action in Iraq has compromised its perceived role as benign hegemon while simultaneously failing to improve its security position.[12]

---

8 Franz Schurmann, *The Logic of World Power*, Pantheon Books, New York 1974.

9 See Glenn P. Hastedt, *American Foreign Policy: Past, Present, Future*, Fifth Edition Prentice Hall, New Jersey, 2003, particularly pp. 125–243.

10 See for example, Louis Fisher, 'Deciding on War Against Iraq: Institutional Failures', *Political Science Quarterly*, vol. 118, no. 3, 2003, pp. 389–410.

11 Michael Cox, 'US Grand Strategy: Implications for Alliance Partners', Keynote Address, *Centre for Defence and Strategic Studies Conference*, Canberra, 1 August 2003.

12 Martin Griffiths, 'Self Inflicted Wounds: The United States Grand Strategy and the War on Terror', *paper presented to the Australasian Political Science Association Conference, University of Tasmania*, Hobart, 29 September – 1 October 2003.

As always, context is important. Until the 1990s, the US was constrained by the Cold War balance of power and sought to use Western institutions to contain Soviet power globally. Thus, the Howard government was dealing with a US superpower feeling unconstrained. Commenting specifically on the Howard government's approach to the US, Chris Reus-Smit identified three concerns. These were: that the government assumed the Bush Doctrine was rational, that it believed it could translate material power into political outcomes and that it could best secure 'Australia's national interests' through uncritical support of the US. As such, this represents a unique posture amongst Australian governments. Where in the past former governments have supported the US alliance; most have done so cognisant of the need for either a balance of power and/or the necessity of institutional constraint.[13] Through the studies in this book, it is clear that in addition to the need for adept management of the US alliance, Australia has interests that are dependent upon international order as supported by a framework of international rules and smooth global political relationships.

Conclusion: Bilateral Fragility but Raised Expectations

That Australia has become more, not less, dependent upon US power also raises the stakes. Material threat perception, plus an orientation tilted by Australia's historical legacy, the cultural cachet, and an overriding desire to retain power motivated the government to raise the stakes in the relationship. Current Australian policy has created an expectation of reciprocity that is more pervasive, but an expectation that may be detrimental to the alliance. That the predictability of US support is unknown except to the extent that it coincides with US interests, has driven Australia to support US global aims, which at times have been at the expense of Australia's own interests. Yet convergence and reciprocity remain context specific.

Integration of defence and trade policy as a consequence of this government's evolving threat mediation choices complicates the relationship for Australia and demands more sophisticated diplomacy. While there is agreement on the general principles of trade in the bilateral relationship, the immediate negotiations continue to evidence a much greater degree of conflict.[14] The annual reviews of the AUSFTA may well enshrine this dilemma. If this conflict were to spill over into the ANZUS security relationship, a vital relationship for Australia, it would be antithetical both to Australia's interests and to the government's quest in upgrading the relationship.

---

13 Chris Reus-Smit, US Grand Strategy and Australia, *Centre for Defence and Strategic Studies Conference*, Canberra, 1 August 2003, p. 1. See also Stuart Harris, US Grand Strategy: Implications for Australia's Relations with Northeast Asia', *Centre for Defence and Strategic Studies Conference*, Canberra, 1 August 2003 and Josef Joffe, 'Hubs, Spokes and Public Goods', *In the National Interest*, 30 October 2002, p. 4.

14 Stuart Harris, 'International Economic Orientations: Australia', in Richard W. Baker and Gary R. Hawke (ed.), *ANZUS Economics: Economic Trends and Relations Among Australia, New Zealand, and the United States*, Praeger, Westport, 1992, pp. 73–90.

Another dimension of this issue is the desirability of any shift from self-reliance to strategic interdependence:[15] the question of the 'more than an ally' status. What might this mean? Over three decades ago Kenneth Waltz pointed to the pitfalls of the interdependence nomenclature in the economic realm. He argued that the rhetoric of interdependence often masked a fundamental dependence and 'subtly obscure(d) the inequalities of national capability'.[16] Given the argument in this book that Australian and US interests need to coincide to ensure reciprocity, it is now more pressing to engage in discussion of the political and strategic appeal of interdependence.

It is axiomatic that mediation choices are complex and the pursuit of long-term interests requirements are more demanding given the electoral process.[17] It is also manifest that times have changed. Any nostalgia for a simple reincarnation of the Hawke–Keating mediation policies would be misplaced too. Their intent that APEC would bind the US to Asia in ways that would ameliorate trade relationships for Australia has unraveled. Instead, policies responsive to the changed regional environment need to incorporate an understanding of Australia's longer-term concerns. That some of these choices may not seem electorally attractive underscores the difficulty of mediation.

One issue requiring attention for Australian governments is the changing regional environment. China's and India's rise add to the conglomeration of great powers in the region. Not only is the mediation question here that of securing Australia's place in East Asia, but it demands an assessment of what choices it can make to assist stability and balance there. Further, former World Bank President, James Wolfensohn, commented on the challenge for Australia as a wealthy country to assist in reducing the disparity and fundamental poverty in the region. He observed that Australia has played some role previously in multilateral negotiations in 'trying to bring along countries that are unable to negotiate and really in a way represent them'. Moreover, he argued that 'unless we have multilateral rule-based systems which cover everybody, you run the risk of rich countries doing deals and leaving out the rest of the world.' With the numbers of those living in poverty set to increase dramatically, particularly in Australia's region, this challenge is exacerbated.[18] It is worth reiterating at this moment, too, that any attempt to maintain both expertise and stability in the region also increases the value of Australia as alliance partner. Ultimately, it may be recognised that Australia has contributed more to the alliance with its mostly effective post-ballot military assistance in East Timor than in its campaign in Iraq.

---

15 As determined by Rod Lyon and William T. Tow in 'The Future of the Australian–US Security Relationship', *Strategic Studies Institute, US Army War College*, Carlisle, December 2003, p. 34.

16 Kenneth N. Waltz, 'The Myth of Interdependence' in *The International Corporation*, A symposium edited by Charles P. Kindleberger, The MIT Press, Cambridge, Massachusetts, 1970, p. 220.

17 Allan Gyngell and Michael Wesley, *Making Australian Foreign Policy*, Cambridge University Press, Cambridge, 2003, p. 256.

18 James Wolfensohn, 'President of the World Bank talks about development', 7.30 Report, *ABC Television*, February 2004.

Consideration of the events in spring 2003 in Australia also provide an opportunity for some final insights on the mediation of threat at the close of this study. At this time, at the completion of the APEC meeting in Thailand, both George Bush and Hu Jintao visited Australia. Howard had attempted to mediate between international and domestic threats through a repositioning of the US alliance at the forefront of Australian policy. During the Bush visit in mid-October 2003, he identified the strength of the cultural and historical connection as it explained both states' pre-emptive military action in addressing a global security threat: a threat perceived to be posed by al-Qaeda in conjunction with regimes in Afghanistan and Iraq. Little was imparted at that time, however, in explaining how the US would assist Australia to overcome its economic vulnerabilities, particularly as it might be informed by the Trade Agreement.[19] By contrast, however, the Chinese President, Hu Jintao, commenting in addition to the political, cultural and security aspects of the Sino-Australian relationship, pointed to the two 'highly complementary' economies and Australia's importance as an economic partner. In 2002, China was Australia's third largest trading partner. Furthermore, at that time it was Australia's fastest growing and fourth largest export market.[20] However, China understood implicitly the Howard government's need to mediate both internationally and domestically, and utilised this politically to secure a favourable bargain on the NW shelf gas deal.[21] Having accommodated US terms in the AUSFTA will there be continued pressure to extend favourable arrangements with China? Therefore, by choosing to focus on short term gains, the government has constrained not only the options but also the opportunity that threat mediation can present in the future.

Throughout this book, I have used the threat mediation thesis to provide an understanding of the Howard government's choices in foreign policy. In this scenario, the national interest as perceived by the Howard government has arbitrated between both the international and domestic. By integrating a traditional material perception of threat bound by cultural preferences and an attentiveness to the domestic environment, including its re-election, the Howard government has clearly chosen to prioritise the US alliance. Its initial attempts to implement the ensuing culturally bound bargaining proved flawed however. Moreover, its endeavours to pursue greater intimacy through the overlay of security and commercial support for the US in effecting bargains have only been successful where Australia's interests have coincided with US preferences. What has been revealed is the structural fragility of this middle ranking US ally's bilateral threat mediation choices over the previous decade.

---

19 President Bush Addresses Australian Parliament, The Australian Parliament House, The White House, news release, October 2003.

20 President Hu Jintao's 'Address to the Federal Parliament of the Commonwealth of Australia: Building a Better Future Together for the China–Australia Relationship of All-round Cooperation', *Embassy of the People's Republic of China in Australia*, 24 October 2003 and 'FM hails success of President Hu's visits', *Embassy of the People's Republic of China in Australia*, 28 October 2003.

21 See Michael Costello's comments on this on 'Friday Forum', transcript, *Lateline, ABC Television*, 24 October 2003, particularly pp. 3–4.

Bibliography

Primary Sources

ABARE (1998a), 'Agricultural Outlook for 1998–9', *Australian Commodities*, vol. 5, no. 3, September, Canberra.

—— (1998b), 'Agriculture Outlook for 1998–9', *Australian Commodities*, vol. 5, no. 4, December, Canberra.

—— (2001a), 'Forecasts and Issues', *Australian Commodities*, March quarter, Canberra.

—— (2001b), 'Minerals and Energy', *Australian Commodities*, vol. 8, no. 4, December quarter, Canberra.

Abbott, Frederick M. (2006), 'Intellectual Property Provision of Bilateral and Regional Trade Agreements in Light of US Federal Law', UNCTAD and the International Centre for Trade and Sustainable Development Project on IPRs and Sustainable Development, Issue Paper No. 12, February.

Abetz, Eric (2000), Parliamentary Secretary to the Minister for Defence, 'Abetz opens Raytheon's new naval and engineering centre', *Media Release*, Parlsec 289/00, 13 October.

ACIL Consulting (2003), 'A Bridge Too Far? An Australian Agricultural Perspective on the Australia/United States Free Trade Area Idea', Commissioned by the Rural Industries Research and Development Corporation, February.

Albright, Madeleine K. (1998), 'US–Australia ties built on shared values, interests', *Address to the Australasia Centre of the Asia Society*, Sydney Opera House, US Department of State transcript, <http://usinfo.state.gov/regional/ea/easec/austasia.htm>.

—— (1999a), 'East Timor Crisis: US others consider "variety of options" re Timor terror', transcript, 7 September, US Department of State, <http://usinfo.state.gov/regional/ea/timor/alb907.htm>.

—— (1999b), 'Indonesia, the United States and Democracy', Secretary of State remarks at the Borobodur Intercontinental Hotel, Jakarta, 5 March, <http://secretary.state.gov/www/statements/1999/990305a.html>.

Armitage, Richard (2003), 'Deputy Secretary of State Armitage delivers remarks at the Asia Society Forum', *FDCH*, Sydney, 13 August.

AusBiotech (2003), 'Growing Australia's biotech through improved access to people and capital: updated recognition for changes to taxation', Canberra, February.

Australian Biotechnology Association (1999), 'Australian Science Capability Review: A Submission from the Australian Biotechnology Association', 16 December <http://www.aba.asn.au/pages/science_cap.htm>. N.B. Renamed in 2001, as AusBiotech, located at <http://www.ausbiotech.org/main.php>.

—— undated, submission to Biotechnology Australia on the discussion paper 'Developing Australia's Biotechnology Future', <http://www.aba.asn.au/pages. biotech_future.htm>, accessed September 2001.

Australian APEC Study Centre (2001), 'An Australia–USA Free Trade Agreement: Issues and Implications', commissioned and published by DFAT, Canberra, August, <http://www.dfat.gov.au>.

Australian Bureau of Statistics (1990–2002), *Yearbook* (various years), AGPS, Canberra.

Australian Science and Technology Council (1993), 'Gene technology: Issues for Australia', *Occasional Paper No. 27*, AGPS, August, Canberra.

Australian Trade Commission, *Annual Reports*, 1996–1999, Canberra.

Barshefsky, Charlene (1997), 'Testimony to the US Senate Finance Committee', 29 January, <http://www.ustr.gov/testimony/barshefsky_6.html>.

—— (1999), 'Toward the Pacific Community: American Trade Policy in Asia', *Speech to the Asia Society,* New York.

Baucus, Max (2002), 'Testimony in the 'Hearing on Lumber and Steel trade Disputes', *Senate Finance Committee, FDCH Political Transcripts*, Washington D.C. 13 February.

Beazley, Kim (1996), 'The case for submarines 7and 8', *Press Release*, Adelaide, 23 July.

—— (2002), 'Reflections on the war on terror', *paper presented at the Australian Homeland Security: Who is Responsible? Conference*, National Convention Centre, Canberra.

—— (2003) 'Self-Reliance before Dependency', *Australian Financial Review*, 14 August, 63.

Berger, Sandy (1999), 'Clinton consults allies on how to 'intensify pressure', *Remarks by National Security Advisor Sandy Berger,* 10 September.

BHP Billiton (2002), 'BHP Steel Vows to Meet Challenge of US S.201 Impact', *news release*, 6 March.

BHP Steel (2002), 'BHP Steel Secures Tariff Exemption for Exports to Key US Customer', *News Item*, 11 March.

Briggs, Peter (1999), Submarine Capability Team Briefing, *Transcript of Press Conference*, Canberra, 23 July.

British Joint Intelligence Committee (2002), 'Iraq's Weapons of Mass Destruction: The Assessment of the British Government', 24 September, <http://www.number-10.gov.uk/output/page271.asp>.

Bush, George W. (2001), 'Transcript of remarks by the President to Steelworkers Picnic at Mon Valley Works', US Steel Group, Pittsburgh, Pennsylvania, *Office of the Press Secretary*, 26 August.

—— (2002a), Address to the UN General Assembly, New York, 12 September.

—— (2002b), 'Fact Sheet: Regarding the Presidential Action on Steel', The White House, *Office of the Press Secretary*, 5 March.

—— (2002c), 'President Announces Temporary Safeguards for Steel Industry', *Statement by the President, The White House, Office of the Press Secretary*, Washington, DC, March.

—— (2002d), 'The President's State of the Union Address', the US Capitol, Washington D.C., Office of the Press Secretary, 29 January.

—— (2003a), 'President Bush Addresses Australian Parliament', The Australian Parliament House, October.

—— (2003b), 'The President's State of the Union Address' at the US Capitol, Washington D.C., Office of the Press Secretary, 28 January.

Bush, George W. and John Howard (2003a), 'Remarks by the President and Prime Minister Howard of Australia in Photo Opportunity', *news release,* Office of the Press Secretary, The Oval Office, 10 February.

Cairns Group, undated, 'Biosafety Protocol Could Erect New Barriers to Trade', *news release,* <http://www.cairnsgroupfarmers.org/ni/reportspapers/biosafety.htm>, accessed March 2005.

Christopher, Warren (1996), 'The US and Australia meet the challenges of the new millennium', *speech by US Secretary of State, transcript*, 29 July.

Clinton, Bill (1999a), 'President's Statement on East Timor: US Role in East Timor Peacekeeping Force', *The White House,* Office of the Press Secretary, 16 September.

—— (1999b), 'The eyes of the world today…are on East Timor', *transcript of President's remarks at CEO Summit Breakfast*, 12 September.

Cohen, William (1999a), Secretary of Defense, 'Countries in region must do their part for peace', *interview transcript*, 29 September, <http://usinfo.state.gov/regional/ea/timor/cohen929.htm>.

—— (1999b), Statement by US Defense Secretary William S Cohen after meeting with General Wiranto, 30 September, <http://usinfo.state.gov/regional/ea/timor/cohen930.htm>. Accessed July 2000.

—— (1999c), Transcript: Defense Secretary Cohen Remarks on Situation in East Timor (Says there is no plan to send US peacekeepers), Pentagon, 8 September, <http://usinfo.state.gov/regional/ea/timor/cohen908.htm>.

Cohen, William and John Moore (1999), *Joint Press Briefing*, Darwin, 29 September, <http://www.defenselink.mil:80/news/Sep1999/t09291999_t09299coh.html>.

—— (2000), 'Transcript of the Joint Press Conference with US Defense Secretary William Cohen and Defence Minister John Moore following the signing of a statement of principles between two allies designed to enhance defence cooperation in the Asia–Pacific and Australian access to US technology', Sydney, 17 July.

Commonwealth of Australia, various years, *Official Yearbook of the Commonwealth of Australia*, AGPS, Canberra.

—— (1987), 'Report on the Iron and Steel Industry', *House of Representatives Standing Committee on Finance and Public Administration*, November.

—— (1989–2003a), Parliamentary Debates, House of Representatives *(CPD), Hansard*, AGPS, Canberra.

—— (1989–2003b), Parliamentary Debates, Senate *(CPD), Hansard*, AGPS, Canberra.

—— (1992), Audit Report No. 22, 1992–93, *New Submarine Project,* AGPS, 1992.

—— (1997), 'ANZUS Alliance', *Joint Standing Committee on Foreign Affairs, Defence and Trade,* Canberra.

—— (1998a), 'Health and Medical Research Strategic Review Discussion Paper', AGPS, Canberra, December.

—— (1998b), 'New Submarine Project', Audit Report No. 34, 1997–8, *The Joint Committee of Public Accounts and Audit*, tabled on 25 March, released in June 1999, AGPS, Canberra.

—— (1999a), Biotechnology Australia, 'Developing Australia's Biotechnology Future', *Discussion Paper*, AGPS, Canberra, September.

—— (2001), 'Australia's Biotechnology Report 2001', with Ernst and Young and Freehills, AGPS, Canberra.

—— (2007), DEST Portfolio, Budget Statement 2007–08, Outcome 5, Canberra, May.

Crean, Simon (2003), *Transcript of speech at the farewell ceremony for HMAS Kanimbula*, 23 January.

Dauth, John (1999), testimony of the Deputy Secretary DFAT (South and Southeast Asia Division, Public Diplomacy, South Pacific, Africa and Middle East Divisions), 'Economic, social and political conditions in East Timor', *Senate Foreign Affairs, Defence and Trade References Committee, Proof Committee Hansard*, 6 December.

Deady, Steve (2002), 'Consideration of Budget Estimates', *Senate Foreign Affairs, Defence and Trade Legislation Committee, Proof Committee Hansard*, Canberra, 5 June 2002, <http://www.aph.gov.au/hansard>.

—— (2003), Speech at International Business Week, sponsored by the Adelaide Office of DFAT, Stamford Plaza, Adelaide, 27 August.

Defence Intelligence Organisation (1999), 'Defence Economic Trends in Asia–Pacific 1999', Canberra, 31 July.

Defence Materiel Organisation (2002), *The Australian Naval Shipbuilding and Repair Sector Strategic Plan,* Commonwealth of Australia, September.

Department of Defence (1986), *Review of Australia's Defence Capabilities*, Report to the Minister for Defence by Paul Dibb, Australian Government Publishing Service, Canberra.

—— (1987), *The Defence of Australia*, Australian Government Publishing Service, Canberra.

—— (1989), *Australia's Regional Security*, Australian Government Publishing Service, Canberra.

—— (1993), *Strategic Review*, Australian Government Publishing Service, Canberra.

—— (1994), *1994 White Paper*, Australian Government Publishing Service, Canberra.

—— (1997a), *Australia's Strategic Policy*, Australian Government Publishing Service, Canberra.

—— (1997b), *Future Directions for the Management of Australia's Defence: Report of the Defence Efficiency Review*, Australian Government Publishing Service, Canberra.

—— (2000a), *Defence 2000: Our Future Defence Forces*, Australian Government Publishing Service, Canberra.

—— (2000b), *Survey of Defence Issues*, Australian Government Publishing Service, Canberra.
—— (2001), 'Federal Court decision allows submarine propeller modifications to go ahead', *Media Release*, Departmental 93/01, 11 April.
—— (2002), *The Australian Naval Shipbuilding and Repair Sector Strategic Plan*, Canberra.
—— (2003), *Australia's National Security: A Defence Update 2003*, Australian Government Publishing Service, Canberra.
—— (2005), *Australia's National Security: A Defence Update 2005*, Canberra.
—— (2007), *Australia's National Security: A Defence Update 2007*, Canberra.
Department of Foreign Affairs and Trade (1986), 'Australia–US relations: ministerial talks-joint communique', *Australian Foreign Affairs Record,* August.
—— (1989), 'Australia–United States Ministerial Talks Joint Communique', *The Monthly Record,* November.
—— (1996), 'Australia–United States Trade and Investment Review: A Partnership in Transition', Commonwealth of Australia, Canberra.
—— (1997a), 'In the National Interest: Australia's Foreign and Trade Policy White Paper', Canberra.
—— (1997b), 'Trade Outcomes and Objectives Statement', Commonwealth of Australia, Canberra.
—— (1998a), 'Merchandise Trade Highlights of 1997–8', AGPS, Canberra.
—— (1998b), 'Trade Outcomes and Objectives Statement', Commonwealth of Australia, Canberra.
—— (1999b), 'Trade Outcomes and Objectives Statement', Commonwealth of Australia', Canberra.
—— (2000), 'Trade Outcomes and Objectives Statement', Commonwealth of Australia', Canberra.
—— (2001a), 'Australia's position on Article 27.3(b)', <http://www.dfat.gov.au/ip/trips_update_index.html>.
—— (2001b), 'A briefing on the WTO TRIPs Agreement and related intellectual property issue', *TRIPs Update, Edition 1,* March.
—— (2001c), *East Timor in Transition 1998–2000: An Australian Policy Challenge*, Canberra.
—— (2002a), 'Background briefing by DFAT Officials on Trade Minister's forthcoming visit to US', 22 January, Canberra.
—— (2003a), 'Advancing the National Interest: Australia's Foreign and Trade Policy White Paper', AGPS, Canberra.
—— (2003b), 'Trade 2003: A statement of outcomes and objectives by Mark Vaile, Minister for Trade', Commonwealth of Australia, Canberra.
—— various years, collection of AUSMIN statements, <http://www.dfat.gov.au>.
Department of Foreign Affairs and Trade, Mark Vaile (2001), 'US to Remove Lamb Tariffs on 15 November', *Media Release*, 1 September 2001, MVT119/2001.
Department of Industry, Science and Resources (2001), 'Biotechnology in Australia: International Reputation and Growth', Canberra.
Department of Industry, Tourism and Resources (2002), 'Pharmaceuticals Industry Action Agenda: Local priority-Global partner', Canberra.

—— (2005), 'Biotech Business Indicators', Canberra, February.
—— (2007), 'Australian Pharmaceuticals Industry Fact Sheet', Canberra.
Department of Trade (1987), 'Australia Reconstructed', *ACTU/TDC Mission to Western Europe, A Report by the Mission Members to the ACTU and the Trade Development Council*, AGPS, Canberra.
Deputy Prime Minister and Minister for Trade, and the Minister for Industry, Science and Tourism (1996a), 'Australia disappointed at US Super 301 Action, Determined to Defend Australian Interests', *Joint Media Release*, Parliament House Canberra, 2 October.
—— (1996b), 'Australian leather exports to the US', *Joint Media Release*, Parliament House Canberra, 20 August.
Downer, Alexander (1999a), 'Australia and the United States: Old Friends and New Priorities', *Speech by the Hon Alexander Downer MP, Minister for Foreign Affairs, to the American Chamber of Commerce*, Sydney 5 August.
—— (1999b), 'Australian Government Historic Shift on East Timor', Minister for Foreign Affairs, *Media Release*, 12 January.
—— (1999c) *Transcript of Door Stop Interview*, Australia's Minister for Foreign Affairs, Washington D.C., 16 June.
—— (2000a), 'Meeting the Security Challenges of the Asia–Pacific Region', *Speech at the Australian Defence College*, Canberra, 31 October.
—— (2000b), *Opening Speech at the Asian Leaders' Forum*, Beijing, 23 April.
—— (2001b), 'The Australia–United States Alliance and East Asian Security', *Speech at the University of Sydney conference*, Sydney, 29 June.
—— (2002), 'The Strategic Importance of a Free Trade Agreement to Australia–United States Relations', Minister for Foreign Affairs, *Speech at the Australian APEC Studies Centre conference on 'The Impact of an Australian–United States Free Trade Agreement: Foreign Policy Challenges and Economic Opportunities', transcript*, Canberra, 29 August.
—— (2003a), 'Speech to the United Nations General Assembly', U.N., New York City, 24 September.
—— (2003b), 'The "Myth" of "little" Australia', *Speech to the National Press Club*, Canberra, 26 November.
Embassy of the People's Republic of China in Australia (2003), 'China considers counter measures to US steel tariffs', 21 November, <http://www.chinaembassy.org.au>.
—— (2003), 'FM hails success of President Hu's visits' 28 October, <http://www.chinaembassy.org.au/eng/58604.html>, accessed December 2003.
European Commission (2002), 'The European Commission's strategy to respond to the US decision to impose protectionist duties on steel imports', DN: MEMO/02/59, Brussels, 18 March.
Evans, Gareth (2002), 'The US vs The World? How American Power Seems to the Rest of Us', *speech transcript, The Foreign Policy Association*, New York.
Federal Coalition (1996a), A Confident Australia: Coalition Foreign Affairs Policy, Melbourne, 10 February.
—— (1996b), 'Meeting the Challenges: The New Global Economy', Liberal and National Party Strategies for the Future.

Field, Peter (1989), 'Encouraging Story for Agriculture', Speech by the Deputy Secretary of Foreign Affairs and Trade to the Pastoral Group Conference of the Victorian Farmers' Federation, Melbourne, *Australian Foreign Affairs Record,* 18 April, 133–36.

Fischer, Stanley (2001), 'Asia and the IMF', *Speech to the Institute of Policy Studies*, Singapore, 1 June, <http://www.imf.org/external/np/speeches/2001/060101.htm>.

Fischer, Tim (1999a), 'Serving Australia's Export Interest – WTO Negotiations on Services', *Speech to the Australian Coalition of Service Industries.*

—— (1999b), 'Trade: Lamb Exports', *Commonwealth Parliamentary Debates, House of Representatives, Hansard,* Question without notice, 24 June, 7451.

—— (2000), *Seven Days in East Timor*, Allen and Unwin, St. Leonards.

Fischer, Tim, The Deputy Prime Minister and Minister for Trade, and the Minister for Industry, Science and Tourism, John Moore (1996a), *Joint Media Release*, 'Australian leather exports to the US', Parliament House, Canberra, 20 August.

—— (1996b), 'Australia disappointed at US Super 301 Action, Determined to defend Australian Interests', *Joint Media Release* Parliament House, Canberra, 2 October.

—— (2000), 'Good, bad and ugly of US–Australia relations', *The Australian*, 5 June, 13.

Glickman, Dan (1999), 'New Crops, New Century, New Challenges: How will Scientists, Farmers, And Consumers Learn to Love Biotechnology. And What Happens if they Don't?', *US Secretary of Agriculture Speech to the National Press Club*, Washington D.C., 13 July.

Goncalves, Tomas (2000), interviewed in, 'The Ties That Bind', Four Corners, *ABC Television*, 14 February.

Gosper, Bruce and Steve Deady (2002), 'Consideration of Budget Estimates', *Senate Foreign Affairs, Defence and Trade Legislation Committee, Proof Committee Hansard, Commonwealth of Australia*, Canberra, 5 June.

Hatakeyama, Noboru (2002), 'Japan's New Regional Trade Policy – Which country comes next after Singapore?', Second annual Whitman International Lecture, *Institute for International Economics*, Washington, D.C., 13 March.

Hawke, Robert J. (1985), 'Australia–US relations', *Speech by the Prime Minister to the Australian–American Chamber of Commerce in Los Angeles.*

Hill, Robert (2002a), 'Beyond the White Paper: Strategic Directions for Defence', *Address to Defence and Strategic Studies Course*, Australian Defence College, Canberra, 18 June.

—— (2002b), Doorstop transcript, Minister for Defence, The Jefferson Hotel, Washington D.C., 10 January.

—— (2002c), interview on *Lateline, ABC Television*, 11 July.

—— (2002d), 'John Bray Memorial Oration', University of Adelaide, MIN 694/02, 28 November, <http://www.minister.defence.gov.au/HillSpeechtpl.cfm?CurrentId=2121>.

—— (2002e), Minister for Defence, interview with Matt Abraham and David Bevan, 5AN, transcript, *Media Release*, MIN 681/02, 27 November.

—— (2002f), 'Replacement combat system for the Collins Class', Minister for Defence, *Media Release*, MIN 479/02, 13 September.
—— (2003), Transcript of doorstop interview with Senator Robert Hill, Commonwealth Parliamentary Offices, Adelaide, 22 January.
—— (2005), 'Special Forces to Deploy to Afghanistan', *Media Release*, 113/2005, 13 July.
Hill, Robert, Minister for Defence, and Senator Nick Minchin, Minister for Finance and Administration (2002a), 'Australian Submarine Corporation – Engagement of capability partner for a scoping study', *Media Release*, Joint 134/02, 9 April.
—— (2002b), 'Electric Boat Corporation signs as capability partner to Australian Submarine Corporation', *Media Release*, MIN 536/02, 3 October.
Howard, John (1995), 'Fair Australia', Address to the Australian Council of Social Service, Sydney, 13 October.
—— (1999a), 'Trade: Lamb Exports to the United States of America', PM (Bennelong), *Commonwealth Parliamentary Debates, House of Representatives, Hansard*, Question without notice, 3 June.
—— (1999b), 'US restrictions on Australian Lamb Exports', Prime Minister, *Media Release*, Tokyo, 8 July.
—— (2001a), 'ANZUS Treaty: Application of ANZUS Treaty to terrorist attacks on the United States', Prime Minister of Australia, *Media Release*, 14 September.
—— (2001b), 'Australia's International Relations – Ready for the Future', *Address to the Menzies Research Centre,* Canberra, 22 August.
—— (2001c), 'Joint statement between the United States of America and Australia', Prime Minister of Australia, *Media Release*, 10 September.
—— (2001d), 'Text of Prime Minister Howard's Letter to President Habibie', 19 December 1998, in DFAT, *East Timor in Transition 1998–2000: An Australian Policy Challenge*, Canberra, 181–182.
—— (2001e), *The transcript of the Prime Minister, The Hon John Howard, MP, Address at reception on the occasion of 50 years of the Australia–United States Alliance*, Opera House, Sydney, 30 May.
—— (2001f), *Transcript of the Prime Minister, The Hon John Howard MP, National Press Club Address,* Canberra, 8 November.
—— (2002a), 'Strategic Leadership for Australia: Policy Directions in a Complex World', *speech transcript*, Committee for Economic Development of Australia (CEDA), 20 November.
—— (2002b), 'PM to push free trade agenda in US', interview transcript with Barrie Cassidy, *Insiders*, *ABC Television*, 2 June.
—— (2002c), *Transcript of the Prime Minister, The Hon John Howard MP address to the Joint Meeting of the US Congress*, Washington D.C., 12 June.
—— (2002d), *Transcript of the Prime Minister The Hon John Howard MP Prime Minister's Closing Address Liberal Party 49th Federal Council, Hyatt Hotel,* Canberra, 14 April.
—— (2003a), *Transcript of the Prime Minister, The Hon John Howard MP, Address to the House of Representatives*, Parliament House Canberra, 18 March.
—— (2003b), *Transcript of the Prime Minister, The Hon John Howard MP, Address to the Nation*, 20 March.

—— (2003c), *Transcript of the Prime Minister, The Hon John Howard MP, Prime Ministerial Statement to Parliament on Iraq*, 4 February.

—— (2005), *Transcript of the Prime Minister the Hon John Howard MP, Joint Press Conference with the Premier of NSW, the Hon Bob Carr MP*, Phillip Street, Sydney, 9 June.

Hu, Jintao (2003), 'Address to the Federal Parliament of the Commonwealth of Australia: Building a Better Future Together for the China–Australia Relationship of All-round Cooperation', *Embassy of the People's Republic of China in Australia*, 24 October.

International Iron and Steel Institute (2001), 'World Steel production, 1950 to 2000', 18 June, <http://www.worldsteel.org/trends_indicators/figures_1.html>.

Japan Maritime Self Defence Force (JMSDF), <http://homepage.eircom.net/~steven/jmsdf.htm>, accessed 13 January 2004.

Keating, Paul (2000), *Engagement: Australia faces the Asia–Pacific*, Macmillan, Sydney.

Kleckner, Dean (1999), 'Recent Developments in US Trade Policy – Implications for the Next WTO Round' *Speech at the National Press Club*, Canberra, 16 April.

Lamy, Pascal (2002), Statement by EU Trade Commissioner Pascal Lamy in reaction to US Measures on Steel, *EU press release*, DN: IP/02/379, Brussels, 6 March.

McIntosh, Malcolm and John Prescott (1999), 'Report to the Minister for Defence on Collins Class Submarine and Related Matters', Commonwealth of Australia, June, <http://www.minister.defence.gov.au//1999/collins.html>.

Meyer, Christopher (2003), interviewed for 'Blair's War', Frontline, *PBS*, 18 March.

Millar, Andrew J. (undated) 'Conventional vs Nuclear Submarines: The Case for Conventional Submarines for Australia', RAN New Submarine Project.

—— (1992–3), 'Profile of the Collins Design', *Australian Navy*.

—— (1999), 'Naval Ships: Collins Class Submarines', *Australian Ships and Ports*, December.

'Collins Class Successes', provided by Andrew Millar to the author in October 2003.

Moench, Lorin jnr. (1998), 'Testimony on behalf of the American Sheep Industry Association', *Committee on Agriculture, Nutrition and Forestry transcript, United States Senate*, Washington D.C. 10 June.

Moore, John (1997), 'New Policies Promote Investment in Australia's Pharmaceutical Industry', Minister for Industry, Science and Tourism, *Media Release (87/97)*, 8 April, <http://www.isr.gov.au/media/archive/april97/87%2D97.html>.

—— (1999a), 'East Timor and Australia's Security', *Speech by minister for Defence*, House of Representatives, The Hon. John Moore, Minister for Defence, *Media Release* 284/99, 21 September, <http://www.minister.defence.gov.au/1999/28499.html>.

—— (1999b), 'Reform of Defence Acquisition', Minister for Defence, *media statement,* MIN 188/99, 1 July, <http://www.minister.defence.gov.au/1999/18899.html>.

—— (1999c), 'Submarine Upgrade Proceeds', Minister for Defence, *Media Release,* MIN 357/99, 9 December.

—— (1999d), transcript of the press conference to launch the McIntosh-Prescott Report, Minister for Defence, *press release*, 1 July, <http://www.minister.defence.gov.au//1999/mt0499.html>.
—— (2000), 'Commonwealth acquires full ownership of the Australian Submarine Corporation' Minister for Defence, *Media Release*, MIN 319/00, 30 October.
Murdoch, Rupert (1998), Speech to the Australian American Association, New York, 2 July.
National Farmers' Federation (1999a), 'Aussie lamb producers have an impact in The White House', *News Release*, NR 72/99, 10 June, <http://www.nff.org.au/nr99/nr072.htm>.
—— (1999b), 'Bad News on Lamb', *News Release*, NR 71/99, 8 June, <http://www.nff.org.au/nr99/nr071.htm>.
—— (1999c), 'It's Official! – White House torn Over Lamb Tariffs', *news release*, NR 90/99, 29 June, <http://www.nff.org.au/nr99/nr090.htm>.
—— (2001), 'Spring finally back in Aussie lamb producers' steps', *NFF Media Release*, NR 107/2001, 1 September, <http://www.nff.org.au/pages/nr01/107.htmNFF>.
Ohff, Hans J. (2001), quoted in Robert Garran, 'Sub deal sinks beneath US secrecy', *The Australian*, 20 December, 2.
Pickering, Thomas R. (1999a), 'Elements of Indonesian military backed killings', Undersecretary of State for Political Affairs Indonesia, 9 September, <http://www.usia.gov/regional/ea/timor/pick909.htm>.
—— (1999b), *Testimony on East Timor Crisis*, Undersecretary of State for Political Affairs Indonesia, 9 September, <http://www.usia.gov/regional/ea/timor/pick909.htm>.
PhRMA, undated, 'Issues around the World, Watch Country: Australia', Washington D.C. <http://www.phrma.org>, accessed September 2001.
—— undated, 'Special 301 watch list for violations of intellectual property rights', <http://www.phrma.org/international/special301/australia/cfm>, accessed October 2002.
Productivity Commission (2001), 'International Pharmaceutical Price Differences', *AusInfo*, Canberra, July, <http://www.indcom.gov.au>.
Raftopoulos, Steve (1998), 'Testimony on behalf of the ASI', *The Subcommittee on Livestock, Dairy and Poultry Committee on Agriculture transcript, US House of Representatives*, Washington, DC, 26 February.
Ray, Robert (1992), Minister of Defence, *CPD*, *Senate Hansard*, 17 December, 5411.
Raytheon (1999), 'US Navy Awards Raytheon $414 Million to Remanufacture Tomahawk Cruise Missiles', *news release*, *media relations*, Arlington, Virginia, <http://www.raytheon.com/press/1999/jul/thawk>, accessed May 2001.
Reith, Peter (2001a), 'Australia and US sign submarine cooperation statement', Minister for Defence, *Media Release*, 12 September.
—— (2001b), 'Kim Beazley's Record', Minister for Defence, *Media Release, MIN 410/01*, 6 October.
—— (2001c), 'Kim Beazley – Not a Good Defence Minister', Minister for Defence, *Media Release, MIN 425/01*, 1 October.

—— (2001d), Minister for Defence transcript of the doorstop interview, Melbourne, *Media Release*, MIN 412/01, 6 October.

—— (2001e), 'Submarines Combat System', Minister for Defence, *Media Release*, MIN 244/01, 9 July.

Rose, Geoff (1997), 'Introduction of Underwater Platform Technology (An Australian Perspective)', *Paper for the Defence Asia Forum 1997 at the World Trade Centre*, Singapore, 16 January.

Roth, Stanley (1999), interviewed by Kerry O'Brien, 7.30 Report, 'World losing patience with violence in East Timor', *ABC Television*, 2 September.

Royal Australian Navy (2001), 'RAN Collins submarines now on track', *Asia–Pacific Defence Reporter*, December/January, 12–13, no author supplied.

Rudd, Kevin (2001), 'ANZUS and the 21st century', *Australian Journal of International Affairs* 55:2, 301–315.

Rumsfeld, Donald (2001), 'US Secretary of Defense holds media availability', transcript, *Federal Document Clearing House*, 23 September.

Scarce, K.J. (2003), 'Measure the Collins-class by performance,' Letters to the Editor, *The Advertiser*, 16 July, 18.

Schacht, Chris and Michael Roche (2000), 'Question and answer exchange', *Foreign Affairs, Defence and Trade Legislation Committee, Senate Hansard*, 29 May, 109.

Schieffer, Tom (2002), quoted in Tim Colebatch, 'BHP Gains Relief from Steel Tariff', *The Age*, 12 March, 3.

Spender, Percy (1950), Minister for External Affairs, The Hague statement, 29 August, in Neville Meaney, *Australia and the World: A Documentary History from the 1870s to the 1970s*, Longman Cheshire, Melbourne, 1988, pp. 639–40.

—— (1969), *Exercises in Diplomacy: The ANZUS Treaty and the Colombo Plan*, Sydney University Press, Sydney.

Svensson, Tore (2003), 'Ask why they are trying to sink our super subs', *The Advertiser*, 16 July, 20.

Thawley, Michael (2001), 'Speech to The Milken Institute', Santa Monica, 20 January, Embassy of Australia in the United States, Office of Public Affairs, Testimony by the Australian Ambassador to the USA, before the International trade Commission, Washington D.C., 6 November, <http://www.austemb.org/Speeches?ITCTestimony2001.htm>.

—— (2003), *Testimony by the Australian Ambassador to the USA, Michael Thawley, before the International Trade Commission*, Washington D.C., 6 February, <http://www.austemb.org/speeches/ITCTestimony2003.htm>.

—— (2005), 'Trade important to US – Australia ties', interview transcript with Leigh Sales, *AM, ABC transcript*, 5 May.

Truss, Warren (2001), 'Lamb levy relief to continue following US decision', Minister for Agriculture, *Media Release*, September.

United Nations, undated, 'East Timor – UNTAET Background'.

—— undated, Secretariat of the Convention on Biological Diversity, United Nations Environment Programme, Cartagena Protocol on Biosafety.

—— (1999a), 'Appendix: Constitutional framework for a special autonomy', 5 May.

—— (1999b) 'Question of East Timor: Report of the Secretary General', A/53/951, S/1999/513, 5 May.

——(2005), Independent Inquiry Committee into the UN's Oil-For-Food Programme (IIC–OFFP), 'Manipulation of the Oil-For-Food Programme by the Iraqi regime', *United Nations*, 27 October.

US Congressional Hearings (1986), 'United States Policy Toward New Zealand and Australia', *Hearing before the Subcommittee on Asian and Pacific Affairs of the Committee on Foreign Affairs, House of Representatives, Ninety-ninth Congress, second session*, US Government Printing Office, Washington, D.C., 25 September.

—— (1999a), '1999 WTO Ministerial in Seattle Washington', *Hearing of the House Agriculture Committee*, 23 June, Washington D.C., accessed from *Federal Information Systems Corporation*, 21.

—— (1999b), 'Indonesia and the Countdown to Elections' US Senate Foreign Relations Committee 1999, *Hearing of the East Asian and Pacific Affairs Subcommittee*, Washington, 18 March.

US Department of Commerce: ITA (2002), 'Product Exclusion Requests Under Section 203', 4 June.

US Department of Defense (2001), *Quadrennial Defense Review Report*, Washington D.C., 30 September.

US Department of State (1996a), 'Australia–US Joint Security Declaration: A Strategic Partnership for the 21st Century', jointly released in Sydney, Australia, 27 July.

—— (1999b), 'East Timor – US–Australian Cooperation', *Statement by James B. Foley*, Deputy Spokesman, 16 September.

—— undated, 'Basic readings in US Democracy, Industrial America: Morrill Act 1862'.

US Embassy in Canberra (1999), 'Decision on US Lamb Imports', *Press Release*, Canberra, 8 July.

US Government Accounting Office (2001), 'Concerns over biotechnology challenge US agricultural exports', *Government Accounting Office Report*, 15 June.

United States International Trade Commission (1999a), Commissioner Carol T. Crawford's assessment in the USITC Report, 'Lamb Meat: Investigation No. TA-201–68, Determination and Views of the Commission'.

——(1999b), 'ITC says increased imports of lamb meat threaten US industry', *news release*, 99–022, 9 February.

——(1999c), 'Lamb Meat, Investigation No. TA-201-68, Determination and Views of the Commission', *USITC Publication No. 3176*, April.

—— (2001a), 'Certain Steel Products Trade Data', 11 December, <http://dataweb.usitc.gov/scripts/steel.asp>, accessed 6 April 2007.

—— (2001b), 'ITC Details Determinations Concerning Impact of Imports of Steel on US Industry', 11 December, <http://www.usitc.gov/er/nl2001/ER1023Y1.PDF>, accessed 6 April 2007.

——(2001c), 'Summary of Commission Remedy Recommendations', 11 December, <http://wwwusitc.gov/er/nl2001/er1207y1c1.pdf>, accessed 6 April 2007.

United States Navy (1997), 'Forward…From the Sea: The Navy Operational Concept', March.

US Steel (2002), 'US Steel chairman Thomas J Usher thanks president Bush: Calls tariffs a bold step that addresses serious injury to American Steel Industry', *US Steel Press Release* 5 March.

USTR (1996), 'National Trade Estimates 1996', Australia, <http://www.ustr.gov/reports/nte/1996/australia.html>, accessed September 2001.

—— (1997a), 'USTR Barshefsky announces results of Special 301 "out-of-cycle" reviews', *Press Release 93–97*, Washington, 27 October.

—— (1997b), 'Building American Prosperity in the 21st Century: U.S. Trade and Investment in the Asia Pacific Region', *Presidential Commission on United States – Pacific Trade and Investment Policy (1997),* Washington D.C.

—— (2000), 'Foreign Trade Barriers: Australia 1999', <http://www.ustr.gov/pdf/2000_australi.pdf>, accessed September 2001.

—— (2001a), '2001 Special 301 Report', <http://www.ustr.gov/html/special.html>, accessed October 2001.

—— (2001b), 'Bush Administration Settles Lamb Safeguard Issue with Australia and New Zealand', *press release*, Washington D.C., 31 August, <http://www.ustr.gov/releases/2001/08/01-66.htm>.

—— (2001c), 'USTR Robert Zoellick Defends Bush Action on Steel Imports', Washington D.C., 6 June <http://usinfo.state.gov/topical/econ/group8/summit01/wwwh01060702.html>.

—— (2003a), 'National Trade Estimates 2003, Foreign Trade Barriers: Australia', <http://www.ustr.gov/assets/Document_Library/Reports_Publications/2003/2003_NTE_Report/asset_upload_file835_6179.pdf>, accessed March 2007.

—— (2003b), 'The US–Singapore Free trade Agreement (FTA): The Intellectual Property Provisions: The Report of the Industry Functional Advisory Committee on Intellectual Property Rights for Trade Policy Matters (IFAC-3)', 28 February, <http://www.ustr.gov/new/fta/Singapore/ac-ifac3.pdf>.

Vaile, Mark (2000), 'Good Outcome for Australia in WTO Pharmaceutical Case', Trade Minister, *Trade News* MVT 22/2000, 29 March.

—— (2001), 'Background: WTO Dispute Settlement – US Lamb', *Media Release*, 2 May.

—— (2002a), 'US Gazettes Australian Exclusion from Steel Import Restrictions', Minister for Trade, Australia *Media Releases*, MVT023/2002,6 April 2002.

—— (2002b), 'US Get(s) Precious Over Steel', Minister for Trade, *Media Release*, 6 March.

Vaile, Mark, Minister for Trade, and the Minister for Industry, Science and Resources, Nick Minchin (2000), 'Settlement reached with US on Howe leather dispute', *Joint Media Release*, MVT64/2000, 21 June.

Vaile, Mark, the Minister for Trade, the Minister for Industry, Tourism and Resources, Ian Macfarlane, and the Minister for Justice and Customs, Senator Chris Ellison (2002), 'Steel Industry Meeting – Communique', *Joint Media Release*, Canberra, 19 March.

The White House (2001), 'Statement by the President Regarding a Multilateral Initiative on Steel', The White House, *Office of the Press Secretary*, 5 June.

—— (2002), Fact Sheet: Regarding the Presidential Action on Steel, *Office of the Press Secretary*, 5 March, <http://www.whitehouse.gov/news/releases/2002/03/20020305-11.html>.

Whitlam, Gough (1966), 'Australia – Base or Bridge?', Evatt Memorial Lecture, Sydney University, Sydney.

Wiltshire, Horden (2001), 'Submarines: an Australian view', in David Wilson (ed.), *Maritime War in the 21st Century: The Medium and Small Navy Perspective*, RAN Sea Power Centre, Canberra, 249–258.

Wiryono, S. (1999), former Indonesian Ambassador to Australia, 'Goodwill should be our mission', *The Australian*, 1 October, 15.

Wolfensohn, James (2004), 'President of the World Bank talks about development', interview transcript, *7.30 Report, ABC Television*, February.

World Trade Organisation, undated, 'The Doha Declaration explained: Trade-related aspects of intellectual property rights (TRIPS) (pars17–19)', <http://www.wto.org/english/tratop_e/dda_e/dohaexplained_e.htm>, accessed 16 March 2007.

—— (2001), 'TRIPs and Pharmaceutical patents: Obligations and exceptions', Geneva, April.

—— (2006), 'Pharmaceutical patents and the TRIPs Agreement', Geneva, September.

Zhou Wenzhong (2000), 'China warns against going all the way with the USA', 7.30 Report interview transcript, *ABC Television*, 25 July.

Zoellick, Robert B. (2001), 'A Time to Choose: Trade and the American Nation', US Trade Representative, *Speech to the Heritage Foundation*, Washington D.C., 29 June.

—— (2002a), 'A Pacific Partnership: Australia and America In a Globalizing World', *Remarks to the Australian American Leadership Dialogue*, Washington, D.C., 10 July.

—— (2002b), 'Globalization, Trade and Economic Security: Remarks at the National Press Club', 1 October.

—— (2002c), 'Press Briefing by US Trade Representative Robert Zoellick', the James S. Brady Briefing Room, White House, 5 March.

—— (2002d), 'USTR Zoellick in Brazil Defends Steel Tariffs Decision', *Speech transcript at the Brazilian Ministry of Finance, Brasilia*, Brazil, 11 March.

—— (2003a), 'Remarks by Robert B. Zoellick, United States Trade Representative on the decision by the President to terminate steel safeguards', December 4.

—— (2003b), Robert Zoellick, 'Zoellick says US trade strategy advocates openness', *Wall St. Journal*, 10 July.

Secondary Sources

Adler, Emanuel and Michael N. Barnett (eds) (1998), *Security Communities* (Cambridge: Cambridge University Press).

Allard, Tom (2004a), 'Going to war secured US alliance, says Downer', *Sydney Morning Herald*, 3 March, 7.

—— (2004b), 'PM was told war would spur terrorism', *Sydney Morning Herald*, 23 August, 1.

Avery, William P. (ed.) (1993), *World Agriculture and the GATT,* International Political Economy Yearbook, vol. 7 (Boulder: Lynne Rienner).

Baker, A.D. (2001), 'World Navies in Review' International Navies Focus, *US Naval Institute Proceedings*, 127:3:1, Annapolis, Maryland, 32–45.

Baker, Richard W. (ed.) (1992), *Australia, New Zealand, and the United States: Internal Change and Alliance Relations in the ANZUS States* (New York: Praeger).

Baker Richard W. and Gary R. Hawke (eds) (1992), ANZUS Economics: Economic Trends and Relations among Australia, New Zealand, and the United States (Westport: Praeger).

Ball, Desmond (1980), *A Suitable Piece of Real Estate: American Installations in Australia* (Sydney: Hale and Iremonger).

—— (1999a), interview with Fran Kelly, 'Academic discusses the relevance of intelligence assessments', transcript, *Radio National*, 21 September.

—— (1999b) 'Strategic Planning for the Defence of Australia in 2015', in Des Ball (ed.), *Maintaining the Strategic Edge: The Defence of Australia in 2015*, Canberra Papers on Strategy and Defence No. 133, SDSC, RSPAS, ANU, Canberra, 1–24.

—— (1999c), 'The US–Australian Alliance: History and Prospects', *Working Paper no. 330*, Strategic and Defence Studies Centre, ANU, Canberra.

—— (2001), 'Silent witness: Australian Intelligence and East Timor', *The Pacific Review*, special edition, 14:1, 43–50.

Barker, Geoffrey (2000), 'Suboptimisation', *Australian Financial Review*, 25 July, 42.

—— (2002), '$12 billion to buy experimental war plane', *Australian Financial Review*, 28 June, 1 and 18.

Barnett, Michael N. (1996), 'Identity and Alliances in the Middle East', in Peter J. Katzenstein (ed.) *The Culture of National Security: Norms and Identity in World Politics* (New York: Columbia University Press) 400–447.

Barringer, William H. and Kenneth J. Pierce (2000), 'Paying the Price for Big Steel', *American Institute for International Steel*, Washington D.C.

Barton, John H. and Peter Berger (2001), 'Patenting Agriculture', *Issues in Science and Technology*, 17: 4, 43–51.

Bateman, Sam (1995), 'Australia's "two ocean" policy', *Business Times*, 29 July 4.

Baume, Michael (2001), 'Steel Battle Requires an Iron Will', *Australian Financial Review*, 4 February, 55.

Beeson, Mark (2003), 'Australia's Relationship with the United States: The Case for Greater Independence', *Australian Journal of Political Science*, 38:3, 387–405.

Beeson, Mark and Ann Capling (2002), 'Australia in the World Economy: Globalisation, International Institutions and Economic Governance', in Stephen Bell (ed.), *Economic Governance and Institutional Dynamics* (South Melbourne: Oxford University Press) 285–303.

Bell, Coral (1988), *Dependent Ally: A Study in Australian Foreign Policy* (Canberra: Allen and Unwin in association with the Department of International Relations, RSPAS, ANU).

—— (1996), 'The Future of American Policy in the Pacific', in Gary Klintworth (ed.), *Asia–Pacific Security: Less Uncertainty, New Opportunities?* (Melbourne: Addison Wesley Longman) 22–34.

Bell, Roger (1997), 'Reassessed: Australia's Relationship with the United States', in James Cotton and John Ravenhill (eds), *Seeking Asian Engagement: Australia in World Affairs, 1991–1995* (Melbourne: Oxford University Press) 207–239.

—— (2007), 'Extreme Allies: Australia and the USA', in James Cotton and John Ravenhill (eds), *Trading on Alliance Security: Australia in World Affairs, 2001–2005* (Melbourne: Oxford University Press in association with the Australian Institute of International Affairs) 23–52.

Bhagwati, Jagdish and Arvind Panagariya (2003), 'Bilateral trade treaties are a sham', *Financial Times*, 14 July, 17.

Booth, Ken and Russell Trood (eds) (1999), *Strategic Cultures in the Asia–Pacific Region* (Basingstoke: Macmillan).

Borgu, Aldo (2003), 'The Defence Capability Review 2003: A Modest and Incomplete Review' (Canberra: *Australian Strategic Policy Institute*).

Brown, Gary (1989), 'Breaking the American Alliance: An Independent National Security Policy', *Canberra Papers on Strategy and Defence No. 54*, Strategic and Defence Studies Centre, Research School of Pacific Studies, ANU, Canberra.

Brown, Gary and Laura Rayner (2001), 'Upside Downside: ANZUS: After Fifty years', *Current Issues Brief, 03, Parliamentary Library*, Parliament of Australia, 28 August, <http://www.aph.gov.au/library/pubs/cib/2001-02/02cib03.pdf>.

Byrnes, Michael (1994), *Australia and the Asia Game* (St. Leonards: Allen and Unwin).

Camilleri, Joseph A. (1980), *Australian–US Relations: The Web of Dependence* (South Melbourne: Macmillan).

Capling, Ann (2001), *Australia and the Global Trade System: From Havana to Seattle* (Cambridge: Cambridge University Press).

—— (2003), 'Democratic Deficit, the Global Trade System and 11 September', *Australian Journal of Politics and History*, 49:3, 372–379.

Capling, Ann and Brian Galligan (1992), *Beyond the Protective State: The Political Economy of Australia's Manufacturing Industry Policy* (Cambridge: Cambridge University Press).

Capling, Ann and Kim Richard Nossal (2001), 'Square Pegs and Round Holes: Australia's Multilateral Economic Diplomacy and the Joint Standing Committee on Treaties', *paper for presentation at the annual meetings of the International Studies Association*, Chicago, 20–24 February.

Cassidy, J.P. (2002), 'Bush steel tariff move impacts "Rust Belt" voters', *The Hill*, 6 March, 4.

Cheeseman, Graeme (1993), *The Search for Self Reliance: Australian Defence Since Vietnam* (Longman Cheshire, Melbourne).

—— (1999), 'Australia: the White Experience of Fear and Dependence', in Ken Booth and Russell Trood (eds), *Strategic Cultures in the Asia–Pacific Region* (Basingstoke: Macmillan) 273–298.

Colombani, Jean-Marie (2001), 'We are all Americans', *Le Monde*, 12 September, 1.

Cook, Ivan (2005), 'Australians Speak 2005: Public Opinion and Foreign Policy', *Lowy Institute for International Policy*, Sydney.

Cooper, William H. (2001), 'RL30461: Trade Remedy Law Reform in the 107th Congress', *CRS Report for Congress*, 12 April.

Costello, Michael (2003), 'Friday Forum', transcript, *Lateline,* ABC Television, 24 October.

Cotton, James (2001), 'Against the Grain: The East Timor Intervention', *Survival*, 43:1, 127–143.

Cotton, James and John Ravenhill (eds) (1997), *Seeking Asian Engagement: Australia in World Affairs, 1991–1995* (Melbourne: Oxford University Press in association with the Australian Institute of International Affairs).

—— (eds) (2001), *The National Interest in a Global Era: Australia in World Affairs 1996–2000* (Melbourne: Oxford University Press in association with the Australian Institute of International Affairs).

—— (eds) (2007), *Trading on Alliance Security: Australia in World Affairs, 2001–2005* (Melbourne: Oxford University Press in association with the Australian Institute of International Affairs).

Cox, Michael (2003), 'US Grand Strategy: Implications for Alliance Partners', Centre for Defence and Strategic Studies, Australian Defence College Conference on United States Grand Strategy: Implications for Alliance Partners, Canberra, 1 August.

Cox, Robert W. (1989), 'Middlepowermanship, Japan, and the Future World Order', *International Journal*, 44:4, 823–62.

Crawford, J.G. (1968), *Australian Trade Policy 1942–1966: A Documentary History* (Canberra: Australian National University Press).

Daley, Paul (2000), 'Howard unwilling on peace force for Timor', *The Age*, 30 January, 1.

Davis, Mark (2002), 'EU attacks Australia on steel stance', *Australian Financial Review*, 17 July, 1.

Day, David (1988), *The Great Betrayal: Britain, Australia and the Onset of the Pacific War 1939–42* (North Ryde: Angus and Robertson).

DeAngelis, Richard (1998), 'Xenophobic Populism and Pauline Hanson's "One Nation": A Comparative Perspective', *Policy, Organisation and Society* 16, 1–27.

DeBats, Donald, Tim McDonald and Margaret-Ann Williams (2007), 'Mr Howard Goes to Washington: September 11, the Australian–American Relationship and Attributes of Leadership', *Australian Journal of Political Science*, vol. 42, issue 2, June 2007, 231–251.

Destler, I.M. (1992), *American Trade Politics*, second edition (Washington D.C. and New York: Institute for International Economics and The Twentieth Century Fund).

—— (1998), 'Congress and Foreign Trade', in Robert A. Pastor and Rafael Fernandez De Castro (eds), *The Controversial Pivot: The US Congress and North America* (Washington D.C.: Brookings Institution Press).

Dibb, Paul (ed.) (1999), 'Defence Strategy in the Contemporary Era', *Strategic and Defence Studies Centre,* Working Paper no. 337, ANU, August.

—— (2003), 'Australia's Alliance with America', *Melbourne Asia Policy Papers* 1:1 (Melbourne: University of Melbourne).

Dibb, Paul and Richard Brabin-Smith (2004), 'Cinderella's reality check', *Australian Financial Review*, 24 February, 62.

Dibb, Paul and Peter Prince (1999), 'Southeast Asia Needs Indonesia and Australia to Make Up', *International Herald Tribune*, 27 October, 8.

Dibb, Paul and Terry Roach (1999), 'Collins: The Submarine We Had To Have', *Australian Financial Review*, 17 February, 17.

Dorling, Philip (1989), 'Origins of the ANZUS Treaty: a reconsideration', *Flinders Politics monographs*, 4, Flinders University, South Australia.

Drahos, Peter, Thomas Faunce, Martyn Goddard and David Henry (2007), 'The FTA and the PBS', Evatt Foundation, <http://evatt.labor.net.au/publications/papers/126.html>, accessed March 2007.

Drysdale, Peter (2001), 'The Impact of the Japanese Economy on Asia and the Pacific: Does Asia Need Regional Trade Arrangements?', *Presentation to IMF–World Bank Conference on Economic Interdependence: Shaping Asia–Pacific in the 21st Century*, Tokyo, 22–23 March.

Dunk, Graeme (2001), 'The Collins combat system', *Asia–Pacific Defence Reporter*, December/January, 14–15.

Dupont, Alan (2001), *East Asia Imperilled: Transnational Challenges to Security* (Cambridge: Cambridge University Press).

Edwards, Peter (2005), 'Permanent Friends? Historical Reflections on the Australian–American Alliance', Lowy Institute Paper 8, Sydney.

Emmerson, Donald (1999), 'Moralpolitik: The Timor Test', *The National Interest* 58, 63–69.

Engel, Matthew (2001), 'US attack opens new phase of war', *The Guardian*, 27 November, 1.

Evans, Gareth and Bruce Grant (1995), *Australia's Foreign Relations in the World of the 1990s*, second edition (Carlton: Melbourne University Press).

Evans, Peter B., Harold K. Jacobsen and Robert D. Putnam (eds) (1993), *Double-Edged Diplomacy: International Bargaining and Domestic Politics* (Berkeley: University of California Press).

Fearon, James D. (1998), 'Bargaining enforcement, and international cooperation', *International Organization* 52:2, 269–306.

Fisher, Louis (2003), 'Deciding on War Against Iraq: International Failures', *Political Science Quarterly* 118:3, 389–410.

Frankel, Glenn (2005), 'From memos, insights into ally's doubts on Iraq War: Blair's advisers foresaw variety of risks, problems', *Washington Post Foreign Service*, 28 June, A01.

Fuhrman, John (2001), 'Political tie not worth more regional flak', *Australian Financial Review*, 6 February, 43.

Garamone, Jim (1999), 'Clinton Says US Would Aid Aussie Peacekeepers in Timor', *American Forces Information Service News Articles*, DefenseLink, US Department of Defense, 10 September.

Garnaut, Ross (2002), 'An Australian–United States Free Trade Agreement', *Australian Journal of International Affairs* 56:1, 123–141.

Garran, Robert (2000a), 'A deadly exercise in stealth', *The Weekend Australian*, 23–25 December 1.

—— (2000b), 'US threat to sink strategic alliance', *The Weekend Australian*, 23–25 December, 1.

—— (2001), 'The Dome', *The Weekend Australian*, 10–11 February, 17 and 20.

Gaull, Gerald F. (1998), 'Biotechnology Regulation in America and Europe: Viewed in a Cultural Framework', *Institute of Economic Affairs*, London, 1 August.

Gillert, Douglas J. (1999), 'US Support Increases to East Timor "Operation Warden"', *American Forces Information Service, News Articles,* DefenseLink, US Department of Defense, 29 September.

Gilpin, Robert (1981), *War and Change in World Politics* (Cambridge: Cambridge University Press).

—— (1987), *The Political Economy of International Relations* (Princeton: Princeton University Press).

Goldsworthy, David (1998), 'The Howard government and purposes beyond ourselves', unpublished draft.

—— (2001), 'An Overview', in James Cotton and John Ravenhill (eds), *The National Interest in a Global Era: Australia in World Affairs 1996–2000* (Melbourne: Oxford University Press) 10–32.

Goldsworthy, David and the Department of Foreign Affairs and Trade (eds) (2001), *Facing North: A Century of Australian Engagement with Asia 1901–1970s*, 1 (Carlton: Department of Foreign Affairs and Trade and Melbourne University Press).

Goldsworthy, David and Peter Edwards (eds) (2003), *Facing North: A Century of Australian Engagement with Asia, 1970s–2000*, 2 (Carlton: Department of Foreign Affairs and Trade and Melbourne University Press).

Grazebrook, A.W. (2000), 'US pressure in RAN submarine competition', *Asia-Pacific Defence Reporter*, August/September, 38.

Griffiths, Martin (2003), 'Self Inflicted Wounds: The United States Grand Strategy and the War on Terror', *paper presented to the Australasian Political Science Association Conference, University of Tasmania*, Hobart, 29 September – 1 October.

Gyngell, Allan and Michael Wesley (2000), 'Interweaving of Foreign and Domestic Policy: International Policy', in Michael Keating and Glyn Davis (eds), *The Future of Governance: Policy Choices* (St. Leonards: Allen and Unwin) 203–229.

—— (2003), *Making Australian Foreign Policy* (Cambridge: Cambridge University Press).

—— (2007), 'Australia and the World: Public Opinion and Foreign Policy', *Lowy Institute for International Policy*, Sydney, August.

Habeeb, William Mark (1988), *Power and Tactics in International Negotiation: How Weak Nations Bargain with Strong Nations* (Baltimore: Johns Hopkins University Press).

Haftendorn, Helga, Robert O. Keohane and Celeste A. Wallender (eds) (1999), *Imperfect Unions; Security Institutions over Time and Space* (Oxford: Oxford University Press).

Harder, Leon T. (1999), 'East Timor and the 'Slippery Slope' Problem', *CATO Institute Foreign Policy Briefing* 55, 20 December.

Harris, Stuart (1992), 'International Economic Orientations: Australia', in R.W. Baker and Gary R. Hawke (eds) *ANZUS Economics: Economic Trends and Relations Among Australia, New Zealand, and the United States* (Westport: Praeger) 73–90.

—— (1998), 'Will China Divide Australia and the US?', The Australian Centre for American Studies (Sydney: The University of Sydney).

—— (2003), 'US Grand Strategy: Implications for Australia's Relations with Northeast Asia', *Centre for Defence and Strategic Studies Conference*, Canberra, 1 August.

Hartcher, Peter (1997), 'Bum note: how the US refused Cabinet's CD deal', *Australian Financial Review*, 9 October.

—— (2003a), 'What Australia won from the war', *Australian Financial Review*, 10–11 May 25.

—— (2003b), 'US calls on Australia to play peacekeeping role', *The Weekend Australian Financial Review*, 5–6 April.

Hartcher, Peter and Geoffrey Barker (2003), 'Tension builds over postwar role', *The Weekend Australian Financial Review*, 5–6 April.

Hartcher, Peter and Colleen Ryan (1996), 'US trade threat to car and textile industries', *Australian Financial Review*, 18 November, 1.

Hastedt, Glenn P. (2003), *American Foreign Policy: Past, Present, Future*, fifth edition (New Jersey: Prentice Hall).

Hemmer, Christopher and Peter J. Katzenstein (2000), 'Collective Identities and the Origins of Multiculturalism in Europe but not in Asia in the Early Cold War', *paper presented at the Annual Meeting of the American Political Science Association, Marriot Wardman Park, Washington D.C.*

Henry, David (2001), Review of Peter Baume's Paper, 'How do decisions on the listing of pharmacueticals influence health and health services in Australia?', Australian Health Policy Institute Commissioned Paper Series, 2001/03, University of Sydney, Sydney.

Hewison, Kevin, Richard Robison and Garry Rodan (eds) (1993), *Southeast Asia in the 1990s: Authoritarianism, Democracy and Capitalism* (St. Leonards: Allen and Unwin).

Higgott, Richard G. (1989), 'The Ascendency of the Economic Dimension in Australian–American Relations', in John Ravenhill (ed) *No Longer an American Lake? Alliance Problems in the South Pacific* (Berkeley: Institute of International Studies, University of California) 132–168.

Higgott, Richard, Richard Leaver and John Ravenhill (eds) (1993) *Pacific Economic Relations in the 1990s: Cooperation or Conflict?* (St. Leonards: Allen and Unwin).

Higgott, Richard A. and Kim Richard Nossal (1998), 'Australia and the search for a security community in the 1990s', in Emanuel Adler and Michael N. Barnett (eds) *Security Communities* (Cambridge: Cambridge University Press) 265–294.

Hubbard, Christopher (2005), *Australian and US Military Cooperation: Fighting Common Enemies* (Aldershot: Ashgate).

Hudson, Philip and Caroline Overington (2003), 'Howard links Iraq war to Bali', *The Age*, 10 March, 1.

Hufbauer, Gary Clyde and Ben Goodrich (2001), 'Steel: Big Problems, Better Solutions', International Economics Policy Briefs, *Institute for International Economics*, Washington D.C., no. 01–9, July.

—— (2002), 'Time for a Grand bargain in Steel?' International Economics Policy Briefs, *Institute for International Economics*, Washington D.C., January.

—— (2003a), 'Next Move in Steel: Revocation or Retaliation?', International Economics Policy Briefs, *Institute of International Economics*, Washington D.C., no. PB03–10, October.

—— (2003b), 'Steel Policy: The Good, the Bad, and the Ugly', International Economics Policy Briefs, *Institute of International Economics*, Washington D.C., January, no. PB03-1.

Huisken, Ron (2004), 'Inquiry into Australia's Defence Relations with the United States: Submission No. 10', Joint Standing Committee on Foreign Affairs, Defence and Trade, Defence Sub-Committee, Australian Parliament, Canberra, March.

—— (2006), 'Iraq: Why a strategic blunder looked so attractive', SDSC Working Paper 399, ANU, Canberra, March.

Ikenberry, G. John (1986), 'The State and Strategies of International Adjustment', *World Politics* 39:1, 53–77.

Jervis, Robert (1976), *Perception and Misperception in International Politics* (Princeton: Princeton University Press).

Job, Brian L. (1997), 'Multilateralism in the Asia–Pacific', in William Tow, Russell Trood and Toshiya Hoshino (eds) *Bilateralism in a Multilateral Era: The Future of the San Francisco System in the Asia–Pacific* (Tokyo: The Japan Institute of International Affairs and the Centre for the Study of Australia–Asia Relations, Griffith University) 160–169.

Joffe, Josef (2002), 'Hubs, Spokes and Public Goods', *The National Interest*, 30 October.

Johnson, Carol (1997), 'John Howard and the Revenge of the Mainstream: Some Implications for Concepts of Identity', in George Crowder, Haydon Manning, David Mathieson, Andrew Parkin and Leonard Seabrooke (eds), *Proceedings of the 1997 Australasian Political Studies Association Conference*, 2, Flinders University, Adelaide, September–October, 409–431.

Katzenstein, Peter (ed.) (1996), *The Culture of National Security* (New York: Columbia University Press).

—— (1997), *Small States in World Markets: Industrial Policy in Europe*, reprinted edition (Ithaca: Cornell Studies in Political Economy).

Kelly, Paul (1999), 'We'll be losers in a lamb war', *The Australian*, 14 July, 13.

—— (2000), 'New messenger, same strategic alliance', *The Australian*, 20 September, 35.

—— (2006), Kelly's term 'Guns and Wheat', *The Australian*, 15 April.

Kelton, Maryanne (2001), 'Sub plots: A Collins-class offset?', *Policy, Organisation and Society, Special Edition, 'An American–Australian Free Trade Treaty?*, 20:1, 131–140.

Kent, Ann (1997), 'Australia and China, 1991–95: Asymmetry and Congruence in the Post-Cold War Era', in James Cotton and John Ravenhill (eds), *Seeking Asian Engagement: Australia in World Affairs 1991–95* (Melbourne: Oxford University Press in Association with The Australian Institute for International Affairs) 170–190.

Keohane, Robert O. (1971), 'The Big Influence of Small Allies', *Foreign Policy* 2, 161–182.

—— (1986), 'Reciprocity in international relations' *International Organization* 40:1, 1–27.

Keohane, Robert O. and Joseph S. Nye (1989), *Power and Interdependence* (Glenview: Scott, Foresman and Company).

Knorr, Klaus (1975), *The Power of Nations: The Political Economy of International Relations* (New York: Basic Books).

—— (ed.) (1976) *Historical Dimensions of National Security Problems* (Lawrence: University Press of Kansas).

Kozaryn, Linda D. (1996), 'More US Training Planned Down Under', *American Forces Information Service News Articles*, August.

Krasner, Stephen D. (1976), 'State Power and the Structure of International Trade', *World Politics* 283, 317–347.

—— (ed.) (1983), *International Regimes* (Ithaca: Cornell University Press).

Kunkel, John (2002), Australian trade policy in an age of globalisation', *Australian Journal of International Affairs* 56:2, 237–251.

La Franchi, Peter (2000), 'Australian Government Strategy for Sub Company Rejected from Within', *Defense Daily International* 1:3, 21 April.

Leaver, Richard (1997), 'Patterns of dependence in post-war Australian foreign policy', in Richard Leaver and Dave Cox (eds), *Middling, Meddling, Muddling: Issues in Australian Foreign Policy* (St. Leonards: Allen and Unwin) 69–90.

—— (2001), 'The meanings, origins and implications of the "Howard Doctrine"', *The Pacific Review*, special edition 14:1, 15–34.

—— (2002), 'Australian Trade Policy: The Return of Imperial Preference', *paper for the Centre for Public Policy* (Melbourne: Melbourne University).

—— (2005), 'The Australia–United States Free Trade Agreement: The Boomerang of Competitive Liberalisation?', Conference on the Evolving Dynamics of Australia–East Asia Relations in the 21st Century, NCCU, Taipei, 3 June.

—— (2007), 'The New Trade Agenda' in Carl Ungerer, *Australian Foreign Policy in an Age of Terror* (Kensington, NSW: UNSW Press).

Leaver, Richard and Dave Cox (eds) (1997), *Middling, Meddling, Muddling: Issues in Australian Foreign Policy* (St. Leonards: Allen and Unwin).

Lind, Michael (2006), *The American Way of Strategy* (Oxford: Oxford University Press).

Lyon, Rod and William T. Tow (2003), 'The Future of the Australian–US Security Relationship', *Strategic Studies Institute, US Army War College*, Pennsylvania, December.

MacIntyre, Andrew (1996), 'U.S. – Australia relations and the rise of South-east Asia', in Roger Bell, Tim McDonald and Alan Tidwell (eds), *Negotiating the Pacific Century: The 'new' Asia, the United States and Australia* (St. Leonards: Allen and Unwin in association with The Australian Centre for American Studies) 66–86.

Malik, J. Mohan (2001), 'Australia and China: Divergence and Convergence of Interests', in James Cotton and John Ravenhill (eds) *The National Interest in a Global Era: Australia in World Affairs 1996–2000* (Oxford: Oxford University Press) 109–129.

Manne, Robert (ed.) (2004), *The Howard Years* (Melbourne: Black Inc. Agenda).

Marris, Sid (2002), 'PM's "win" leaves BHP in the queue', *The Australian*, 12 March, 1.

Martin, Roger and Robert Garran (2000), 'US early warning on defence', *The Australian*, 11 October, 2.

Matthews, Trevor and John Ravenhill (1987), 'ANZUS, The American Alliance and External Threats: Australian Elite Attitudes', *Australian Outlook* 41:1, April.

—— (1991), 'Adrift in an Alien Sea? Australian Perspectives on the World', in Richard W. Baker (ed.) *Australia, New Zealand, and the United States: Internal Change and Alliance Relations in the ANZUS States* (New York: Praeger) 159–182.

McAllister, Ian (2004), 'Attitude Matters: Public Opinion in Australia Towards Defence and Security', APSI, Canberra, August.

McAllister, Ian and John Ravenhill (1998), 'Australian Attitudes Toward Closer Engagement with Asia', *The Pacific Review* 11:1, 119–141.

McCausland, Jeffrey D., Douglas T. Stuart, William Tow and Michael Wesley (2007), *The Other Special Relationship* (Carlisle: Security Studies Institute).

McDougall Derek and Peter Shearman (eds) (2006), *Australian Security after 9/11: New and Old Agendas* (Aldershot: Ashgate).

McQueen, Humphrey (1970), *A New Britannia: An Agreement Concerning the Social Origins of Australian Radicalism and Nationalism* (Melbourne: Penguin).

Monk, Paul (undated) 'Defence: the Seamless Challenge', Austhink, <http://www.austhink.org/monk/seamless.htm>. Accessed 12 July 2005.

Moravcsik, Andrew (1993), 'Introduction: Integrating International and Domestic Theories of International Bargaining', in Peter B. Evans, Harold K. Jacobson, Robert D. Putnam (eds) *Double-Edged Diplomacy: International Bargaining and Domestic Politics* (Berkeley: University of California) 3–42.

Muradian, Vago (2000), 'Top US Admiral Lauds Quality of Australian Collins Subs', *Defense Daily International* 1:30, 27 October.

Murdock, Clark A. (2001), 'The Navy in an Anti-access World', in Sam J. Tangredi (ed.) *Globalization and Maritime Power* (Washington D.C.: Institute for National Security Studies, National Defense University) Chapter 25.

Nairn, Alan (1999), 'US Complicity in Timor', *The Nation*, 27 September, <http://www.thenation.com/doc/19990927/nairn>.

Nossal, Kim Richard (2004), 'Upper Hand Down Under: American Politics and the Australia–US Free Trade Agreement', *Paper prepared for the annual meeting of the Australian and New Zealand Studies Association of North America,* Toronto, 20–21 February.

Nye, Joseph S. (2000), *The Paradox of American Power: Why the World's Only Superpower Can't Go It Alone* (New York: Oxford University Press).

O'Donnell, Lynne and Sid Marris (2002), 'Beijing warns on sub sales to Taiwan', *The Australian*, 22 April, 7.

O'Neil, Andrew (2003), 'Issues in Australian Foreign Policy: January to June 2003', *Australian Journal of Politics and History* 49:4, 540–557.

—— (2007), 'Ambitious strategic policy misfires, *The Advertiser*, 10 July, 20.

Overington, Caroline (2007a), *Kickback: Inside the Australian Wheat Board Scandal* (Crows Nest: Allen and Unwin).

—— (2007b) 'Mr Not Responsible', *The Australian*, 7 May, 7.

Phelps, David (2001), 'What's Wrong with the Steel Industry Again?', American Institute for International Steel, at the *Cato Institute Policy Forum*, 20 February 2001, <http://www.freetrade.org/pubs/speeches/cf-022001.html>, accessed May 2002.

Plane, Terry (2001), 'Reith shows two faces in one day on Collins subs – Election 2001: 2 days to go', *The Australian*, 8 November, 3.

Plume, Janet (2002), 'Decision time on steel; Restrictions on imports would have spillover effects on carriers and ports', *Journal of Commerce*, 7 January.

Quinlivan, Beth (2001), 'Hype and high hopes', *BRW*, 6 April, 69.

—— (2004), 'Peptech's Happy Holiday', *Business Review Weekly*, 29 January, 38.

Ravenhill, John (1998), 'Cycles of Middle power activism: Constraint and choice in Australia and Canadian Foreign Policies', *Australian Journal of International Affairs* 52:3, 309–27.

—— (2001), 'Allies but not friends: the economic relationship', *Australian Journal of International Affairs* 55:1, 249–260.

Renouf, Alan (1979), *The Frightened Country* (South Melbourne: Macmillan).

Reus-Smit, Christian (2001), 'Lost at Sea: Australia in the turbulence of world politics', *Working Paper*, 2002/4, Department of International Relations, Research School of Pacific and Asian Studies, Australian National University, Canberra, July.

—— (2003), 'US Grand Strategy and Australia', *Centre for Defence and Strategic Studies, Australian Defence College Conference on 'United States Grand Strategy: Implications for Alliance Partners'*, Canberra, 1 August.

Reuters (2003), 'US wants Australian peacekeepers in Iraq – reports', *The New York Times*, 30 April.

Richelson, Jeffrey T. and Desmond Ball (1990), *The Ties That Bind: Intelligence Cooperation between the UKUSA Countries – the United Kingdom, the United States of America, Canada, Australia and New Zealand*, second edition (North Sydney: Allen and Unwin).

Risse-Kappen, Thomas (1996), 'Collective Identity in a Democratic Community', in Peter J. Katzenstein (ed.) *The Culture of National Security* (New York: Columbia University Press) 357–399.

Roach, Terence (2000), 'Opportunity knocks for the Collins class', *Asia–Pacific Defence Reporter*, October/November, 38–39.

Robertson, David (1997), 'Reciprocity and Protectionism in Australia's Trade Policy', *Agenda* 4:2, 135–42.

Robinson, Gwen (1991), 'Pressure to buy US', *Asia–Pacific Defence Reporter*, July, 16.

Rosen, Howard F. (1989), 'The US–Israel Free Trade Area Agreement: How Well Is It Working and What Have We Learned?', in Jeffrey J. Schott (ed.) *Free Trade Areas and US Trade Policy* (Washington, D.C.: Institute for International Economics) 97–119.

Rothstein, Robert L. (1968), *Alliances and Small Powers* (New York: Columbia University Press).

Ruggie, John Gerard (1995), 'At Home Abroad: Abroad at Home', *Millennium* 24:3, 507–526.

——(1998), *Constructing the World Polity: Essays on International Institutionalization* (London: Routledge).

Ryan, Michael P. (1998), *Knowledge Diplomacy: Global Competition and the Politics of Intellectual Property* (Washington D.C.: Brookings Institution Press).

Rycroft, Matthew (2005), 'Iraq: Prime Minister's Meeting, 23 July', 2003, as reported by David Manning, 'The secret Downing Street memo: Secret and strictly personal – UK eyes only', *Times Online*, 1 May.

Schott, Jeffrey J. (ed.) (1989), *Free Trade Areas and US Trade Policy* (Washington, D.C.: IIE).

Schurmann, Franz (1974), *The Logic of World Power* (New York: Pantheon Books).

Scott, Richard (2000), 'Final countdown for new Collins combat system', *Jane's Defence Weekly*, vol. 34, no. 2, 12 July.

Scott, Richard and Ian Bostock (2000), 'Final countdown for new Collins combat system', *Jane's Defence Weekly* 34:2, 12 July.

Seabrooke, Leonard (2001), *US Power in International Finance: The Victory of Dividends* (London: Palgrave).

Segurra, Alejandro E. (2000), 'Biosafety Protocol for Genetically Modified Organisms', *Congressional Research Service: Report for Congress, RL30594*, 5 July.

Sell, Susan K. (1998), *Power and Ideas: North–South Politics of Intellectual Property and Antitrust* (Albany: State University of New York Press).

Shanahan, Dennis (1999), 'US fury at our failings', *The Australian*, 17 September, 1.

Shishkin, Philip (2003),'Russia's backing of US's war on terror won't extend to Iraq', *The Wall St Journal Europe*, 3.

Shonfield, Andrew (ed.) (1976), *International Economic Relations of the Western World 1959–1971,* 1, Politics and Trade (London: Oxford University Press).

Snape, Richard, Jan Adams and David Morgan (1993), *Regional Trade Agreements: Implications and options for Australia* (Canberra: Department of Foreign Affairs and Trade, AGPS).

Snape Richard H., Lisa Gropp and Tas Luttrell (1998), *Australian Trade Policy 1965–1997: A Documentary History* (St. Leonards: Allen and Unwin).

Snyder, Glenn H. (1984), 'The Security Dilemma in Alliance Politics', *World Politics* 36:4, 461–495.

—— (1997), *Alliance Politics* (Ithaca: Cornell University Press).

Solomon, Russell Keith (1993), 'Political Economy of Australia's Trade Policy – Making Towards the United States', *unpublished Ph.D thesis (*Sydney: University of Sydney).

—— (1999), 'Bargaining with the strong: New Zealand and Australia's bilateral trade relations with the United States and the European Union', *Political Science* December, 512, 149–163.

Spencer, Stephen (1997), 'US expert warns against Tomahawk purchase', *AAP Newsfeed*, 7 October.

Starke, J.G. (1965), *The ANZUS Treaty Alliance* (Melbourne: Melbourne University Press).
Stewart, Cameron (2001), 'Top US spy unit sent to Pine Gap', *The Australian*, 28 January, 1.
Stokes, Donald E. (1991), 'US Political Change and the ANZUS Relationship', in Richard W. Baker (ed.), *Australia, New Zealand, and the United States: Internal Change and Alliance Relations in the ANZUS States* (New York: Praeger) 109–26.
Stokes, Geoff (1994), 'Toward a national trade strategy: Recovering bilateral strategies in trade promotion', *Australian Quarterly* 74 :95.
Strange, Susan (1983), 'Cave! Hic Dragones: a critique of regime analysis', in Stephen D. Krasner (ed.) *International Regimes* (Ithaca: Cornell University Press) 337–54.
—— (1988), *States and Markets* (London: Pinter).
The Australian (2002), editorial, 7 March.
Thomas, John R. (2000), 'An Examination of the Issues Surrounding Biotechnology Patenting and Its Effect Upon Entrepreneurial Companies', *CRS Report for Congress*, 31 August.
Thomson, Mark and Simon Harrington (2002), 'Setting a Course for Australia's Naval Shipbuilding and Repair Industry', *An ASPI Policy Report*, Budget and Management Programme, August, Canberra.
Tow, William T. (ed.) (1998), *Australian–American Relations: Looking Toward the Next Century* (South Yarra: Australian Institute of International Affairs in association with Macmillan).
—— (1999a), 'Assessing US Bilateral Security Alliances in the Asia Pacific's "Southern Rim": Why the San Francisco System Endures', *Asia/Pacific Research Center Discussion Paper* (Standford: Institute for International Studies, Stanford University).
—— (1999b), 'The Future of Alliances: AUSMIN as a "Case Study", in Des Ball (ed.) *Maintaining the Strategic Edge: The Defence of Australia in 2015*, Canberra Papers on Strategy and Defence 133, SDSC, RSPAS, ANU, Canberra.
—— (2001a), 'Alliances and Coalitions', in Marianne Hanson and William T. Tow (eds) *International Relations in the New Century: An Australian Perspective* (South Melbourne: Oxford University Press) 17–37.
—— (2001b), 'Australia and the United States', in James Cotton and John Ravenhill (eds) *The National Interest in a Global Era: Australia in World Affairs 1996–2000* (South Melbourne: Oxford University Press) 171–192.
—— (2003), 'US Bilateral Security Alliances in the Asia–Pacific: Moving Beyond the "Hubs and Spokes", *paper presented to the Australasian Political Science Association Conference, University of Tasmania*, Hobart, 29 September – 1 October.
Tow, William and Henry Albinski (2002), 'ANZUS – Alive and Well after Fifty Years', *Australian Journal of Politics and History* 48:2, 153–173.
Tow William T., and Leisa Hay (2001), 'Australia, the United States and a China growing strong: managing conflict avoidance', *Australian Journal of International Affairs* 55:1, 37–54.
Tow, William T., Russell Trood and Toshiyo Hoshino (eds) (1997), *Bilateralism in a Multilateral Era: The Future of the San Francisco Alliance System in the Asia–*

Pacific (Tokyo: The Japan Institute of International Affairs and the Centre for the Study of Australia–Asia Relations, Griffith University).

Treadgold, Tim (2002), 'US Tariffs A Kiss of Death for BHP Steel', *Business Review Weekly (Australia)*, 14 March, 14.

Viviani, Nancy (1990), 'Foreign Economic Policy', in C. Jennet and R. Stewart (eds) *Hawke and Australian Public Policy: Consensus and Restructuring* (South Melbourne: Macmillan).

Vogt, Donna U. and Mickey Parish (1999), 'Food Biotechnology in the United States: Science, Regulation, and Issues', *CRS Report to Congress*, 2 June.

Walker, David (1999), *Anxious Nation: Australia and the Rise of Asia, 1850–1939* (St. Lucia: University of Queensland Press).

Wallace, Christine (1996), 'The Fischer king? Not likely', *Financial Review*, 29 January, 21.

—— (2004), 'Lobbyists, negotiators stunned by Bush rebuff', *The Australian*, 25 February, 2.

Wallender, Celeste A., and Robert O. Keohane (1999), 'Risk, Threat, and Security Institutions', in Helga Haftendorn, Robert O. Keohane and Celeste A. Wallender (eds), *Imperfect Unions: Security Institutions over Time and Space* (Oxford: Oxford University Press) 21–47.

Walt, Stephen M. (1985), 'Alliance Formation and the Balance of World Power', *International Security* 9:4, 3–41.

—— (1987), *The Origins of Alliances* (Ithaca: Cornell University Press).

—— (1997), 'Why Alliances Endure or Collapse', *Survival* 39:1, 156–79.

Walters, Patrick (2000), 'US technology is sub plot', *The Defence Review* in *The Australian*, 28 June, 2.

Waltz, Kenneth N. (1970), 'The Myth of National Interdependence', in Charles P. Kindleberger (ed.) *The International Corporation*, symposium papers (Cambridge MA: MIT Press) 205–223.

Warley, T.K. (1976), 'Western Trade in Agricultural Products: The Failure to Liberalize Agricultural Trade', in Andrew Shonfield (ed.) *International Economic Relations of the Western World 1959–1971*, 1, Politics and Trade (London: Oxford University Press) 396–404.

Welfield, John B. (1981), 'Australia and Japan in the Cold War', in Peter Drysdale and Hironobu Kitaoji (eds) *Japan and Australia: Two Societies and their Interaction* (Canberra: Australian National University Press) 385–418.

—— (1988), *An Empire in Eclipse: Japan in the Postwar American Alliance System* (London: The Athlone Press).

Wendt, Alexander (1994), 'Collective Identity Formation and the International State', *American Political Science Review* 88:2, 384–96.

—— (1995), 'Constructing International Politics', *International Security* 20:1, 71–82.

Wesley, Michael (2001), 'APEC's mid-Life's Crisis? The Rise and Fall of Early Voluntary Sectoral Liberalization', *Pacific Affairs* 74:2, 185–207.

Wesley Michael and Tony Warren (2000), 'Wild colonial ploys? Currents of thought in Australian foreign policy', *Australian Journal of Political Science* 35:1, 9–26.

Wettern, Desmond (1991), 'US defence industries seek new markets' *Asia–Pacific Defence Reporter*, 33–34.

White, Hugh (2002), 'Australian defence policy and the possibility of war', *Australian Journal of International Affairs* 56:2, 253–264.

—— (2003a), 'Beyond the War on Terror: Australian Defence Policy in an Age of Uncertainty', *Address to the National Press Club*, 1 October.

—— (2003b), 'Mr Howard goes to Washington: The US and Australia in the Age of Terror', *Comparative Connections, Pacific Forum CSIS*, 2nd Quarter: Occasional Analysis: Australia–US Relations.

—— (2003c), 'Why fewer and bigger is bad for defence', *The Age*, 24 November.

—— (2006), 'Old, New or Both? Australia's Security Agendas at the Start of a New Century', in Derek McDougall and Peter Shearman (eds), *Australian Security after 9/11*, Ashgate, Aldershot, 13–28.

Wilkinson, Marian (1999), 'Why we kept Timor secrets from the US', *Sydney Morning Herald*, 13 August, 3.

—— (2000), 'Timor: The Quest for Justice', *Sydney Morning Herald*, 29 January, 35.

Wilson, David (ed.) (2001), *Maritime War in the 21st Century: The Medium and Small Navy Perspective* (Canberra: RAN Sea Power Centre).

Wolpe, Bruce (2000), 'Australia and America: Renewal and Reinvention', *Australian Journal of International Affairs* 54:1, 11–14.

Woodard, Garry (2000), 'Australia's foreign policy after Timor', *Canadian Journal of International Affairs* 55:1, 1–14.

Woodward, Bob (2002), *Bush at War* (New York: Simon and Schuster).

Woolner, Derek (2002), 'Fighting terrorism: Alliance and national interest', *Dissent* Autumn/Winter, 33–36.

Wright, Lincoln (1999), 'Secret Defence Papers Show 'conspiracy' at Highest Level', *Canberra Times*, 24 November, 1.

—— (2000a), Lincoln Wright, 'Secrets Blow About Building Site', *Canberra Times*, 23 August, 3.

—— (2000b), 'US adviser apologises for stupid metaphor', *Canberra Times*, 20 September, 5.

Wright, Tony (2003), 'The Road to War: War in Iraq Week 2', *The Bulletin*, 8 April, 36.

Young, Thomas-Durrell (1986), *Australian, New Zealand, and United States Security Relations, 1951–1986* (Boulder: Westview Press).

Zartman, I. William (1971), *The Politics of Trade Negotiations between Africa and the European Economic Community: The Weak Confront the Strong* (Princeton: Princeton University Press).

Zysman, John (1983), *Government, Market and Growth: Financial Systems and the Politics of Industrial Change* (Ithaca, Cornell University Press).

No author supplied (1999), 'Ali Alatas looks back on 11 years of Indonesia's foreign policy', *Jakarta Post*, 2 November, 5.

No author supplied (2000), 'German Government Spurs Defense Industry Alliances', *Defense Daily International*, vol. 1, no. 32, 10 November.

No author supplied (2001), 'RAN Collins submarines now on track', *Asia–Pacific Defence Reporter*, December/January, 12–13.

Index

Made in United States
North Haven, CT
14 December 2022

28724032R00135